KRISTEVA, PSYCHOANALYSIS AND CULTURE

Examining Julia Kristeva's contention that contemporary Western society is witnessing a crisis of subjectivity due to the failure of the paternal function, Gambaudo places Kristeva's thesis within the context of Freudian psychoanalytic thought and shows how Kristeva defends her position against a cultural climate privileging scientific and cognitive answers to aesthetic concerns.

Gambaudo argues that while Kristeva's position might be construed as defensive and a reactive clinging on to paternal modes of organisation of subjectivity, it also offers a unique and visionary analysis of subjectivity that rescues the paternal project from its decline. Eschewing a traditional emphasis on Kristeva's feminism, this book's primary interest is located at the intersection between psychoanalysis and culture, specifically analysing the superseding of Oedipus by narcissistic organisation.

ASHGATE NEW CRITICAL THINKING IN PHILOSOPHY

The *Ashgate New Critical Thinking in Philosophy* series brings high quality research monograph publishing into focus for authors, the international library market, and student, academic and research readers. Headed by an international editorial advisory board of acclaimed scholars from across the philosophical spectrum, this monograph series presents cutting-edge research from established as well as exciting new authors in the field. Spanning the breadth of philosophy and related disciplinary and interdisciplinary perspectives *Ashgate New Critical Thinking in Philosophy* takes contemporary philosophical research into new directions and debate.

Kristeva, Psychoanalysis and Culture

Subjectivity in Crisis

SYLVIE GAMBAUDO
Durham University, UK

ASHGATE

Published by
Ashgate Publishing Limited
Gower House
Croft Road
Aldershot
Hampshire GU11 3HR
England

Ashgate Publishing Company
Suite 420
101 Cherry Street
Burlington, VT 05401-4405
USA

Ashgate website: http://www.ashgate.com

British Library Cataloguing in Publication Data
Gambaudo, Sylvie
Kristeva, psychoanalysis and culture : subjectivity in crisis. - (Ashgate new critical thinking in philosophy)
1. Kristeva, Julia, 1941- 2. Subjectivity 3. Psychoanalysis - Philosophy 4. Narcissism
I. Title
194

Library of Congress Cataloging-in-Publication Data
Gambaudo, Sylvie, 1965-
Kristeva, psychoanalysis and culture : subjectivity in crisis / Sylvie Gambaudo.
p. cm. -- (Ashgate new critical thinking in philosophy)
Includes bibliographical references and index.
ISBN: 978-0-7546-5561-9 (hardcover) 1. Kristeva, Julia, 1941- 2. Subjectivity. 3. Psychoanalysis and culture. I. Title.

B2430.K7544G36 2007
150.19'5092--dc22

2006037933

ISBN: 978-0-7546-5561-9

Printed and bound in Great Britain by Antony Rowe Ltd, Chippenham, Wiltshire.

Contents

List of Figures

A la mémoire de mon frère
Matthieu Gambaudo
09.07.1968 - 28.04.2006

Introduction

'Our century is at once a technical apotheosis and a time of great human distress' (Guberman, 1996: 269). For Julia Kristeva, the contemporary subject is experiencing a time of crisis. She proposes the increasing difficulties the subject is faced with as a problematic staging a changing relationship of the subject with parental categories. She sees a weakening of the subject's connection with the paternal function counteracted by the strengthening presence of the maternal abject within that subject. These findings lead her to examine contemporary identities and to question the possibility of change and of renewal of subjectivity. In spite of today's technical apotheosis, 'science [...] still does not know how those mysterious "qualitative leaps", that transform "inorganic matter" into "living matter" and then into "living spirit", are generated' (Kristeva, 1998d). Julia Kristeva believes that human civilisation is now caught between adapting human life to conform to our technical understanding of it or to give life a sense beyond this technical image. 'I am one of those who think that in spite of the technical era in which we live ... there exists a life of the psyche which to me is still the essential value of our civilisation' (Smith, 1998: 1). Against a cultural backdrop favouring technique to the soul, Julia Kristeva's work invites her reader to revisit the path followed by the human subject that led him/her to a position of distress. In the chapters that follow, I am proposing an interpretation of Kristeva's work that will emphasise two themes of particular significance in understanding the crisis in contemporary subjectivity: the failure of the paternal function and the intensification of the maternal disposition.

Reading Kristeva necessarily implies one's engagement with psychoanalysis. Kristeva's work is both embedded in and a divergence from Freudian legacy. Freudian theory can roughly be described as a series of theoretical constructs articulated around the study and mapping of the unconscious and an interpretation of human psychosexual development. Even today, the use of 'unconscious' is what differentiates a Freudian analysis from any other analysis. Anne-Marie Smith (1998) points out that Kristeva's theorising on subjectivity, be it cultural, sexual or political, is subjected to her 'commitment to an ethics of identity and difference which is clearly psychoanalytic and Freudian' (Smith, 1998: 7). As Smith points out, many of the misinterpretations of Kristeva's work stem from critics neglecting her Freudianism.[1] They, in an attempt to provide more empirical answers to a

1 Smith points out that the understanding of Kristeva's *oeuvre* rests on positioning Kristeva's work within the psychoanalytic frame and that the related concepts of foreignness and femininity are also crucial in her work. Hence, Smith also dedicates part of

questioning of "human", reject psychoanalysis as unscientific and by-pass Kristeva's commitment to a Freudian discourse.

On the other hand, her work is also a departure from tradition when she proposes the re-assignment[2] of the paternal function to the maternal disposition. Like Smith, Doane and Hodges (1992) insist on a repositioning of Kristevan thinking within the psychoanalytic frame; but they also emphasise Kristeva's often neglected indebtedness to Object Relation Theory. Julia Kristeva's work can be positioned on both sides of this theoretical debate. As early as 1974, with the publication of *La Révolution du langage poétique*, she introduces and develops the idea that in his/her separation from the maternal realm and subsequent existence in paternal society, the subject is not as clearly cut off from the maternal as the more traditional Freudian approach suggested. In this, Kristeva follows Melanie Klein and her supporters. Klein had already introduced the idea of a primitive 'subjectivity', antecedent to the encounter with the Oedipal father:

> Some of my conclusions about the earliest stages of infancy are a continuation of Freud's discoveries; on certain points, however, divergencies have arisen, one of which is very relevant to my present topic. I am referring to my contention that object relations are operative from the beginning of post-natal life. (Mitchell, 1991: 204)

Freud's theories on infant object relation remained for Klein inconsistent, at times alluding to the pre-Oedipal subject's 'libidinal attachment to an object' (Mitchell, 1991: 205) and at other times conceiving of the infant's libidinal energy as operating '*in vacuo*' (Mitchell, 1991: 206).

Laplanche and Pontalis (1988) succinctly outline Freud's ambivalence vis-à-vis a possible structuring of the pre-Oedipal subject:

> As for the possibility of a preoedipal *structure*, Freud's own position was always reserved. He did acknowledge that he had been late in recognising the full implications of the primal link to the mother, admitting that the findings brought forward on the preoedipal phase in girls -particularly by women analysts- had taken him by surprise. But these facts, Freud felt, could still be explained without necessarily having recourse to a frame of reference other than the Oedipal one. (Laplanche and Pontalis, 1988: 285)

---

her critique to a discussion of the translation of Kristeva and how it links to foreignity and sexual identity.

2 In psychoanalytic theory, the paternal function is traditionally assigned to the Oedipal phase of development, that is the time the child gains the ability to symbolise, evidenced in the capacity to speak. Kristeva believes that before the Oedipal phase, some form of symbolisation is already manifest in the pre-linguistic baby. She proposes a re-assignment of the paternal function to a time anterior to Freud's Oedipal phase and consequently is considering an earlier Oedipal dynamic linked to, but different from, Freudian logic. I will develop this aspect of Kristeva's work in chapter four in particular.

Although alert to other theorists' findings in pre-Oedipality, Freud's theoretical framework remained firmly based upon the Oedipal model he had created. Klein brought a new insight by positing the infant's capacity to relate to an object '*ab initio*' (Mitchell, 1991: 206). She did not dispute Freud's Oedipal frame, but where Freud envisioned the onset of the Oedipal phase between the ages of three and five, Klein believed it began earlier in infancy. Consequently, both theorists worked within the same framework but with different material: Freud dealt with patients' linguistic production and attempted the mapping of the unconscious as *process*; Klein focused on young children and psychotic patients' extra-linguistic material and 'finding the unconscious *content* of the phantasies and the work of the unconscious ego' (Mitchell, 1991: 24; italics are mine). Part of the Kleinian legacy was first to propose the unconscious as content, rather than the unconscious as process, and bring to light extra-linguistic material, second to construct this material as part object and constitutive of the symbolic subject.

Julia Kristeva's work takes its place in the psychoanalytic theoretical continuum initiated by Freud and Klein. With terms such as *poiesis* and *semiotic*, she puts forward the reminiscence of a time preceding the subject's access to language within linguistic production. In so doing, her work bridges two theoretical factions so far kept apart. Doane and Hodges (1992: 57) suggest that on one side of the debate are the French psychoanalytic group who, loyal to the Freudian model and influenced by Lacan, focused on the concept of the 'dead father'[3] and the impact of symbolic castration upon the subject. This is echoed by Kristeva:

> One hears people say that psychoanalysis is dead, and in some ways they are not completely wrong. Many psychoanalysts and analytic societies are in the process of self-destructing, both in the guise of an excessively dogmatic obedience to the letter of Freud's text and of sectarian splinterings around the remains of Lacan. (Guberman, 1996: 173)

Against a stagnant devotion to the dogmas of the fathers of psychoanalysis are the followers of Melanie Klein who analyse the centrality of the maternal object, the loss of which engenders the subject's anxiety and depression. From her debut until now, Julia Kristeva has increasingly been filling the theoretical gap that separates the two factions, demonstrating the presence of maternal time within symbolic production. She is thus firmly anchored in the Freudian model of subjectivity on the one hand and on the other draws from Object Relation Theory to access and elucidate pre-linguistic material.

While her work is secure in the past findings of psychoanalytic thought, Julia Kristeva has also been demonstrating her originality and has been recognised as one of the important figures not only of psychoanalysis but also of contemporary

---

3 The concept of the dead father is a theme I will develop in chapter two.

thought. With regards to the crisis of subjectivity, Kristeva's treatment of parental categories is perhaps the most disputed. The Freudian and Kleinian models tended to enhance the role of one parent in the process of subjectivation: the father for Freudians, the mother for Kleinians. In bringing together the two models, Kristeva reconsiders biological categories and the manner in which they impact the subject, and rewrites these earlier findings from a figurative base. The traditional approach stages a pre-Oedipal 'family' dynamic, that is a triad constituted by the infant, the pre-Oedipal father and mother. The role of the latter two is, in early psychoanalytic theory, played by the actual mother and father. Kristeva's work is a continuation of this theoretical legacy, but also accounts for a contemporary reality where the definition of sexual categories is being questioned and modified. Hence, Kristevan theory testifies to a struggle to move away from biologism and towards a metaphorisation of parental categories.[4]

First, we observe that, since Freud, theorists have been seeking an appropriate terminology to describe the subject's process in relation to the family dynamic. This family is decreasingly the marker of a biological reality and increasingly defined according to its functions. In Kristeva, we find the father has evolved into a 'paternal function', the mother into a 'maternal abject'. Moreover, this shift in terminology from biology to function, also indicates a change of focus from parental figure to subject. Contemporary psychologists in general, and Kristeva in particular, consider that the baby has, as yet, no unified apprehension of its world and that the parent is experienced as fragmented.[5] Theorists refer to the parent under different terms to convey the fragmented experience of the infant. The parent is divided up into morsels and theorising occurs on the disconnected fragments that qualify as active components of the subjectivation process. Melanie Klein for instance speaks of 'the breast' as the infant referent for the whole of its mother: the part object refers to the whole. Theory attempts to mirror the infant's pre-subjective world by operating a depersonalisation of the subject into a scattering of pre-objects, closer to the pre-subjective reality of the infant's world and away from biological totalisation.

Second, where the division of parental labour followed a biological logic (the mother deals with pregnancy, birth and child rearing while the father earns a living to support them), the current cultural climate increasingly erases this biological

---

4 This struggle is felt especially in the dialogue with and amongst her followers and detractors. Both sides have repeatedly asked her to assign her terms 'paternal function' and 'maternal disposition' to sexual categories. In response, Kristeva has been increasingly separating parental functions (which she defines) from the biological body (which she considers in its psychical imprints and in its symbols, not as a 'pure' biology). See in particular Guberman (1996).

5 But note that over the past decade, the alleged fragmented apprehension of the infant's world has been increasingly questioned. See for instance the work of Daniel Sterne (Sterne, 1985).

division: 'the role of the father has changed in modern families: monoparental families, many couples are not married and take the risk of having an unstable bond, etc' (Kristeva, 1998a: 95). The traditional nuclear family is facing socio-cultural changes and is struggling with first a blurring of the differences between parental roles: reversal of parental roles ('the father often assumes his own femininity and certain tasks traditionally reserved to the woman' Kristeva, 1998a: 95), and condensation of both roles into one person (single-parent families); second, we observe a displacing of those roles onto entities other than the actual parent: social institutions, like schools and social workers, take the place of the missing/inadequate parent. From a theoretical viewpoint, the fading out of traditional parental agencies translates into an increasing use of terminology that enables the theorising of parental categories when those categories have collapsed on the biological level. The growing lexicon of the 'theorised parent', suggests a cultural reality whereby biological parenting is being replaced by a metaphoric parent and is apparent in Kristeva's work also: the parent is a *function*, a *role*, a *disposition* or a *metaphor* for the individual or group occupying the parental place.

On the other hand, Kristeva's construct of parental categories as metaphors is one of the areas where she is most strongly criticised. Within the context of this research, we shall be describing her account of the functions played respectively by the paternal and maternal agencies. Kristevan theory posits a paternal function performed by the mother before the subject's entry into the father's society. This maternal function, which would precede and prepare the subject for his/her encounter with the paternal function, is construed in different ways. On the one hand, 'critics who embraced her semiotic "chora" were suspicious of this return to the father' (Oliver, 1993: 69) and saw in Kristeva's work a disappointing "race back into the arms of the Law" (Oliver, 1993: 69): the paternal within the maternal is seen as the recreation, on the maternal body, of the primacy of the father over the mother. On the other hand, those 'who dismissed Kristeva as essentialist because of her semiotic "chora" were not surprised by this strong father to counterbalance the strong mother' (Oliver, 1993: 69). In short, her theorising on parental functions attracts accusations of both phallocentrism and gynocentrism.

In response, Kristeva rightfully points out that while the characteristics of the oedipal parents may change, it matters that the oedipal triangle be somehow maintained: 'it is not necessary to call them mother or father - what is necessary is to have three terms, if you prefer call them X and Y, why not? But I'm not sure that changes much.' (Oliver, 1997: 335). In a time when gender identity is increasingly difficult to define, Kristeva's work does not offer to draw biological hierarchies between father and mother in relation to the child but insists on the necessity to retain the three terms that frame the process of subjectivation. The ambiguity in her terminology stems from a cultural reality blurring gender categories, rendering the separation of parental roles difficult. We are witnessing a contamination of one parental category by the other and vice-versa, which for Kristeva 'is due to the crisis of the paternal function' (Oliver, 1997: 335). Faced with the increasing difficulty in defining gender roles on the one hand and a better apprehension of pre-linguistic material, Kristevan theory presents us with the possibility to apprehend the contemporary subject from this changed perspective, that is in relation to the paternal function and the maternal disposition.

This enquiry will open with an overview of Julia Kristeva's recent work, in particular her contention that the contemporary subject is experiencing a time of crisis. She is concerned, in a first stage, about the robotisation of the human or the increasing absence of what used to define the human. In a society eager to replace psychical vitality, once observed and described by Freud, with ready-made formulae, the answer to the subject's quest for an enhanced quality of life can be found in the media or at the pharmacy. In his review of *La révolte intime* (Kristeva, 1997a) Michel Contat sums up:

> This world of prefabricated images, this teleworld has us hooked, like the drug addict to his drug, and it is not pleasure, pure ecstasy or the diminishing of our psychical suffering that these "spectacular" images flog, but a life substitute excluding thought while cancelling the body. (Contat, 1997: 6)

In a society where TV characters or Prozac tablets can 'cure' human discomfort and where 'what is revolutionary is the product to clean the washing machine' (Kristeva, 1996c) Kristeva queries the very possibility of revolt. In the traditional sense of the term, the revolter upsets and overthrows an unsatisfactory system with the hope for a better one. In promoting revolutionary salvation in a given consumer product, 'We promote value X against prior values and we promote a new product like an absolute that will solve all problems. It is the same spirit which carries Stalinism or fascism: a dogmatism that stops the process of revolt.' (Kristeva, 1996c). The contemporary subject's anxiety, revolt and salvation are in consumerism and euphoric discourse: advertisement slogans for instance but also the emphatic speeches of the likes of Jean-Marie LePen. But 'proposing a product or a Front National type solution' (Kristeva, 1996d) is a denial of individual and social anxiety in the face of socio-symbolic instability. Noticing the anxieties of the contemporary subject and the absence of adequate help in a social system substituting the psychical mechanisms of revolt with pre-codified formulae, the potential for revolt of the individual and of society is under question. To identify the winner in the dispute 'uneasy thinking against calculation thinking' (Kristeva, 1996c) we need to follow the subject's trajectory backwards, from the moment of crisis back to its cause. The following chapters relate this journey back to the root of crisis.

The first chapter will present the recent work of Julia Kristeva and propose a general view of the crisis in subjectivity within both Freudian and Kristevan theories. Freudian theory remains the reference point against which Kristeva defines the subject and analyses the crisis of subjectivity. An understanding of her texts means positioning the debate within the psychoanalytic frame generated by Freud. At one end, and the subject of the second chapter, is the traditional psychoanalytic frame, positing the paternal function as the key factor in the genesis of the subject. At the other end is the narcissistic subject, envisioned beyond the demise of the paternal function, a thematic we will return to in chapter eight. Between these two extremes, we find Kristeva's analysis of the contemporary subject. As we will see in the second part, recent research shows an overall shift of interest away from Freud and towards theories on the maternal. The re-assignment of the Oedipal frame to a pre-Oedipality is emblematic of a cultural preoccupation concerning the maternal/paternal roles in psychoanalytic research. This re-orientation of the Freudian model indicates a limitation in Freudian patriarchal thought. Since the 1980s, Kristeva's work has been suggesting a 'failure of the paternal function' that I describe in chapter three, and invites a revisiting of parental categories as psycho-societal functions, with particular emphasis on the reassignment of the paternal genesis to the maternal realm (chapter four). This shift from paternal to maternal entails a closer encounter with the subject's pre-linguistic experience. This translates in the withering away of the traditional Oedipal subject and the emergence of a narcissistic type of subject closely connected with what Kristeva describes as the maternal abject (chapter five). The proximity of abject contents brings the risk of the subject's ultimate dependence upon the maternal. The threat that the maternal abject represents to the social subject is paralleled by an increase in research in the pre-Oedipal reality of the human subject.

What Kristeva regards as a crisis in subjectivity is evidenced further in the multiplication and diversification of therapeutic methodology. We are witnessing a division between pro-Freudian and anti-Freudian theorists, the former operating a return to the Freudian subject (Kristeva) and the latter departing from the Freudian model and towards a more cognitive approach. Against the saturation of psychoanalytic tradition, Kristeva also recognises the existence of a 'living, fruitful psychoanalytic discourse [...] competing and conflicting with two contemporary trends' (Guberman, 1996: 173): the media and neurosciences. In the first instance, Kristeva has consistently been objecting against the appropriation and bastardisation of analytic discourse into an image of the human that erases its complexity and suffering. In the second instance, although she is favourable to the furthering of neuroscientific research, Kristeva has been objecting to the trend of replacing psychical work with pharmaceutical answers. In her opinion, the replacing of analytic work by chemical substances translates in individual responsibility being taken away. The drug becomes the acting agent instead of the human subject. Post-Freudian theory is then confronted with a contemporary propensity for immediacy, efficacy and the spectacular. The final part of this study will assess the belief that post-Freudian psychoanalytic research and practice are increasingly solicited by a new type of subject: the narcissist. I will first return to the history of narcissism in Freud (chapter six) and then turn to contemporary debates concerning Freudians' bias towards the Oedipal model (chapter seven). Today, some claim that this new subject functions in osmosis with a social organisation that has transformed narcissism into a new commodity. But the commodification of narcissism also transpires in post-Freudian theory. Kristeva is critical of the popularisation of the Freudian legacy and its use for capitalist advancement: 'You are worried, it is a pathology; you are no longer worried, you become a buyer, a pure stabilised being who will be manipulated like a robot' (Kristeva, 1996c). But the divergence away from the Freudian subject can also be construed as a contemporary cultural process attempting to assist an impaired paternal function and consolidate a narcissistic subject while by-passing the increasing threat of the maternal. The debate over the contemporary faces of narcissus will be the theme of the concluding chapter.

Chapter 1

Kristeva, Psychoanalysis and Culture: An Overview[1]

In 1992, Julia Kristeva painted a somewhat pessimistic picture of contemporary society, saying that, 'the moment of militancy is over and we are living in a therapeutic age in which we must face up to our problems' (Kristeva, 1992: 20). In the five years that followed, Kristeva committed herself to offering a psychoanalytic diagnosis of these problems, culminating in the publication of three texts: *Les nouvelles maladies de l'âme* in 1993, *Sens et non-sens de la révolte* in 1996 and *La révolte intime* in 1997. Her analysis is articulated around the two recurring themes of absence and revolt. The failure of the symbolic/paternal function and the return to archaic/maternal processes has brought about a situation of crisis. Human beings are experiencing a splitting of subjectivity, with a growing divide between two opposite poles.

On the one hand, men and women are craving to become more efficient social performers with homogenised personal needs satisfied by manufactured sensations. This mass consumption has engendered schizoid social subjects whose identity crises have found their way into popular culture, in the alluring problematic of the *replicant* that films like *Blade Runner* (Scott, 1991) initiated. On the other hand, the singularities of human experience are displaced and transformed into social 'diseases', symptomatic of repression and homogenisation: the collapse of ideologies of revolt, the fragmentation of the family unit, resurgence of fundamentalism and extremism, may be aetiologically linked to the spread of stress related illnesses. In turn, sufferers of these *fin de siècle* diseases find fast and efficient relief in pills, ready-made images or euphoric discourses of damnation/salvation.

Kristeva presents us with no less than the future of the human race. Throughout her 1990s work, we read that we are now faced with a choice: withdrawal from the human or reassessment and rehabilitation of the possibility for revolt and survival. Before we delve further into Kristevan crisis, we can pause a moment on the trajectory that led the author from her 1960s structuralist research on the limits of signification to her 1990s post-feminist stance on the human subject.

---

1 Parts of this chapter were published as 'Absence and Revolt: the Recent Work of Julia Kristeva'; See Gambaudo (2000a).

Kristeva's Trajectory

Linguistics, Semanalysis, Intertextuality

As early as 1969, Kristeva begins focusing on 'the history of thought applied to this unknown which constitutes it' (Kristeva, 1981: 323). At the start of her work, she enthusiastically believes that the 20th century, self-assured in the knowledge it has gained in linguistics, is now ready to move beyond mere systemic understanding of the human. She believes we are witnessing 'a complete mutation of the sciences and ideology of this technocratic society' (Kristeva, 1981: 326), a mutation from symbolic tradition to new frameworks. *Le langage, cet inconnu* describes that century (and Kristeva's) distancing from traditional linguistics and attraction to the psychoanalytic model. Since language cannot be totalised and fully studied, then it must not be studied outside its subject. Instead, Kristeva proposes to construe human communication as a split system of words on the one hand and transverbal articulations on the other. The domain of dreams, of poetry, of the unknown dimension of communication, transverbal articulations are known on the level of words that attempt to order and name this unknown. She says:

> The West, reassured by the mastery it achieved over the structures of language can now confront these structures to a constantly evolving and complex reality to find itself faced with all the omission and censorship which enabled it to construct this system: this system was but a refuge: language without a reality, signs, mere signifiers even. Having been sent back to these very concepts, our culture is forced to question again its own philosophical matrix. (Kristeva, 1981: 326-7)

The enthusiasm in 1969 is in sharp contrast with the pessimism of the late 1980s. For in questioning its philosophical matrix, at the turn of the 20th century, Kristeva repeatedly deplores the withdrawal of the subject behind a wall of typified formulas, images, words, etc. Far from leaving the refuge of systemic thinking, the West reinforced that construction even further. We see the separation between words and transverbal articulations and repeated attempts at totalising modes of representations, shutting out the possibility of considering the unknowable dimension of language as both transcendence and origin of the system. In other words, not only can the human be known, but also the human can be controlled through the manipulation of what expresses it, language.

If the framework is refined and the tone changes, her discontent today echoes her 1969 criticism. Against the reductionist bias of traditional linguistics Kristeva proposes, at her début, to redress the balance. She applies her theoretical views to the aesthetic field of literature and attempts to demonstrate how a reading that does not sacrifice the transverbal dimension of language can enhance our apprehension of text and subject. Whether she calls it 'semiotic analysis' or 'semanalysis' (Kristeva, 1978) or 'semiotic practice' (Kristeva, 1974a: 188), her theoretical framework firmly challenges traditional literary criticism. It is also a 'method' or 'signifying practice' to approach text that entails two things: first, to show the functions of the aesthetic discourse; second, to remain aware of such a construction of text and of its limits. It is, in other words, a meeting, or better a 'hybridisation' of two discourses. On the one hand is the traditional structuralist discourse actively seeking the symbolicity of communicative operations. On the other hand, is the transformational process itself, that is the attempt on Kristeva's part to describe the movement of communication, from the body that initiates it to the symbol that stands for it, the 'subject in process':

> [A]nalysis should not limit itself simply to identifying texts that participate in the final texts, or to identifying their sources, but should understand that what is being dealt with is a specific dynamics of the subject of the utterance, who consequently, precisely because of this intertextuality, is not an individual in the etymological sense of the term, not an identity. In other words, the discovery of intertextuality at a formal level leads us to an intrapsychic or psychoanalytic finding, if you will, concerning the status of the "creator", the one who produces a text by placing himself or herself at the intersection of this plurality of texts on their very different levels – I repeat, semantic, syntactic, or phonic. (Kristeva, 1985: online)

The concept of intertextuality that Kristeva develops from 1966[2] takes after Freud's model of language.[3] It first positions the production of language, from body to symbol, on an unconscious or psychic level, thus challenging traditional linguistics. Second it adds to Freud's 'displacement' and 'condensation' a further dimension to the analysis of language and the subject, that of *process*. Her interest rests not only with the finished product, the condensation and/or displacement of psychic activity, but also with the very passage from one sign system to another.[4] In this passage, text is the result of a complicated process Kristeva positions on two axes: horizontally, words are shared in 'real time' by both speaker and addressee; vertically each unit of the text is the result of the speaker's belonging to a given environment that is both anterior and synchronic to him/her. Intertextuality is this crossroad where text takes its place amidst a mosaic of other texts. Kristeva's intertextuality exceeds then the traditional Freudian view of language as the product of 'castration'. In her logic, language (in its wider sense of text) is not solely the manifest content of a wider picture of the subject, the biggest part of which has been repressed and hidden from view. She makes of Freud's model a more permeable structure where she seeks to show the process of symbolisation and repression. This does not mean that her work marks the end of repression and the beginning of a theory where the subject can fully be known. On the contrary, her discursive practice insists on the repression of corporeality as 'it' is

2 Kristeva first presented her work on intertextuality in 1966 at one of Roland Barthes's seminars. She further develops it in *La Révolution du langage poétique* (1974a).

3 Freud's model of language will be described later in this chapter.

4 See Smaller (1985) 'Intertextuality: An Interview with Julia Kristeva'.

transformed. What is repressed is contained in this "it". Not only do transformational processes repress corporeal elements but maybe more importantly for an understanding of Kristevan logic, repression is the repression of the very process of repression. The repression of process is for her one of the markers of Western society. Western society 'represses the *process* that occurs within the body and the subject [...]. [Because] this mode of capitalist production has organised language into idiolects, it has made of them closed untransmittable units' (Kristeva, 1974a: 11). Against the repression of the subject and its body and to redress the balance, Kristeva proposes to ground the subject and its production into a materiality she finds in language.

> What we call *signifiance* is precisely this unlimited creation that is never closed, this constant work of drives towards, in and through language, towards, in and through exchange and its protagonists: the subject and its institutions. This heterogenuous process [...] is a structuring and destructuring *practice*, touching on social and subjective *limits*, and – under those conditions only - it is jouissance and revolution. (Kristeva, 1974a: 15)

Several themes are introduced here. In retrospect these form the foundation of Kristeva's later work. First, Kristeva makes clear that she does not separate the subject from its institutions. Rather, institutions, that is any production, social, cultural, the individual's objects, should be treated like a language: neither can be considered in separation from their subject. Both the subject and its objects are enmeshed into a constant exchange where the one is projected onto the other and the other is symptomatic of the one. Hence the structuring, destructuring, empowerment and limitations of the one is also all that in the other.[5]

Second, in her insistence to expose the powers and limits of a semiotic practice, we recognise a theme that will remain present throughout Kristeva's oeuvre: a dedication to describing how her theoretical framework empowers the speaker but also limits the capacity for construction. Those limits are indeed set out by Kristeva from 1969 and more strongly with her adoption of Freudian psychoanalysis as a frame of reference. In short, phallicism structures and empowers, the feminine destroys and limits. The adoption of such a framework will warrant her the status of misogynist amongst a certain group of feminist critics, as we will see below. In spite of repeated criticism, Kristeva remains firm in her conviction that femininity is a negativity. To talk about femininity is to speak from outside the psychoanalytic frame. From semanalysis to psychoanalysis, the Kristevan framework considers no other dimension of human subjectivity than phallic. Hence terms such as 'the transverbal', 'the semiotic', 'the feminine', etc. should only be apprehended from without traditional psychoanalysis or, at best, as the expression of a 'not-

---

5 We will return to the idea of the social/cultural as symptom of subjectivation in chapter three.

something'. This brings us to the second aspect and 'phase' of Kristeva's trajectory, that of her uneasy relationship with feminism.

Feminism, Psychoanalysis

Kristeva is famous in Anglo-American circles for her views on sexual identity and her work on women's position in social organisation. Along with Cixous and Irigaray, Toril Moi sees her as one of the three authoritative figures of French feminism, the 'new holy Trinity of French feminist theory' (Oliver, 1993: 163) as she put it. Moi's tongue-in-cheek comment is a fair assessment of a certain Anglo-American bias regarding 'French feminism', evidenced in their selection of these three writers over and above a multiplicity of other feminist work in France. At the same time, defining Kristeva as one of the three pillars of French feminism tends to fence Kristeva's work within the 'French feminist philosopher' (Moi, 1985: 11) category that has given Kristeva's work exposure beyond French intellectual circles but has also limited the understanding of the scope of her work.

Kristeva's theoretical position on identity goes well beyond gender identity, or rather, she proposes a framework that can be applied to sexual difference as well as to other fields. She clarified her position in 1996 by stating:

> I believe that much of what has been written in the United States about my conception has been inaccurate. People have either defined and glorified the "semiotic" as if it were a female essence or else claimed that I do not grant enough autonomy to this "essence", this "difference". I hear in such reductive statements traces of the old-age debate between the "universalists" and the "differentialists". I have the impression that American feminists cling to differentialism and fan the flame of a war between the sexes that is no doubt quite real. My goal is to inscribe difference at the heart of the universal and to contribute to what is much more difficult than war: the possibility, with a little bit of luck, that men and women, two human species with sometimes conflicting desires, will find a way to understand each other. (Guberman, 1996: 269)

The key to understanding, and possibly misunderstanding, Kristeva's feminism lies in her own use of the term 'sexual difference'. Where most view sexual difference as that which differentiates man from woman (biological and environmental), Kristeva's 'sexual difference' refers to a very specific process, a Freudian one, namely that of the individual's sexual development. Sexual difference does lead to an understanding of gender difference, but more widely, it leads to a logic of differentiation. The only claim to a feminist practice that Kristeva makes in 'Women's Time' (1990b) is to refuse to define the essences of 'man' or 'woman'. Such definitions are fruitless as both terms belong to metaphysical categories. Instead, the gender debate, along with any debate founded on a binary logic (race, class, etc.) must be brought back to a re-assessment of what created it in the first place. This corresponds to 'an *interiorisation of the founding separation of the sociosymbolic contract*' (Belsey and Moore, 1990: 215). Through an analysis 'of the potentialities of *victim/executioner* which characterise each identity, each subject, each sex' (Belsey and Moore, 1990: 216), Kristeva is urging her readers against the fabrication of scapegoats -this patriarchal society- and victims -women, foreigners, etc. Her views go beyond a mere attack on liberal/radical feminists (or 'universalists' and 'differentialists' as she calls them) perpetuating 'unconsciously the very oppositions they are trying to undo' (Guberman, 1996: 107). Throughout her work, and more particularly in the last ten years,[6] questions of sexism are also the questions of racism, class conflict, etc. These questions, traditionally separated into individual struggles, become symptoms of one common psychical constitution, that of the human subject which, as diverse as they appear, form a kind of blueprint of Western culture. However, if the symptoms of sexual difference she describes pertain to Western culture, the structuring of the individual through sexual difference does not.

With the publication of *Des Chinoises*, in 1974, Kristeva notices that in spite of cultural differences opposing the capitalist West and communist China, both cultures are faced with the same difficulty regarding subjectivity: 'the search for legitimisation through the paternal function, the impossible relationship of the daughter with the mother, the suicidal call of polymorphous jouissance in front of a crumbling social contract' (Kristeva, 1974b: 224). This leads her to believe in the universality of sexual difference, reminiscent of Freud's belief in the universality of the Oedipal triangulation. The difficulties experienced by individuals are rooted in a crisis in the family structure, itself regulated by sexual difference. Crisis is the crisis of the traditional family triangle, mother, father, individual. Crisis is the effect of the collapse of religious values and the withering away of 'God' as socio-symbolic instance. After the collapse of the symbolic father (God), Man, in his biological fragility, is now threatened. This theme of the collapse of the symbolic and threat of biology prevails throughout Kristeva's work and increasingly so at the turn of the century. She will return in a quasi obsessive way to the importance of phallic organisation, the subject's relationship with 'an abstract instance, say symbolic, which is not necessarily a sexual partner, or a psychoanalyst, or a Party, but a *social practice*: political, aesthetic, scientific' (Kristeva, 1974b: 224). In this, Kristeva makes herself the advocate of Freud (and Lacan) and shows the limit of her own practice. Yet, she also steps away from the definition of woman as biological category based on reproduction and insists that the phallic frame of reference necessitates the re-defining of woman in relation to the symbolic instead of the biological. In 1974, Kristeva predicts that after the crisis of man's identity will come the crisis of woman's, 'which will be the true revolution of industrialised humanity, freed from the anxiety to procreate and to produce: neither man, nor woman, nor uni-sex: a whirl of clashes and laughter' (Kristeva, 1974b: 225). In

6 The publication of *Les nouvelles maladies de l'âme* in 1993 marks the turning point in Kristeva's work.

Des Chinoises, Kristeva is the most outspoken about her hopes and expectations regarding the future not only of individuals and of society but also of gender identity. Her 'mission' is clear:

> [...] to build a society whose acting power, is represented by no one: no one can appropriate it if no one is excluded from it, not even women – these last slaves, necessary support to the master's power, and whose marginalisation from power ensures that it is representable and to be represented (by the fathers, the legislators). (Kristeva, 1974b: 228)

The symbolic must be preserved and the other of the symbolic, the feminine, even if multiple and subversive, must be included. But for men, women and the gender debate, neither the erasure of difference between the sexes, nor the 'war' opposing the sexes will bring the struggle to an end. Instead when society discovers that 'neither Man nor Woman exists or need each other' (Kristeva, 1974b: 224), society will have moved on to another type of ethical understanding whereby the subject will be the outcome not of biological or metaphysical categories but of a universal triangular structuring taking multiple forms, another family structure whose social ethics 'depends directly on the economy and function of sexual difference' (Kristeva, 1974b: 226). This fantasy of an Oedipal society whose members would be aware of the power and limitation of their own construction reveals her desire 'to inscribe difference at the heart of the universal' (Guberman, 1996: 269). Substituting terms, we could say that the aim is to inscribe the feminine at the heart of the phallic, or to shake the Freudian model from within, with the theoretical concept fragmenting its unity without basically destroying it.

In the past ten years, Kristeva's use of the Freudian model as the organising structure of the subject in relation to its socio-cultural objects has become increasingly prevalent. Since the publication of *Les nouvelles maladies de l'âme*, the work published has increasingly dealt with cultural illustrations, or symptoms, of what former theoretical work previously explained in a heavily jargon-laden style. Kristeva has not significantly altered her theoretical position since her début, but refined and deepened her framework to a certain limit and made that framework more available to the uninitiated. This limit corresponds to the limit of the Freudian model itself that Kristeva has consistently claimed as her own. The publication of the late 1990s lecture series at the UFR 'Sciences des textes et documents' of the university of Paris VII Denis Diderot testifies to these two points. On the one hand, Kristeva wished for a 'discours direct', a less elitist style accessible to intellectual circles beyond psychoanalysts and theoreticians. On the other, the very title 'Pouvoirs et limites de la psychanalyse' (powers and limits of psychoanalysis) demonstrates Kristeva's awareness of the Freudian framework and of her willingness and resistance to go beyond that framework. It is partly commendable that she could show such dedication to one theoretical framework and push its boundaries to the extent that she has. It is also to be deplored that while hinting often at this 'other scene', and expressing her curiosity towards the possibility of another mode of exchange that would not be phallic, she could never bring herself to leave the Freudian model and radically re-think subjectivation outside this Freudian framework as others have done.[7]

If difference is to be considered, it will be from within the universal, the symbolic, but certainly not from without. If a 'feminine identity' must be considered, the emphasis on biology and physiology is always 'a symbolic effect of the way the subject experiences social cohesiveness, power and language' (Guberman, 1996: 104). The legacy of the female body can only be envisaged from a symbolic or phallic logic, that is as a negativity, a lack or an absence. The effect of a symbolic or phallic reading of the reality of female biology/physiology is counter-balanced by what she calls the 'maternal function' or 'woman effect'. The maternal

> [...]'entails a specific relationship to both *power* and *language* or, if you will, to the power of language. This particular relationship is based not on appropriating power and language, but on being a source of silent support, a useful backdrop, and an invisible intermediary. I have called this modality of the linguistic (and social) functioning of language the "*semiotic*" (Guberman, 1996:104)

This is the closest Kristeva comes to giving a definition of 'feminine identity'. More socially engaging then a nothingness, femininity or 'the woman effect', rather than womanhood, is support through silence, a kind of background or foundation towards the useful, the invisible that lies in-between two instances: the feminine and the symbolic. Here lies the difficulty in assessing Kristeva's feminism. Support, foundation and transition are always of and towards the socio-symbolic contract. Hence the feminine is maintained as silence and invisibility but is also given a social function within the symbolic. This feminine positioning is available to both men and women and when it does not lead to psychosis, the feminine leads to an aesthetic practice.

> What we call 'art' is characterised by a more patent immanence of the semiotic to the symbolic. Art transforms language into rhythms and transforms 'aberrations' into stylistic figures. Art is the incestuous side of language, as reflected in its dependence on the mother's body and its relationship to the pre-oedipal stage. (Guberman, 1996: 109-10)

Aesthetic practice is open to both sexes, but Kristeva has tended until recently[8] to emphasise the aesthetic practice of the feminine of man with works of art (writing,

7 See for example the work of Bracha Lichtenberg Ettinger (1992) or Deleuze and Guattari (1984).

8 After years of analysing exclusively male artists, Kristeva turned her attention to the possibility of a 'génie féminin' in women. See Kristeva, 1999, 2000 and 2002. But in this 1975 interview, her resistance vis-à-vis the idea of female artists is more pronounced.

painting, etc.) and that of the feminine of woman with maternity and maternal. 'The maternal function has to do with the pre-oedipal process and thus aesthetic practice' she says. 'The incest taboo, which is constitutive of the social order as well as the order of language, is in the end a mother taboo for both the boy and for the girl' (Guberman, 1996, 110). However, males have an easier time finding a substitute for the forsaken mother than heterosexual females who must become exiles from and rivals of the maternal continent. Kristeva sees aesthetic practice as a sublimation of incest in the form of the aesthetic product. Hence, women find it harder to sublimate because their identity rests upon an inimical relationship with the maternal. Women 'are more fragile than men because identifying with such fetish-objects as books and fame offers derisive support against the violence of this relationship and this fundamental frustration' (Guberman, 1996: 111- 2). For women, maternity can then become the means to move from pre-Oedipal to social and safely deal with issues of hostility towards the mother.

This separation of the sexes in the face of the feminine is in contrast with a point we highlighted earlier. In 1974, Kristeva wished for a society founded upon an Oedipal dynamic that would not fabricate marginal groups. This is perhaps where her work shows an ambivalence and opens a theoretical impossibility; for how could a theory founded upon the castrating moment be anything else than a platform for the dualism between what is kept and what is discarded? This question we will leave open but note, to emphasise Kristeva's phallicism once more, that with her increasing interest in psychoanalytic theory and practice, this openness regarding her own 'fantasy' of a future fades away, leaving the place to a harder core psychoanalytic discourse refusing to describe 'symptoms' other than those of psychoanalytic and literary practices (Kristeva, 1977b, 1980, 1983 and 1987a). Although her refusal to become descriptive has contributed to refining and avoiding the trivialising of her theoretical stance, it has also created misunderstandings when non-Freudians failed to analyse her work in the light of its metaphoric bias. To be clear, Kristevan crisis is rooted in the sense of loss initiated by the Oedipal frame, initially common to both sexes and later detected in culture under the guise of marginalisation. Given that psychoanalysis is Freudian, that is phallocentric, by definition, it could be argued that Kristeva is correct in positioning debates on the place of the feminine outside psychoanalysis. This can be said also of her early enthusiasm for a triangulation that would avoid marginalisation and its excesses. Another thesis would have been to argue that the articulation of a psychoanalysis founded on a non-phallic, say 'matrixial' logic, to borrow Ettinger's terminology, does not so much invalidate the Freudian frame as reflect it. Yet, our argument will show that Kristeva's work paves the way to such a reflection on the ante-phallic (as opposed to anti-phallic). So, even if she refuses to forsake the 'primacy of the phallus', she also initiates the retro-active shortcomings of phallic theory. Crisis should be read accordingly. Kristeva's work has a place as part of a process, that of psychoanalytic research. What is proposed, through a description of this process, is a reading of subjectivity as transition or crisis of the psychoanalytic subject. In Kristeva's work the subject and its objects are not separate. Likewise, we should not separate psychoanalysis (or the psychoanalyst) from its (her) objects and offer a deconstructive analysis of psychoanalysis. Instead, Kristeva's trajectory within psychoanalysis can be followed, from the defining moment of the 'subject' to its narcissistic limits.

The Contemporary Subject and the Freudian Scene

The publication of *Les nouvelles maladies de l'âme* (Kristeva, 1993) marks a turning point in Kristeva's work. The book is a collection of essays written between 1979 and 1992 showing the author's growing interest in the symptoms of a society in transition. With this collection, she attempts to define the 'new maladies of the soul' and to defend a psychoanalytic oriented position promoting the importance of language in maintaining the good health of civilisation. The analysis of our new 'maladies'[9] is inspired by the contemporary difficulty to translate and frame the space of the psyche. To understand Kristeva's theoretical framework we need to return briefly to Freud.

Freud considered that psychic life is 'doubly determined -by the biological domain and by the symbolic domain' (Guberman, 1996: 85). This is not new; as far back as the Antiquities, disciplines such as medicine and philosophy have often conceived of the diseased body as separate from biological fate. Freud, however, emphasises the notion of illness as doubly-bound. Illness is both physical, related to a given biological terrain, and a response to the 'mal à dire' (the difficult to tell), a 'failed' translation of psychical activity. What is perhaps unique with psychoanalytic theory is its emphasis on the presence of the body at all levels of rationalisation. However accomplished the thought, the psyche and its libidinal weight always precede and inform it. Thought is indebted to this 'heterogeneous stratification of the psyche' (Kristeva, 1997b, online). Freud's model can be conveyed diagrammatically.

9 'Maladie': sickness/maladie but also 'mal à dire' (cf. Lacan), the difficult to tell; hence, what we find difficult to represent in language is translated into a 'mal', a disease.

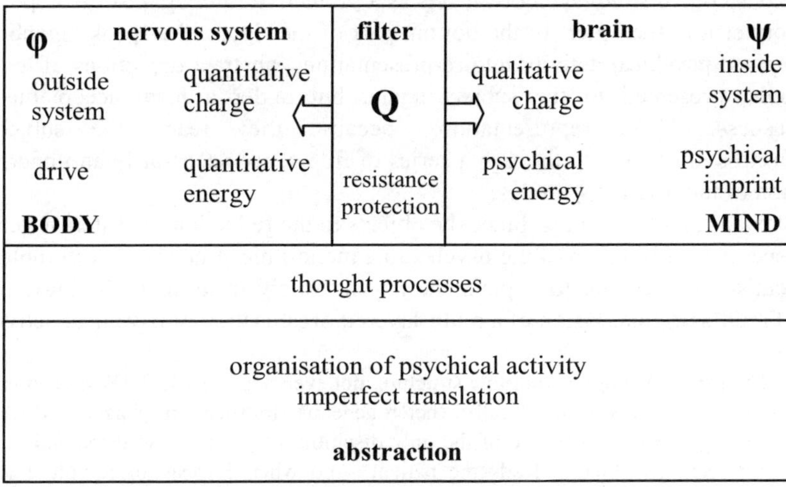

Figure 1.1 Diagrammatic interpretation of language production

In an attempt to represent the processes at play within the human subject in the production of language, Freud first imagined a topography of the human mind divided into three zones: the unconscious, pre-conscious, conscious model or first topic. Each zone would correspond to a positioning of mental processes as highlighted in figure 1.1. The top part of the figure, corresponding to the individual's unconscious processes, depicts Freud's supposition that within the individual exists a system permitting the apprehension of the world: a sensing of the outside through the nervous system (system φ) and more significant in Freud, its psychical translation (system ψ). From stimuli to psychical imprint, the information perceived by the individual (charge Q) is transformed from quantitative to qualitative. The translation of 'Q' rests on processes of filtering and resistance, aiming at protecting system ψ from damage. This movement of charge 'Q' Freud will later name 'drive'. In system ψ, information takes the form of psychical representations which inscribe in the mind 'mnesic'[10] traces, that is to say psychical imprints which are at the basis of future organised memory. The processes at work between systems φ and ψ pertain to the human encounter with their world, mediated by the body and processed by the psyche. The middle zone, corresponding to the preconscious, translates psychical processes into symbols and interacts with both the unconscious and the conscious. In the translation of

10 'Mnesic' refers to material upon which memory can be organised. In Freud's understanding, mnesic traces remain relatively constant once imprinted in the psyche while memory is an organisation of those traces into a changeable narrative. Amnesia points to a breakdown in the relationship unconscious/conscious while anamnesia is the recapture of that relationship.

unconscious contents into symbols, it acts as a protective filter against the impulses of the former into the latter. In the bottom part of the figure, the speaking subject has organised psychical activity into re-presentations, abstract depictions of things and words, presented to the subject again, but under a form acceptable to consciousness. These representations, because they reach the subject's consciousness after passing through a series of filters, are necessarily an imperfect translation of the original stimulus.

Kristeva argues two things. First, she objects to the reduction of system φ/ψ, the heterogeneous stratification of the psyche, to a monolithic structure. She complains that scientists are seeking to explain the psyche solely in terms of biology, thus erasing Freud's original vision of a multi-layered organisation of psychical activity.

> The psyche is not a monolithic structure, not even a biology [...]. [W]e economise on this complexity that I call a 'heterogeneous stratification of psychical life' - that psychoanalysis is one of the only disciplines to claim nowadays, and in the windings of which it leads the patient. And when I speak of re-volt, I refer precisely to this journey, capable of accessing this heterogeneity of psychical experience. (Kristeva, 1997b)

Second, not only is the φ/ψ system replaced by a biological structure, but the part of the psyche where conscious interacts with unconscious (the pre-conscious in Freud's first topic) is also replaced by ready-made images and calculations.

> [S]ome [...] assert that man would be solely determined by genetics. Too often, we find ourselves driven from a spectacular vision of man, due to this society of the spectacle and technique, which reduces him to a dependence upon images or economic calculations, to a completely basic materialism reducing him to the biological. (Kristeva, 1997b)

Hence, the processes at play between systems φ and ψ are no longer the source of stimulation out of which we generate signification. Instead, the translation of charge Q from quantity into quality is being provided by ready-made outside stimuli. These stimuli take various forms according to the cultural setting (at least in western culture). Kristeva frequently returns to three: spectacularised images, consciousness-altering drugs, and the hypnotic discourses of fundamentalism. In the economy of system φ/ψ and of its translation into symbols, the subject no longer has any need to entertain any relations with the body, the senses and affectivity, as noted by Michel Contat:

> Kristeva's intellectual battle [...] is a battle against cognitivism which pretends to know of the mind only its relationship with knowledge, that is to say, a relationship with its own asexuality, not a relationship to the other, through the body, the senses, affectivity. (Contat, 1996, in Smith, 1998: 74; my translation)

Contat is suggesting that in the encounter body/world and in its translation by the psyche, the subject necessarily confronts the other than themselves, which is at the basis of differentiation: sexual, identifying with the other. In the event of this translation being replaced by a custom-made one, the subject is provided with an interpretation of the other based on a mirroring of the subject's own needs. In retreating from encountering the other as difference, the subject meets the same, their reflective image, that is an undifferentiated narcissistic 'other'.

Moreover, Contat suggests that Kristeva is fighting against the reduction of the mind to a cognition. The manufacturing of images is an acknowledgement and a response to a society in crisis: 'the moment of militancy is over and we are living in a therapeutic age in which we must face up to our problems' (Kristeva, 1992: 20). What Kristeva is deploring, is the form given to 'therapeutic'; society is facing up to a calculation of the human problem rather than an 'aesthetic and moral battle' (Smith, 1998: 74). Contemporary answers to 'crisis' rest on an understanding of 'crisis' limited to what is known of it. The human has become the sum of its parts. As advancement in technology enhances our understanding of human biology and neurobiology, so is the subject becoming a gathering of scattered organs upon which highly specialised techniques can apply 'cure'.

> It would even seem that in some documents of the European Community, they do not talk of "citizens", of "subjects" or of "persons", but of "patrimonial persons": all this to say that we are taken into account (quite!) only as owners and what is new, owning not only material goods (a few centuries accumulating capitals have got us used to this clerical definition), but also owning our organs. (Kristeva, 1998a: 103)

Hence, away from the old Freudian process of filtering, resistance, frustration and pain, the new 'patrimonial person' would then be riddled to enjoy a future of fast, efficient relief from the affliction of human-ness.

> And who can revolt, if the human person is deconsidered, deconsiders him/herself or suffers from an unbearable fragmentation? [...] you can see how impossible it is for this "patrimonial person", disseminated in his/her eventual goods and more or less desirable organs, to live life a free subject, asking questions, reconsidering and changing his/herself. (Kristeva, 1998a: 102-3)

If the unconscious relationship between body and mind is becoming increasingly poor to the point where revolt is no longer conceivable, we can imagine a future where the primary dynamics generating subjective and collective meaning will have become obsolete. Instead, the 'human' subject will be the locus of technological implant of knowledge, that is to say a new form of subjectivity and society that science fiction[11] has already described.

11 See Dick (1997). Philip K. Dick describes a world where humans strive to replace their capacity to emote with technological devices they control. The dynamics body/mind

Between narcissism and robotisation, the human subject is found facing up to a new set of representations: on the one hand the manufacture of their desire, on the other the proliferation of modern diseases such as insomnia, stress, anxiety, psychosis, depression and relational problems. While psychical activity is replaced with pre-fabricated psychical representations of the self, the subject is invaded by signs of the degenerating body. '[T]he pulverisation of identity' (Kristeva, 1998c: 7) is evident in artistic productions (from cinema to the museum). Contemporary spectators are offered images of violence and carnage as representations of the contemporary subject, which they identify also to.

> Instead of a kind which produces totality, created by art practices aspiring to a kind of completion, [...] we notice a cult of the fetish, of kitsch, of ugliness, of installation. These all function as forms of fragmentation which belong to a logic of non-identity [...]. They touch part of our personalities which are already pulverised and dissolving. (Kristeva, 1998c: 8)

The less active the psyche, the more diseased the body marks the reality of the contemporary subject whose unconscious processes do not find enough release in the 'pressure valve' that is language production.

In replacing the subject's psychical activity with ready-made representation, Kristeva believes the subject loses the ability to separate dream from reality. Where stimuli follow their 'normal' path, the subject generates their own images, which characterise the real. Where images generative of subjectivity have been constructed outside the subject's body, the subject consumes pre-processed representations operating like real images and mistaken for the real. As the subject loses the need to create their own images, the very ability to psychically conceive of their self is also lost: it is then the subject's authority upon their own subjectivity that Kristeva sees withering away. Instead, the contemporary subject is authored by the discourse pertaining to a given cultural climate or anchors their scattered identity onto the hypnotic discourse of fundamentalism.

> In our reality of crisis, many believe they can 'get out of it' by subscribing to an 'identity', preferably the most fundamentalist, the one that replaces individual questions with solutions for the mass, the clan. 'I do not know who I am, but I belong with them' [..]. (Kristeva, 1996b)

The dissolution of subjectivity translates in the frustration of the desire to be. Kristeva notices that in the denial of their being, the subject has operated a shift from the desire to be to the desire to belong. 'This shift from being as the foundation of identity to belonging forces a desire to adhere to a group, to an ideology, to a sect [...]' (Kristeva, 1998c: 8). As in the case of media images,

---

are generated by pre-programmed technical operations preferred to the disdained imperfection of human psychical activity.

subscribing to a sectarian group is another aspect of the subject's inability to author their own subjectivity.

These compensatory measures confirm the new living conditions of the contemporary subject: confronting their own impotent discourse. Drives and affects are not represented, their inexpressibility leaving the human subject with the impossibility of verbalising the body. In speaking a language which denies the body its expression and its potency, we are left with a somatic body. The somatic body is automatic, mindless and entirely imprintable, a diseased body from which the ability to represent unconscious drives has been suppressed, and which 'produces' non-organic diseases as an alternative 'language' to language which no longer carries individual desires.

The Failure of the Paternal Function

Having defined and analysed, in *Les nouvelles maladies de l'âme* (Kristeva, 1993), what constitutes the new cultural maladies of individual and collective psychical space, Kristeva then concentrates on the possibility of change in/of society. *Sens et non-sens de la révolte* (Kristeva, 1996a) and *La révolte intime* (Kristeva, 1997a) first propose a theoretical framework questioning and defining the sense of 'revolt' and second illustrate the powers and limits of 'revolt' and of psychoanalytic interpretation. From the psychoanalytic base, the conditions necessary for revolt to take place are exposed. Put on the Freudian stage, the human subject is now experiencing difficulties in verbalising the body. Kristeva demonstrates how in a culture favouring ready-made representations of the human, the subject's capacity to represent drives and affects is increasingly disabled. The resulting split body/mind is engendering on one side a language emptied of its connectedness with the body and on the other a body transforming energy (charge Q) into stress-related illnesses. The markers of the contemporary subject are then impotent discourse and somatic body.

There is a correlation between, on the one hand, drive activity (the psychical transfer of quantitative energy into qualitative energy described earlier) and its symbolic representation, and on the other the maternal and paternal functions. Kristeva has been insisting from her debut that the maternal function prepares the future subject for the paternal function. The maternal is the space where the child begins to encounter the outside world. They experience the satisfaction of bodily needs but also face the frustration of those needs. The maternal figure, in many cases the actual mother, acts as the regulator of this constant fulfilment/disappointment of bodily needs. In the transfer from quantity into quality, she participates in inscribing within the child's psyche the dialectic experience at the basis of symbolic representation. Hence, the maternal and paternal functions are two moments of birth of the human subject.

> The father gives birth, it is true, but in a quite metaphoric sense: he ensures the

> "paternal metaphor", the accomplishment of this transfer of the drive into signification that the mother constantly prepares [the child] for. (Kristeva, 1998a: 97)

The transfer from drive to signification, or from maternal to paternal functions, is enabled through 'the loving father'. The loving father is a Kristevan term also found in Freud as the 'father of individual prehistory' and in Lacan as the 'imaginary father'. In Freud, the 'father of individual prehistory' is a form of archaic father who is neither the oedipal father nor the phallic mother but holds characteristics of both parents. Freud imagines a stage, in subject formation, anterior to the oedipal stage; the pre-linguistic infant starts detaching itself from the dyad mother-child and transfers its desire to a third entity: this transfer would be a direct response to the mother's desire for an other than the baby: the child's father, her father, an extra-familial other or a symbolic other. Lacan will further develop this with his concept of the 'mirror stage'. For Freud, this 'degree zero' of identity - the infant goes through a primary identification with an imaginary loving father - prefigures and announces the future oedipal triangulation which will finalise the process of subjectivation. In Kristeva's work, we find an insistence on the 'loving' aspect of the paternal function within the maternal, as opposed to Freud or Lacan who focus on its sternness. Hence, the Kristevan loving father is a stabilising source both nurturing and securing the maternal function.

The loving father represents the maternal connection with the symbolic, a true paternal metaphor within the maternal. The mother's relation to her father or to her work, for instance, act as a symbolic other authenticating the mother's participation to the socio-symbolic order. The child, wanting to be the focus of the mother's desire, attempts to occupy the place of the loving father. The desire to be in the place of an other than itself prefigures the subsequent identification with the paternal function. In other words, the presence of the paternal within the maternal introduces a third party, other than the mother/child dyad, and sets in motion an Oedipal dynamic on a pre-Oedipal level. This Oedipal dynamic degree zero, or 'Oedipus prime' as Kristeva terms it in *Sens et non-sens* (Kristeva, 1996a: 208), prepares the child to Oedipus proper by inscribing on a psychical level the dualism regulating symbolic representation.

> The father is a guarantor of the symbolic [...]: we are dealing with a new regime, a leap into the psychical representation that the child elaborates through the depressive stage (separation with the mother), through identification with the loving father of individual prehistory, and that he consolidates with Oedipus (the ordeal of phallicism and castration). (Kristeva, 1998a: 97)

The notion of crisis resides here. Kristeva finds that the increasing difficulties faced by the subject in leaping from maternal to paternal are generated by the failing or absence of the paternal function on the Oedipal level. Seeking to understand the root cause of such a crisis of Oedipality logically leads to an analysis of failure in its archaic form on the maternal level. However, such an understanding does not lead to cure.

Kristeva doubts the possibility of revolt in modern society. In Freud's infamous *totemic meal* argument as founding moment of civilisation,[12] revolt can take place on the condition that a dominant unified power be present. This can be in the form of one person (a leader, an authority figure) or a group standing for the One (a political party representing one unifying voice). The paternal entity acts on two levels; on the one hand, it castrates the individual in their desire to break the uniformity of one prescribed identity, forbidding the transgression of paternal prohibition. On the other hand, the subject identifies with paternal power and desires to appropriate this power.

Kristeva argues that the potential for transgression of paternal law and appropriation of its authority, is now threatened. Transgression is a two-fold process: on the one hand it is about the individual questioning their identity and their position in relation to an illusory outside social norm; on the other hand individual commitment to an identity has consequences on the whole social edifice: to define oneself as different and deferred from that 'norm' exposes it as illusory and unnatural; society is then threatened by the precariousness of its existence. The unnatural, illusory and precarious aspects of existence are projected onto the individual in a process of scapegoating the stranger to cultural norms. Hence, society displays a prohibitive attitude towards certain cultural groups.

Two factors participate in hindering transgression. The absence of an authority, the laws of which could be transgressed nullifies the potential for transgression of that law. Second, as we saw earlier, individuals are apprehended as amalgamates of organs and images that they often do not own. The sense of 'person' is altered to such a degree that there is no unified base from which to revolt.

In the first case, the 'failure of ideologies of revolt' (Kristeva, 1996a: 20) has given way to a new world order resting between banality and theatrical performance. As a Bulgarian native, Kristeva is sensitive to the predicament of post-communist eastern countries. She often cites their example to demonstrate how the collapse of Communism has translated into an absence of clearly defined boundaries vis-à-vis socio-political organisation But the collapse of ideologies of revolt does not solely pertain to the East. The western quasi-obsession with 'political correctness' is another example. Political correctness demands that we recognise and treat all differences (ethnic, sexual, etc.) with an attitude of fairness. To the extreme, this equals a levelling of differences that normalises the individual

12 In *Totem and Taboo* (Freud, 1996) Freud imagines an original society organised around the absolute rule of the father. The father has sole access to the women of the group. The sons, envious of his power, kill and eat the father but then are ridden with guilt and, to avoid further murders, renounce on possessing the women who were at the source of their wish for parricide. Hence are established the prime taboos of social organisation: parricide and incest.

into a subjective sameness. For Kristeva, each subject is a deviation from the norm (itself a fluid and changing concept) and as such presents a subjective singularity making each individual unique in their relation to the paternal function. By granting equality amongst all 'deviations' in subjectivity, the paternal function first suppresses the singularity of the individual (Kristeva, 1997a: 22) and ensures the impossibility of revolt against itself. Hence the contemporary paternal function is characterised by a 'vacancy of power'; the function of paternal figures is no longer to enforce laws but to take measures that will ensure their own survival. Western democracies are becoming more and more bureaucratic, with bureaucratic set-up being answerable to itself but not to the people it is supposed to serve, a new form of totalitarianism (Kristeva, 1991). To sum up, the absence of a clear definition of paternal norms leads to the impossibility to locate and encounter the ab-normal. Social subjects then find themselves homogenised into identities of equals, incapable of revolt against the foundations of authority, which becomes corruptible instead of transgressable.

In the second case, it is the locus of revolt which is threatened; revolt takes place on the unified body of the individual, which it fragments and renews, and which confers *jouissance*[13] to thc subject in revolt. But contemporary western society views the subject in terms of 'patrimonial entity' (Kristeva, 1996a: 56) whose value as an individual, once guaranteed by human rights, has become a marketable, technological entity. Examples are plentiful. Neurosciences have gained recognition and value precisely because, in their analysis, the subject's disease can be reduced to a biological process. In the field of psychology, cognitivism enables us to define and know the logics and patterns of human behaviour, and thus to change them (Kristeva, 1997a: 22). Philosophy tends to equate the organic with a pre-verbal, pre-social animality (Kristeva, 1997a: 81-5). We can then suggest that control of the organic subject, defined, refined or transplanted, is in fact a displaced attempt at controlling what threatens the unity of the symbolic subject: the modification of organs would lead to the modification of identity, a manufactured identity strangely comparable to that of science-fiction's androids.

If the locus of revolt is now dispersed, Kristeva warns against the dangers of adopting a deconstructive approach to an already fragmented self: 'One does not deconstruct before having constructed' (Guberman, 1996: 56). Deconstruction is an operation upon already constructed subjectivity, through the supplementary force of, for example, pre-linguistic or extra-linguistic interruption, creating a space for *jouissance*. However, when the sense of subjective and social unity has

---

13 '*Jouissance*' (sensory/sexual enjoyment) is not 'pleasure' in the sense that we consciously give it. 'Jouissance' belongs to the semiotic, unconscious space which, according to Freud, knows no frontiers, and so no dualism: pain and pleasure are both *jouissance*. It is only with language and socialisation that we learn to differentiate between 'good' pleasure (a stroke) and 'bad' pleasure (a slap).

been dispersed, neither the individual nor the collective can easily reassemble, even around the deconstructive principle, so that the possibility of revolt and its jouissance is zero.

Kristeva also warns against the danger of a precipitated rallying around euphoric discourses of damnation or salvation emanating from groups presenting a sectarian or dogmatic attitude (political or religious fundamentalism for instance). 'It sometimes happens that we need to hold on to an ideal, to a prosthetic authority, which becomes more dogmatic than the real father.' (Kristeva, 1996b: online). Between the deconstruction of an already failing paternal function and its hasty reconstruction, Kristeva insists on the urgency to re-think the idea of 'the revolt-culture' (Kristeva, 1996a: 19). Since it is the very existence of culture which is threatened in the present crisis of the paternal function, it has become urgent to theorise a form of culture where revolt has a space. As a psychoanalyst, Kristeva unsurprisingly advocates the re-actualisation of revolt through psychoanalysis, as it offers the patient the possibility to recapture their memory not as a transgressive act but as an act of reconstruction of their past (anamnesia). The process can work because the analyst functions as the normative referent, the paternal entity incarnating prohibition and boundaries against which (and whom) the patient can re-assemble, and begin to articulate their own boundaries. However, Kristeva is also aware that the difficulties and impasses faced by the contemporary subject are also the difficulties faced by psychoanalysis. The analytic scene traditionally rests on a deconstructive type of work against the silent sternness of the analyst and the risks of annihilation and dogmatism highlighted above are also the pitfalls analysts must avoid. Hence, if the saving powers of psychoanalysis are to be salvaged, it will be through a rethinking of contemporary pathologies and a distancing from the purely traditional approach to analysis.

Reassignment of the Paternal Function to the Maternal Disposition

Kristeva observes and analyses the effects of modern living in clinical cases and she notes a dissociation between conscious representation and the expression of affects: the affective charge has been repressed from conscious memory, producing a discourse devoid of desire.

> The language of the depressed person is not psychotic. But it rests upon a denial of the signifier which results from the dissociation of the affect from language. It speaks, but it does not touch me. Affect remains in suffering, so all I can do is weep. The work of the analysis is to reconnect language and affect. (Kristeva, 1998c: 16)

The repression of affects had been identified by Freud who also suggested the return of repressed contents in the form of symptoms. However, in Freud's work, the disconnection language/affect translated in the disabling of his analytical ability. If the markers of the contemporary subject are, as suggested earlier, impotent discourse and somatic body, in Freudian terms, the markers of the contemporary analyst are also an impotent interpretation and a patient's process arrested at the level of somatisation. In short, the failure of the paternal function means that contemporary Freudian psychoanalysis is doomed to failure. The analysis of impotent discourse is where Kristeva distances herself from the Freudian model:

> My major disagreement with Freud in this field [depression and melancholia] lies in the attention that I pay to language. In certain cases, the discourse of the melancholic is so impoverished that one wonders on what could one base an analysis. (Kristeva, 1998c: 16)

While also questioning the possibility to interpret patients' discursive material, she remains confident in the curative potential of psychoanalysis, provided contemporary analysts remain attentive to the reality of today's patients rather than loyal to an outdated psychoanalytic tradition.

Kristeva adds to Freud's return of the repressed another dimension. Faced with contemporary patients presenting an increasingly disabled psychical apparatus, she pioneers new analytic skills, enabling her to hear and interpret the material presented by these new subjects. The collapse of the contemporary subject in verbalising internal matters can be analysed as a collapse of the relationship with the paternal function. The understanding of subjectivity was gathered around a strong paternal image which held the individual and the social unified. The crisis the contemporary subject is facing can be explained through an analysis of a crisis in the paternal function on the one hand. On the other, the failing paternal function is counter-balanced by a resurgence of the subject's experience with the maternal. Although new patients seem unable to represent unconscious contents, their 'language' show traces of the affective charge. The originality of Kristeva's work rests not only on her identifying these traces but also on analysing the carriers of these traces as distinctive and representative of the subject's present situation. Alongside the fabricated image that the contemporary subject impersonates, unconscious contents pertaining to the subject's crisis can be found on 'semiotic vectors'.[14] The inability to verbally associate linguistic symbols with affect indicates a break-up between the subject and the paternal function, a suspension of the psychical exchange between unconscious and conscious. The recognition of semiotic contents on vectors such as the voice, gestures or the gaze, and which are

---

14 In *Les nouvelles maladies de l'âme* (Kristeva, 1993: 159), Kristeva draws a distinction between the semiotic and linguistic signification: within semiotic activity, sensory vectors such as sound, colour, smell, carry the sense of the drive and of affect and are organised within the primary process (unconscious); on the other hand, signification is achieved through linguistic signs which are organised according to logic and syntax (conscious).

not subjected to the arrested process unconscious/conscious, points to a new reality and interpretation of subjectivity. Contents identifiable on semiotic vectors tell the story of the subject prior to the collapse of the paternal function. Those vectors have in common non-verbal, non-symbolisable qualities reminiscent of the individual's pre-linguistic time. In locating them in the person's pre-history, Kristeva also positions them before the Freudian unconscious/conscious model, that is before the subject's Oedipal encounter with the paternal function and the acquisition of language. Those contents are thus not subjected to the unconscious/conscious modalities, but irrupt into the linguistic stream, existing alongside it: semiotic that is not yet unconscious but already constitutive of the unconscious. Hence, the presence of semiotic contents can be interpreted as the marker of the subject's reactualisation of a time anterior to language, that is a return of the subject to maternal time and a reactualisation of maternal time within the subject. Kristeva's intuition of the dissociation between subject and paternal function and of the return to the maternal disposition is transferred, through the analytic work performed with the patient, into conciliative discourse.

The interpretative discourse of the analyst is two-fold. On the one hand, psychoanalytic discourse is a system of representation, that is to say a theoretical, normative construct of reality within which psychical activity occurs and can be known. On the other hand, the relationship between the analyst and the patient mobilises the affect and psychical representations of both protagonists and through the process of transference and counter-transference[15] creates a space where the desire and *jouissance* of the patient are respected and maintained. Throughout *Les nouvelles maladies de l'âme*, Kristeva analyses the role of transference in the psychoanalytic process, but also emphasises the importance of the 'countertransferential mode of listening' (Guberman, 1996: 88) that is required to understand these new *maladies*. In dealing with modern illnesses of the soul, psychoanalysts must acknowledge the newness of these cases that call for a refinement of their methods. In order to understand these new patients, analysts have to loosen their formerly distant attitude and instead, within limits, manifest to their patients a more invested identification with their illnesses. That is to say, they must allow and acknowledge, within the dynamic of counter-transference, the re-actualisation of their own unconscious wishes in response to the analysand's

15 The notions of 'transference' and 'counter-transference' are to be understood in the sense given by J. Laplanche and J.B. Pontalis (1988). Transference, 'a process of actualisation of unconscious wishes' (Laplanche and Pontalis,1988: 455). Unconscious wishes are actualised in a re-play of early events experienced in childhood. These events and the manner in which the child managed them then act as proto-types for future management of similar situations. The patient in psychoanalysis seeks to examine and change the way they manage such actualisation.

Counter-Transference is 'The whole of the analyst's unconscious reactions to the individual analysand - especially to the analysand's own transference.' (Laplanche and Pontalis, 1988: 92).

transferential process. As a consequence of this two-way process, analysts can better apprehend the new *maladie* and renew both the patient's and their own psychical creativity. In this, Kristeva reinstates her belief in the potential offered to all of us by poetic language, which both breaks and renews the social contract. She gives the example of Paul (Kristeva, 1993: 157-70), a young child whose relationship with other speaking subjects was traumatic. His refusal to move from the maternal semiotic space to the socio-symbolic sphere meant that the analysis was resisted. It was discovered that Paul was sensitive to the semiotic vector of music and singing in the sessions with Paul and his mother solved the problem of resistance to symbolic language. In this example, the adults' 'operas' were the locus where symbolic constraints were broken by poetic/musical language and thus the child's relationship with another speaking subject rendered possible. At the same time, the boy's relationship with the social contract could be established, inaugurated by his entry into the discourse of the analyst.

The double aspect of the psychoanalytic tool, normative and affective, has crucial consequences and is in line with the spirit of Kristeva's *œuvre*; she insists on the *poiesis* of the analytic process itself, and argues that this transcends purely theoretical constructs. Psychoanalysis is therefore able to offer the reality of authoritative discourse (symbolic) in balance with transgressive elements (semiotic). More precisely, it highlights 'the necessity of structuring narcissism' (Kristeva, 1998c: 10) and rebuilding the lost ability to relate to the other. The example of Paul exemplifies how the child's subjective development can be arrested in the pre-Oedipal, narcissistic moment of fusion with the mother. Kristeva goes further by suggesting the same problematic in the adult. Although most adults have successfully entered the symbolic sphere, an increasing number have done so at the expense of a disconnection language/affect. The difficulties faced by Paul in acquiring language are equalled in the difficulties of contemporary subjects to recapture their affects. Both find their process arrested where 'normal' process assumes a leap from the maternal to paternal function. 'Thus what is needed is a reassurance or reconstruction of both narcissism, personality and, of course, the subject for there to be a relation to the other' (Kristeva, 1998c: 10). Faced with a changing problematic, the 'maladies of the soul', Kristevan psychoanalysis proposes to link the somatic body and the psyche, by focusing on the moment of crisis: 'I would argue that we must heal our shattered narcissism before formulating higher objectives' (Kristeva, 1998c: 11). In other words, a momentary distancing from Oedipus is needed, in order to accompany the contemporary subject back and through the pre-Oedipal, that is the narcissistic phase, with a view to reconstructing the Oedipal bond. Under these conditions only can the analytic process offer the possibility of finding and translating into language the lost desire of the contemporary subject.

The Possibility of Revolt

> I understand the term revolt etymologically. It means not only political revolution,

> for we also speak of the earth's revolution around the sun, which implies a sense of return, a sense of displacement. In the etymological analysis of the root of the word itself there is also the dimension of unveiling. [...] I understand it also in the Proustian sense of a search for the past - time, anamnesis, a moment when thought is that language which returns to the past, in order to displace us towards progress. It is the past which prepares a renaissance, a rebirth. (Kristeva, 1998c: 6)

'Revolt' is to be interpreted in its relation to movement in space and especially in time. Etymologically, philosophically, in literature and psychoanalytically, 'revolt' indicates a sense of 'return'. Although a cultural perception of revolt entails social destabilisation through the overthrow of the status quo, Freud understood revolt as constancy in the subject's identity and the process of subjectivation as destabilising the subject's being. His vision of the movement of revolt as the constant in the subject, locates the subject against a background of forces of de-stabilisation and division, through which the subject experiences meaning. The fragmented, conflicted 'being' described at the beginning of this chapter, faces the reality of a void and within that the possibility for change, for a trans-formation: on the one hand the re-presentation of the body/mind exchanges in the form of language as an attempt to fill the void, on the other the repression of unsymbolisable elements keeping the void intact and revolt a constant. It is in this incessant movement of revolt that Kristeva envisions the potential for a *reconduction*[16] of identity.

Hence we find in both Freud and Kristeva's work that revolt is related to the notion of return as re-collection: a return to and of memory or a retrospective return experienced as a constant questioning of the self and its truth. In an attempt to understand the formation of identity and map the processes and exchanges at play in the subject, Freud proposed three models of language. In his first model, Freud notices a gap or maladjustment between the biological and the symbolic. The human subject forms a biological reality from birth and the symbolic self only arises with the recognition of modes of mediation/reality construction (representation, language, the constitutive dishonesties of the image). The body and the self are therefore out of phase from the start and the organisation of the psychical apparatus translates this constantly frustrated imperative to fill the gap between the unspeakable original being and its pale wordy expression as self-identity.

Freud's second model has language play an intermediate role between conscious and unconscious, with the latter under the dominance of the former. Language is then positioned in the pre-conscious zone and would enable the speaking subject to have access to the unconscious, unlock the unknown and subject the unconscious to the rules of language, even possibly filling the gap

---

16 In French, *reconduction* means both 'renewal' and 'continuation of'. Here, both meaning and identity are 'reconduits', renewed and continued.

constitutive of the neurotic self. Kristeva sees a certain 'linguistic optimism' (Kristeva, 1996a: 91) in Freud at this stage of his work. As she puts it: 'Freud tends to erase the irreducible alterity of the unconscious in relation to the conscious' (Kristeva, 1996a: 90) which is 'invested with [...] unconscious logics' (Kristeva, 1996a: 90). This second model of language enabled Freud to arrive at an understanding of language as 'a process of *signifiance* founded on the negative' (Kristeva, 1996a: 115), while the dualism present of conscious and unconscious within the subject could work to enable the subject to overcome amnesia, return to the original trauma and cure neurosis. Later on, Freud distanced himself from his second model. However, it remains important in understanding the role assigned to drive activity, in particular its rejection (negativity) and the concept of heterogeneity in Kristeva's work (Kristeva, 1974).

In the third model elicited by Kristeva, Freud finds two forms of trace present in the psyche: those referring to irrepresentable acts (traumatic acts in childhood) and those psychical representations deriving from key processes: identification of the subject with the paternal function, in more general terms, the structuring of subjectivity. Between the two, *signifiance* takes place. Here Freud still uses the idea of language as an intermediate between unconscious and conscious but no longer defines it in relation to consciousness; instead, he envisages unconscious representations as referring to 'material which remains unknown' (Kristeva, 1996a: 105), whereas pre-conscious representations 'would be associated to verbal representation' (Kristeva, 1996a: 105). In other words, conscious representation is possible only if the material transformed exists as memory traces in the unconscious, and in reverse, conscious representations can be internalised and take the form of hallucination or error. Hence, language can no longer be considered as a reliable bridge between conscious and unconscious, but the impossibility of iteration allows it to become the place of symbolisation, meaning that error, resistance and hallucinations are at least partially constitutive of the subject's symbolic universe. In parallel, Kristeva points out that in the act of revolt, the revolter remains the subject of and subjected to acts of language and to its errors. There appears to be no escape from the place of *signifiance* and therefore from negativity.[17]

---

17 Freud's optimistic views considered that *signifiance* rests on the rejection of drive activity (negativity) as it is transformed into language. The conscious would then be the place where unconscious processes can be translated and known. Although Freud modified this second model, his concept of 'negativity' permits an understanding of the dissociation between drive activity and linguistic activity. Kristeva repeatedly returns to this dissociation, which she sees as a marker of modern day subjectivity. We shall return to this throughout this piece. Negativity also remains central in the work of the followers of Lacan. Lacan's idea of the unconscious being structured like a language refers to this second model. But Lacanian and post-Lacanian psychoanalysis do not recognise the importance of the drive. Lacanians consider that since the drive can be known through language, any mention of 'something' outside language is a myth. Kristeva also points out that if the

Kristeva argues that 'signifiance is made accessible to psychoanalytic experience through three modalities [...]: identification, [...] idealisation, [...] sublimation' (Kristeva, 1996a: 115- 6). We have seen earlier the difficulties encountered by the subject vis-à-vis identification and idealisation: in a social climate where the guarantor of the symbol, the paternal function, is failing, idealisation and identification are also failing. Freud's third term, 'sublimation', clarifies the way language takes place within a process of negativity or rejection of drive activity. In sublimation, the subject can become the object of the life drive (Eros) through a process of identification with the 'father of individual prehistory'. The object of Eros is the self; sublimation deals with a narcissistic libido rather than a sexual libido; in this process, the death drive and the life drive are disassociated:

> [...] the ego cuts itself from erotic impulse [...]. Such a transformation [...] frees the death drive. [...]. In other words: the *death drive* is thus, *from the start*, inscribed in the *process of subjectivation*, or in the constitution of the ego, as an initial and indispensable stage in the *mutation of the drive into signifiance*. (Kristeva, 1996a: 120- 1)

Under the threat of the death drive, the subject operates a transformation of the quantitative charge of the drive (physical/body) into a qualitative charge (psychical/mind), that is to say *signifiance*. Because this process of rejection of the drive activity repeats itself, it becomes a negativity: negativity is at once a positive assertion of the symbolic and a denial of the content of the drive.

Freud's concept of sublimation can be linked with a certain aesthetic practice whereby the object of narcissistic desire is language itself: literary and theoretical practice, analytic work, etc. By positing negativity as the basis for *signifiance* and *signifiance* as the space for change and transformation, Kristeva exposes the contemporary definition of revolt as flawed. Two examples can be put forward here: revolution as a non-sense of revolt and a certain type of psychoanalytic practice that limits the power of revolt. In revolution, revolt as being reduced to an act contesting a given societal and/or political order in the hope of replacing it with another society/political order. The psychoanalytic field is also witnessing a trend towards understanding revolt as the expression of the patient's unfulfilled desires; the role of the psychoanalyst is then to help that patient overcome frustration and attain their goal (career enhancement for example). 'The best outcome of analysis is not the adaptive normalisation which does occur in some schools of analysis, in the United States and France, for instance. The best outcome is a recognition of permanent conflictuality' (Kristeva, 1998c: 15).

---

unconscious is under the control of the conscious, then a 'mathematisation' of the unconscious is possible. This leads to a cognitivist approach whereby the unconscious is considered in terms of automatic acts. For this reason, Kristeva remains critical towards cognitivism and insists that it offers an understanding of 'unawareness' rather than of the unconscious.

The effect of an analysis aiming for adaptive subjectivity is to arrest the process of revolt, by equating it with the wish for a better future and abandoning revolt once that future has become reality. This concept of revolt transforms revolt into norm, even dogma. Kristeva's aim is not to arrest the process of *signifiance* and revolt, but on the contrary to question and open language to *signifiance*. 'Thus the ideal result is that you are enabled to transform what cannot be analysed into some form of creativity. It could be maternity, friendship, teaching. It could be writing' (Kristeva, 1998c: 15). Hence, the rehabilitation of the role of negativity (as opposed to negation) is paramount in the making of the subject and of society. Kristeva's work is a plea to re-think the very sense of revolt without which this culture is in danger of becoming a culture for robots.

Conclusion

From her début, Kristeva proposes a shift of emphasis from the traditional, Saussurian model of linguistic towards a 'speaking subject in process'. The former she finds suppresses aspects of human communication in order to present language as a unified product to which the subject is assimilated and through the study of which he or she can be known. Instead, she shows that language is made of two dimensions, symbolic and semiotic, the one classifiable, the other exceeding order. Her early work seeks to explain the passage from the one to the other and describes how the symbolic act is both the transformation and repression of the subject's corporeality. Because it suppresses the excessive dimension of language, modern linguistics misses out on the analysis of what oppresses individuals and makes them foreign to themselves and their environment. In retrospect, Kristeva's endorsement of the psychoanalytic model as that which will enable her to succeed in her enterprise has proved both fruitful and a limitation. The development of what could be termed a 'theory of marginality' has impacted theoretical understandings of marginalisation (sexism, racism, etc.) and facilitated the move towards a third wave of feminism (French feminism). But, loyal to Freud's idea of the 'primacy of the phallus', Kristeva has also refused to consider an economy of the subjects that would be based on anything other than the father. The demise of the primacy phallus (or paternal function) is where post-Freudian theorists now see a contemporary crisis. To understand crisis, we must go back to Freud's model of language production.

The Freudian model is based upon a series of stages beginning with the individual's perception (nervous system), through protective filters controlling the influx of stimuli, to their organisation into abstract representations. Psychical health depends upon how well the individual negotiates the movement between what can be known (conscious representation) and what should remain hidden (unconscious repression). Hence, the process of 'meaning-making' is founded upon separation: rejection of unwanted information and transformation of the world as perceived into the verbally known. In short, castration, in the sense of having one's corporeal potency rejected and/or replaced, is prime to becoming a meaningful subject. For post-Freudians like Kristeva, this primacy is today threatened. The Freudian model is reversed in such a way that corporeality is no longer the site from which meaning is generated and castration no longer negotiated. Instead, ready-made (that is already censored) information is supplied to individuals by outside sources (the media mainly but also consciousness-altering chemicals, stereotyped language, etc.) who use it as a source for 'identity-making' without the necessity to deal with the awkward body/mind contingency. This reversal, or replacement of 'castration', translates in an increase in psychosomatic illnesses (the body expresses itself in ways other than verbal) and a decrease in the importance given to the paternal function.

Faced with the fading away of the paternal role, Kristeva advocates a reassessment of its function. In this, she distances herself from tradition. Freud's work was dependent upon his patients providing him with the material necessary for analysis, namely speech. The Freudian patient's speech showed the process of castration: it was constituted of linguistic material per se and repressed material passing through censorship as affect. In the post-Freudian world, castration is avoided and speech appears devoid of affect. The (psycho)analysis of how the patient battled with body/mind constraints and came to 'make meaning' is not possible. Without the involvement of some paternal agency (castration), Freud's psychoanalysis is itself disabled. To put it bluntly and as Freud admitted himself, he could treat neurosis but failed in the treatment of psychosis. And psychosis is on the increase if we believe post-Freudians. The difference between the two comes down to the question of the Oedipus Complex. For Freud, the Oedipal phase makes the subject and their neuroses while psychosis is the sign of a failed Oedipus. But while Freud considered other, pre-Oedipal founding moments, he discarded the possibility of a pre- or ab-Oedipal subjectivity. To find an answer to the contemporary subject's enigma, post-Freudians must reconsider Freud's firm stand vis-à-vis Oedipus and the primacy of the phallus.

Kristeva proposes to 'treat' crisis and revive the Freudian model through a compromise. Psychoanalysis must, in the first place, leave aside its dogmatic allegiance to Oedipus and re-trace the subject's evolution that led to the failure of the Oedipal model. Her study shows that, contrary to Freud's belief pre-Oedipality can be analysed. Through a theorising of the semiotic, she finds traces of the subject's 'lost' corporeality in spite of the disconnection body/mind and in spite of the absence of affect. But this innovation in psychoanalytic theory also serves the traditional model, for her method is ultimately the structuring of the pre-Oedipal material and the re-instating of Oedipus as founding moment.

Chapter 2

The Genesis of the Subject: The Paternal Function

The Traditional and the Kristevan 'Family'

In *Le féminin et le sacré* (Kristeva and Clément 1998b), Catherine Clément suggests that the separation between maternal and paternal function in contemporary society begins with the separation between maternity and paternity. Maternity is the mother's unquestionable domain, with gestation and birth giving her indubitable maternal claim upon the newborn. Paternity, however, is more problematic. Paternity claims rely solely on the mother's word and that uncertainty on the father's part regarding his paternity has given rise to an array of cultural events aiming at reassuring him and securing his claims over the child's paternity.

> For to accede to paternity, fathers need a good "rehab" session. No society without solemn moments when the child is passed over to paternal law. Initiation rites of all kinds, circumcision, excision, seclusion in forests, bodily scarification… (Kristeva and Clément, 1998b: 137)

If the child's link to the maternal appears unproblematic, the connection with the paternal requires the active enactment of a 'second birth' which Clément seems to deplore while Kristeva defends 'these 'baptisms' and other acceptation rites of children in the symbolic line of the father.' (Kristeva and Clément, 1998b: 165). Whether the separation of parental interest in the child is to be deplored or praised will not be discussed here. But we can note that the debate is very much alive amongst Anglo-American researchers in particular. Under the general terms of 'French Feminism', discussions on the relationship between biology, gender identity and parental functions are found. Kelly Oliver (2000) for instance deplores like Clément the segregation of the sexes into one parental role, which imprisons the mother into a corporal role and the father in a disembodied, cultural role. In the view of Clément's suggestion of a patriarchal 'snatching away' from the mother of the child by the father, we can also note that Kristeva's praise of the re-birth of the child into the paternal function is founded upon a different, more metaphoric, understanding of parental categories. It is this metaphoric understanding of 'father' and 'mother' that interests us.

In *From Klein to Kristeva*, Doane and Hodges (1992) accuse Kristeva of constructing the mother from a biologically determined stance and ignoring cultural reality when assessing identity crisis: 'Rarely in recent psychoanalytic feminism has femininity seemed more detached from cultural determinants than it does in Kristeva's account' (Doane and Hodges, 1992: 76).[1] They describe how, in *Soleil noir*, Kristeva (1987) locates the source of melancholia in women to a loss of the maternal she describes as the 'Thing'. Doane and Hodges's analysis of Kristevan logic is interesting because it epitomises the interpretative differences (and misunderstandings) that separate continental and Anglo-American thought.

Anne-Marie Smith (1998) has described the cultural differences between a French readership and an Anglo-American one, differences that give rise to misunderstandings of Kristevan theory.

> The French Lacanian tradition reads Freud as a study of language and Kristeva must be situated firmly in this context. It is impossible to comprehend the full import of her work if one leaves out its Freudianism. (Smith, 1998: 8)

Badinter (1981) further describes the difference between a Freudian and Anglo-American feminist interpretation of women's predicament. While Anglo-American feminists such as Kate Millett believe 'that the answer is to be found in the nature of patriarchal society and in the situation it forces on women (Badinter, 1981: 294-5), Freud preferred 'an etiology of childhood experience based upon the biological fact of anatomical difference'' (Badinter, 1981: 295). The debate then can be reduced to patriarchal culture versus the mother as source of women's discontent. When Doane and Hodges object to a Kristevan practice proposing 'a discourse that refuses to discuss the social, political, and economic situation of women (except as symptoms of an archaic relation to a maternal object)' (Doane and Hodges, 1995: 77), they indeed bracket out the essence of the Kristevan spirit, that any cultural aspect is indeed a symptom of the early development of the human subject, 'a representation and an emotive, aesthetic issue' (Smith, 1998: 11). Thus, for Kristeva, to discuss the social, the political or the economic situation is to discuss the process by which an individual (male or female) or a group have come to position themselves within the maternal/paternal dynamic. Smith (1998) firmly believes that the source of misunderstanding is to be found in the cultural difference that separates an Anglo-American and a French tradition. Anglo-American thought rests upon a protestant or puritanical tradition interested in testing a theory (like Freudian theory) 'against the demands of empiricism' (Smith, 1998: 8). Such a tradition resists the 'unabashed avowals of desire and seduction and distinct forms of identification [...] as narcissistic or uncritical and needs to turn [them] into either abstraction or plain speech' (Smith, 1998: 8). Such a need

1 To define Kristeva as a 'feminist psychoanalyst' is to ignore her suspicion and avoidance of feminist groups. In her words: 'I have many problems with the feminist movement because I am uncomfortable with all militant movements. [...] Let's just say that I found that these groups often adhere to the very dogmas they opposed. As a result, I never joined any of the feminist groups' (Guberman, 1996: 7).

translates (figuratively and actually) in a misuse of Kristeva's terminology. Smith's work has useful example that elucidate the translation difficulty.

When she discusses sexual development, Kristeva's use of the pronoun 'il' ('he') to refer to the young individual does not necessarily mean that her research addresses the subjectivation of the male child only. More often than not, it is a generic pronoun encapsulating both sexes (one reason could be that the French 'enfant', 'child', from the latin 'infans' is classed as a neutral noun, which in French is assimilated to the masculine; hence a masculine article or pronoun indicates sometimes a male child, sometimes a female child, sometimes both). There is also a confusion in Anglo-American interpretations of Kristeva (Doane and Hodges, Oliver for instance) between reality and its representation. Doane and Hodges assume that the terms 'feminine' and 'maternal' connote 'woman' while 'masculine' and 'symbolic' pertains to men. As Smith put it, 'French feminists do not problematise the feminine in the same way. Cixous and Irigaray, for example, are more concerned with the cultural importance of representing and imagining femininity in its alienable difference than with arguing with parity' (Smith, 1998: 10). Such linguistic differences make interpreting Kristeva's work difficult for an English speaking readership because the interpreter must transpose such elusive terminology into an either/or dialectic that is not present in the original text.

One could think that the ambiguity could, partly at least be lifted by a clarification over terminology. Yet Kristeva has frequently refused to do so. At times, her work has even encouraged such ambiguity, but few critics have pondered upon the reasons for Kristeva's insistence on creating ambiguities in the text. To be sure, the debate over biological and metaphorical categories resides in rendering ambiguity significant. To return to Doane and Hodges, these critics fail to understand the full weight of terminology. When they attempt to clarify the role of the mother in cases of melancholia, they assimilate the terms 'Thing' and 'mother'. In Kristeva's logic, the use of 'Thing', as opposed to 'thing' or 'object', attempts to dissociate the actual object of loss (the mother) from its affective reality for the infant. At that stage of her work (in 1987), Kristeva, as a psychoanalyst, analyses early experience of loss in a baby who does not yet have any apprehension of a totalised other than itself, but is engaging with pre-objects experienced on an affective level. Thus any attempt to refute Kristevan logic with comments such as 'the mother is defined as *the* problem for her female patients' (Doane and Hodges, 1992: 76) shows a misunderstanding of the psychoanalytic dynamics that animate the infant's pre-linguistic experience on the one hand, and a misreading of Kristevan terminology on the other.

Second, Doane and Hodges insist that Kristeva assumes the link between the mother and the lost object' (Doane and Hodges, 1992: 76) and object to her making of the mother an *origin* to be explained rather than an *effect* of the analyst's own representational practice.' (Doane and Hodges, 1992: 77). They object that the origin of melancholia may not be found in the biological origin of the melancholic woman, but in the cultural (political, economic, psychoanalytic, etc.) construction of that 'woman'. Although their criticism fairly records the often neglected impact of the social context upon the subject's predicament, they fail to understand Kristeva's psychoanalytic viewpoint whereby the analyst's job is not to change the world to make it a better place for the analysand but to empower the analysand to position themselves symbolically (through language) within a given socio-symbolic reality. This symbolic act is in Kristevan psychoanalysis unique to each analysand and the attempt to universalise female analysands' predicament as a collective oppressed by patriarchy is to misunderstand the very dynamic of the psychoanalytic scene.

Finally, Doane and Hodges tend to read the terms 'mother' and 'father' as the actual flesh-and-blood parents of the subject. Although the terms are often ambiguous, sometimes referring to the actual parents, sometimes referring to their symbolic function, to read accounts of subjectivity solely from 'a tradition which associates the maternal with enclosure or domesticity' (Smith, 1998: 11) and the paternal as the patriarchal oppressor is to opt for a separatist logic which can but misinterpret Kristeva's work. Analysing the 'imaginary father', they fail to consider it from a symbolic viewpoint:

> Kristeva, then, restores the father as a savior, though she is careful to mitigate his power: "the father of individual prehistory" is not the stern, oedipal father and is associated with the mother's desire (understood as the mother's desire for the phallus). This new and improved father does not prove especially liberatory for women. The father of individual prehistory is said to enable a woman's "triumph over the death-bearing mother", a locution that strongly enforces stereotypical sexual differences (*Black Sun* 79). (Doane and Hodges, 1992: 66)

'The father of individual prehistory' is not a Kristevan term but a Freudian one; Doane and Hodges choose to ignore the importance of the Freudian legacy in Kristeva's work and omit to assess Kristeva's re-interpretation of Freud's expression, an exercise which would have clarified Kristeva's position regarding the relationship between 'the father of individual pre-history' as parental metaphor and its enactment in the actual parents. In short, the aim of Doane and Hodges's analysis is to prove that Kristeva's construction of parental categories comes down to associating 'mother' with deadly and 'father' with triumphant. Consequently, Kristeva is made a participant in women's oppression. The analyst's imaginary partakes in a patriarchal conspiracy against women and is the real source of their oppression. Doane and Hodges's work bears the question of how to read Kristeva's work. John Lechte (1991) attempts to answer this question:

> What is sometimes difficult to grasp in Kristeva's work, and perhaps more difficult for an Anglo audience to accept, is the fact that, for the theorist of the semiotic, there is no clear separation between art, society, and language on the one hand, and the individual subject as the outcome of the interaction between the semiotic and the symbolic on the other. This means, for one thing, that Kristeva does not separate out the (western) societal category of 'family' from the dynamic psychoanalytic triad of mother-child-father. As Kristeva sees it, the category 'family' and the societal beings, mothers, fathers

> and children are exclusively of the symbolic order. Moreover, society itself is a product of the symbolic. (Lechte, 1991: 130- 1)

Lechte stresses that Kristevan terminology borrows some of its terms from everyday language but does not use these terms in their common sociological understanding. When the family is described, terms may refer to the societal beings mother, father and child but more importantly describe a dynamic staging three 'protagonists': the maternal (the energy generated by the activity of the drive), the paternal (the symbolic activity giving form to this energy) and the subject (the product of the former two). The subject may be an individual; it may not. A speech without limits can testify 'to a mother who is entirely accessible' (Lechte, 1991: 131); 'the precision and order of every paragraph' in utterances can suggest too visible a father. The product of maternal/paternal is not confined solely to speech. In a work of art such as Pollock's painting 'Blue Poles' 'the rhythms and flows of 'Blue Poles' are equivalent to 'Pollock's battle against the symbolic father''. (Lechte, 1991: 131). The notion of 'subject' is not so much the actual individual but its enactment in language, art, generally any space of signification. The subject is thus found in any production generated by the interaction maternal/paternal: language, social organisations, art, etc. Here lie the reasons behind Kristeva's refusal to separate on the one hand the question of subjectivity from the psychoanalytic framework, and on the other societal 'events' (politics, history, art, etc.) from the process of subjectivation. In this sense, we could go further than John Lechte and consider that society is not so much the product of the symbolic as a product of the interaction maternal/paternal, a symptom of subjectivity. Indeed Kristeva's treatment of subjectivity goes further. Each individual subjectivity is also the site of monumental history.

> In *Civilisation and its Discontents*, Freud tries to explain the preservation of the memory-trace [...] namely that the psyche is an entity with 'a long and copious past...in which nothing that has once come into existence will have passed away and all the earlier phases of development continue to exist alongside the latest one'. But Freud belonged to an era with a different conception of psychic space, and while Kristeva follows Freud in many things, she believes that the peculiar nature of life today is working to erase the memory-trace and hence, psychic depth. (Smith, 1996: 191)

Memory-trace is being erased by two factors: the replacing of psychic activity by ready-made images the aim of which is to compensate for the impoverishment of psychical activity. We have then a potentially irreversible situation where 'the universal banality which she [Kristeva] feels is growing today, fed by the increasingly sophisticated powers of the media to disseminate a shallow, pleasure-seeking discourse' (Smith, 1996: 192) makes up for an increasingly disused psyche. Banality (or the ordinary) is the normative effect such discourse has on the subject. Kristeva is suggesting the universalisation of subjectivity due to the fast advances in information technology and the attraction provided by the media in their supplying the subject with instant gratification. The new universal subject is then the opposite of the singular, the original, which constitutes the essence of Kristevan subjectivity. To resist this normalisation of the human subject, and move beyond the crisis it constitutes for contemporary subjectivity, entails several things: the individual must step away from this act of 'collective subjectivation' and return to a more individual approach to development. This means a return to and of the memory-traces initiated by Freud and further elaborated by Kristeva in her analysis of the maternal function. It also means a recognition of the father's death and its mourning. In effect, the failure of the paternal function drives the subject to return to a time anterior to that failure in order to reconstruct its subjective history, that is they[2] must first mourn the loss of the paternal before encountering the maternal.

Kristeva attempted to illustrate the need to recognise the father's death in her second novel *Le vieil homme et les loups* (1991). The narrator mourns the death of two father figures (the character of the old man and her own father) who die because their 'world that separated good and evil is failing' (Smith, 1996: 194). Failure means the collapse of personal ideals and beliefs about themselves and others: the two characters are rejected as the embodiment of a successful paternal function around which the social sphere can be constructed. The 'father' or paternal function is thus 'killed' by a new social order that no longer recognises a certain ethics of life socially valuable.

> Thus what gives the novel its revelatory thickness and gives it a shape resistant to the crushing forces of media-fed banality is the personal act of mourning, and in particular, the act of mourning a father. (Smith, 1996: 197)

Kristeva is proposing an historical journey upstream in order to recapture the moment of failure and transcend it. As Smith put it 'if there is no longer a wall between good and evil, how can this difference be maintained?' (Smith, 1996: 199). The answer lies in a revisiting of what constitutes differentiation in the human subject, that is the pinpointing and study of the moment (or moments) the individual becomes a symbolic subject.

Kristeva's work implies that the subject is subjected to a form of 'imprinting' of human histories upon themself. A study of her texts, *Sens et non-sens* in particular, suggests three. Neither she, nor her critics gather the three different historical timeframes we are proposing now. My suggestion in considering the possibility of subjectivation as the symptom of three 'histories' helps to clarify the position of the contemporary subject within a historical continuum. Such an interpretation of history justifies the idea of a Genesis of the paternal function and its preservation as the only viable function in 'saving' the subject in crisis. Furthermore, the crisis of subjectivity could also be interpreted as the end of paternal time and the rise of

2 Smith (1996) points out that Kristeva often sees women as privileged in their potential to grieve: 'Sons, Kristeva seems to imply, are still too busy trying to put the father to death, but women keep believing and investing in the personal' (Smith, 1996: 199).

another social and subjective organisations we cannot name. Although Kristeva acknowledges this different interpretation, she has tended to refuse to discuss it in detail as she believes subjectivity is first and foremost founded upon the triadic Oedipal structure. Any suggestion of another type of structure - triadic with the maternal founding socialisation or dyadic with the erasure of difference maternal/paternal - is for her not analysable because it is the domain of speculation and/or science fiction.

Within the context of this second chapter, we are interested in how the cult of the paternal (commonly referred to as 'patriarchy') has come to prevail in religious and psychoanalytic discourses. The first historical clue we will consider again later is the idea that the cult of the paternal would be born from the destruction of a previous social order gathered round the cult of the maternal (the Minoan-Mycenaean civilisation). Paternal order succeeded maternal organisation and human beings would have kept an unconscious collective memory of this first historical event that marked the history of subjectivity. Subjectivation would then be a re-enactment of the genesis of the paternal function triumphing over the maternal. In turn, this collective memory of the superseding of the maternal by the paternal becomes a pattern, which every human is born into. We then find a second apprehension of historical imprint upon the subject, one that suggests that the paternal function precedes birth and the newborn's innate ability for symbolisation, an ability that parental functions will activate. We will return to the importance of this pre-programming of the newborn in chapter four. Finally, Kristeva's work describes the subject from their individual history. Following Kleinian theory, she puts forward maternal time as preceding and preparing the child for the paternal function. However, Kristeva's does not, like her predecessors (Freud, Lacan, Klein), divide maternal and paternal into two distinct either/or spheres the subject would find themself in. As Lechte (1991) explains:

> The limit of phenomenological research is that it always, and inevitably, refers back to an ultimate unity, a posited subject of experience, a Cartesian subject in fact which is already an 'I', already the result of the distinction between subject and object.' (Lechte, 1991: 134)

Kristeva posits the idea of 'subject' from a different angle on two accounts: first, she agrees that the process of subjectivation requires some identification to a symbolic function posited before the symbolic subject can exist, as suggested above. In fact, part of the 'success' of symbolic birth rests on the pre-existence of a 'good enough' paternal function through which the subject forms identifications. In analysing the crisis of the contemporary subject, Kristevan theory makes of the failure of the paternal function to provide stable enough paternal agencies the corner stone of that crisis. Second, while positing an already-there of the paternal function, Kristeva adds a second term, the semiotic, as the foundation of this function.

> In summary, the semiotic is both a kind of material base for the symbolic and *sui generis*. It cannot be grasped in conceptual thought […]. (Lechte, 1991: 132)

The semiotic is at once part of symbolic production and an 'entity' in its own right, existing before symbolic production can occur. With the symbolic and the semiotic, we add the third of the Kristevan triadic family, the subject. More to the point, this subject is the expression of the interaction symbolic/semiotic.

Kristevan theory is then changing the problematic regarding the paternal and the maternal. Rather than simply have the former preceding or triumphing over the latter, the boundary that separate the two terms is permeable: the maternal already contains the paternal function and the paternal function operates before the maternal function sets in motion. Moreover, the positioning of the one within the other becomes a fertile dynamic producing so to speak more 'subjectivity'. Following such logic, it becomes difficult to consider the paternal/maternal/subject as a source of oppression as Doane and Hodges see it. Their work, as we saw, epitomises the quasi impossibility to read Kristeva from a non-psychoanalytic (and possibly a non-Kristevan) base for the differences in understanding such a reading causes. In Kristeva's own words:

> […]generative theory concentrates its attention on what we have called a *symbolic* functioning, sustained by a cartesian subject foreclosed to the signifier. In consequence, this theory is not interested in the *process* of the subject which may be glimpsed in the semiotic processes of condensation and transposition. (Kristeva in Lechte, 1991: 142)

A reading of Kristeva's work will then report on symbolic functioning[3] understood as the consequence of a process that precedes it. More precisely, the analysis of pre-symbolic 'mechanisms' describes the crisis Kristeva believes the contemporary subject is experiencing. Such an analysis implies, as we saw, embracing the psychoanalytic spirit. I am therefore proposing to pause a little longer on psychoanalytic narratives in contemporary culture, precisely its origin and current situation vis-à-vis patriarchy.

---

3 In analysing Kristeva's work, the terms symbolic, social, Oedipal and paternal are so closely related that they can be considered as interchangeable. Similarly, the terms semiotic, archaic, pre-Oedipal and maternal are used as near equivalents.

The Paternal Function in Religious and Psychoanalytic Narratives

A Common Discourse

In *The Religious and Romantic Origin of Psychoanalysis*, Suzanne Kirschner (1996) demonstrates the religious origin of psychoanalysis. She shows clearly the commonalities between the religious and psychoanalytic metaphors, hence defining the capture of the one discourse by the other. 'In its earliest form, that narrative chronicles man's creation, fall out of unity with God, and redemption via reunion with God' (Kirschner, 1996: 4). This early narrative pictures a collective search for the ideal redeemed self: mankind's fall and salvation through God. It was followed by a more internalised narrative concomitant with the rise of Protestant mysticism. With Protestantism the Judaeo-Christian search for salvation is transformed into an individual quest for self idealisation through 'visions of the soul's election by God or reunion with him' (Kirschner, 1996: 5). This internalisation and individualisation of the religious narrative and of its ideals was further secured and secularised through the Romantic movement: Romanticism is typified by the 'mal du siècle' (Peyre, 1979: 107) coined by Alfred de Musset (1993), that is a 'Romantic-type' hero contemplating their existential angst in their search for ideals: 'suffering, frustration, and various forms of moral "evil"' (Kirschner, 1996: 7) mark the Romantic hero's struggle to form identifications. Today, Kirschner believes that what defines Anglo-American culture, '[t]he ideals of self-reliance, self-direction, and even intimacy are articulated in terms that recapitulate several Judaeo-Christian images of salvation' (Kirschner, 1996: 5) and are found in a fourth type of narrative: the psychoanalytic narrative. Kirschner's study clearly leaves out classical Freudian psychoanalysis, found for instance in France and South America, to concentrate on Anglo-American culture.

In the light of the contemporary return to and of religion elicited by Kristeva, Kirschner's historical positing of psychoanalysis after religion could be questioned. Michel Monroy (2000) enumerates the many similarities between the mechanisms experienced in a psychotherapeutic setting and those found in sects, in recruiting and creating a dependence on the leader. Certain contemporary religious groups, in particular American born, will today use the findings of ego psychology (cognitive in particular) to the advantage of their particular religious message.[4] The recruiting is founded upon a research and knowledge connected to the context of

4 For instance, the use of positive assertions in which the 'ego-terms' (I, me, etc) are replaced by terms referring to God, hence shifting ego assertion to faith assertion. In both cases, we are dealing with a linguistic programming of the self towards a chosen aim, symbolised in the ideal other with whom 'I' wishes to identify. See: Monroy, Michel (2000). The importance of identification with this other is central to an understanding of the contemporary crisis of identity. In Kristeva's opinion, it is this identification with the other which has become problematic. This point will be emphasised further throughout the thesis and more particularly in chapter three and the final chapter.

psychotherapy and 'the therapeutic methods are wrongly attributed to the master's discoveries' (Monroy, 2000: 47). Monroy's study echoes Kristeva's concern about the return of fundamentalism, be it religious, social or political and about the appropriation of the psychoanalytic tool, albeit with a deviated hypnotic objective rather than a desire to facilitate subjectivation. Monroy finds that few survivors of sects seek psychotherapeutic help, partly because they distrust a system that rests upon the same mechanisms as the one they fled. Compared with Kirschner's views, we have then a reversal where religion is now following psychoanalysis.

Whether the religious discourse precedes or follows psychoanalysis is not the question we are asking here. The interest lies in the recurring subordination of the one discourse by the other. Both narratives are testimonies of a trans-historical human search for identification with a form of strong paternal agency. Kristeva argues that the weakening of the paternal function, which will be discussed in chapter three, is counterbalanced by the emergence of groups whose common denominator is a gathering around a strong paternal agency and against a common enemy. Examples are plentiful: the small-scale sects, the official political groups such as the French National Front, the BNP, the more sinister terrorist groups, etc. For both religion and psychoanalysis, the paternal is the subject's 'maker'. This search for a paternal function, and the reasons for searching, forms the basis of both narratives. But, Kristeva believes that the human subject is today failing to find a suitable paternal function, causing a crisis in subjectivity. A comparison between the religious and psychoanalytic discourse highlights the differences that separate the two in their understanding of 'paternal function' and shows why Kristeva dismisses religion as solution and advocates psychoanalysis.

Similarities and Differences

Kristeva published in 1985 a long essay clarifying, like Kirschner did (1996), the similitude between religious and psychoanalytic discourses, but also claiming the autonomy of the psychoanalytic narrative from the religious one. Speaking of the experience of analysis, she states:

> In substance, the subject in analysis, or the analysand if you like, says this: "I am suffering from an archaic trauma, often sexual, deep down a narcissistic wound, that I relive by displacing it upon the person of the analyst. Here and now, the all-powerful agent (father or mother...) of my being well or unwell, is him. This invisible drama, enactment of the deep sense of my discourse, supposes that I grant the analyst considerable power; but the trust I give him implies above all the love I feel for him and that I pre-suppose he feels for me." (Kristeva, 1985: 11)

If the subject identifies with an 'all-powerful agent', it takes many forms: analyst, father, mother, the loving God of the New Testament (I, Jn, IV, 8). The diversification of the form taken by the 'all-powerful' translates the individual's capacity to identify as a repetitive act, a faculty arching back to the earlier generic event of primary identification.

> Freud saw, at the dawn of psychical experience, a primary identification consisting of the "direct and immediate transference" of the forming ego towards the "father of individual prehistory" [...] whose permanence ensures the prime stabilisation of the subject [...]. (Kristeva, 1985: 38)

The 'father of individual prehistory', by virtue of its potency, stability and permanence, enables the individual to become a subject. Because it belongs to the pre-nominal experience of the individual, it also has the capacity to be displaced onto actual agents named father, mother, analyst, god, party, etc. With the 'father of individual prehistory', Freud and Kristeva are attempting to describe a psychical mechanism by which the individual can endow, through transferential processes, another entity with the power of life and death. Hence, the dynamic which animates religious fervour or analytic transference stems from the same psychical mechanism, identification with what Kristeva often refers to as the 'paternal function'.

The term 'paternal function' refers to two moments of the individual's capacity to identify and is represented through two figures of the religious/psychoanalytic narrative. First, a primary moment when the pre-linguistic subject identifies with the 'father of individual pre-history' or the loving God of the Bible. The paternal function enables an archaic type of identity and subjectivity, preceding identification 'proper' and preparing the individual for it. Succinctly, the infant in maternal care attempts to 'be' the sole centre of interest for the mother. It notices that the mother is also fulfilled by other 'agents' than the child (by her partner, her job, etc.) and tries to become this other agent. What fulfils the mother, and is other than the child, is the paternal function. In its attempt to emulate the other, the infant learns the process of symbolisation of its self. Kristeva also identifies a secondary moment of the paternal function when the subject symbolically re-enacts primary identification on a linguistic level, that is the paternal function enables the displacement of deeper archaic identification onto agents the subjects can now name.

A further distinction between the two moments of the subject's encounter with the paternal function can be made. Where the pre-linguistic paternal function represented a stable, loving agent (held by maternal care), its transference onto the linguistic sphere infers a displacement onto the Oedipal scene and the subjection of the individual to paternal law that Freud and Lacan have described. Both theorists make the concept of the 'dead father' central to their understanding of human subjectivity. Freud (1996) believed that social organisation (for males at least) rested upon an historical event during which the sons, envious of their father's exclusive right to all the women, decided to kill him and eat him. Riddled with guilt, they then forbade themselves sexual encounter with these women, the source of their murderous act. The symbolic pact rests on the murder of the father who has become more powerful for being dead and introjected.[5] In fear of the dead father's authority, the brothers give up their desire to possess the father's women. The prohibition of incest thus constitutes a first law founding the social contract shared by the sons. In order to avoid further murders, the sons also impose interdiction on parricide for future generations. While Freud suggested the event as historically viable, Laplanche and Pontalis amongst many remain dubious and prefer to analyse it as a mythical tale: 'The Oedipus complex is not reducible to an actual situation - to the actual influence exerted by the parental couple over the child. Its efficacy derives from the fact that it brings into play a proscriptive agency (the prohibition against incest) which bars the way to naturally sought satisfaction and forms an indissoluble link between *wish* and *law* (a point which Jacques Lacan has emphasised)' (Laplanche and Pontalis, 1988: 286). Where Freud posits the desire for incest and parricide as the corner stone of his interpretation of the subject, Lacan adds a further dimension: 'Only the dead father, [...] can assume the position of the phallus, and thereby ensure the continuation of the law' (Lechte, 1991: 51). By virtue of his absence, the dead father acts as a constant reminder of the sons' wish to take his place and of the consequences of that wish. The dead father stands then both as the wish for satisfaction and as interdiction of its enactment, in other words, the dead father represents both the wish for incest and its suppression. Lacan interprets Freud's idea of the 'dead father' not so much as a potentially real event, but as a discursive support explaining the relationship between the subject and the paternal function. So, where Freud considered the actual father, in Lacanian theory, the father becomes a symbol of what he stands for and that Lacan terms 'phallus'. More precisely, the phallus stands for the gap between wish and its fulfilment. On the one hand, the subject wishes to have the phallus (kill the father and appropriate the women); on the other, parricide means the destruction of the phallus. To have the phallus equals not having it. Hence, for Lacan, the phallus represents a void between two irreconciliable 'truths', that he believes is played out in language production. While social membership rests on the wish for and interdiction of actual incest and parricide, the speaking subject re-enacts this on a symbolic level. Speech acts are on the one hand an attempt at filling in the void between the subject and the phallus, an effort at possessing it. On the other hand, these speech acts can never reconcile the dychotomy having/not having because to speak of oneself is also to speak of the not-oneself.[6] This very impossibility sets the phallus or dead father at the heart of human signification. Speaking is both an act

5 The killing and eating of the father are the means by which the sons satisfy their desire. Introjection is the process by which this outside event is integrated within the subject's ego. Hence, the desire for incest, parricide and cannibalism become founding aspects of the subject.

6 Being and saying that 'I am' are not equivalent: although 'I am' expresses partly one's being, it also exposes the difference or gap between the two. Lacan is theorising on the quintessential question of 'humankind': how can we reconcile biology and social, the unconscious and the conscious (Freud), the 'in-itself' and the 'for-itself' (Sartre), etc?

signifying the life of the subject and its death. To return to Lechte's reading of Lacan, 'the phallus as the signifier of an absence is evocative of death; but the idea of death comes to the subject through language itself. This signifier of death, therefore, is also a sign of life' (Lechte, 1991: 45). Lacan, like Freud, thus envisions the concept of the dead father and his law as the starting point from which the social subject is articulated.

It is interesting to note that for both Lacan and Freud, even if the wish for incest with the mother is the source of the subject's desire for the paternal function, the maternal is not the site of the subject's desire. For both, the maternal is the primordial site of infant desire, because the infant sees the mother as the one who can fulfil its desire for unity. However, the child realises that the mother is herself subject to the same symbolic law (interdiction of parricide and incest) and furthermore that her social standing[7] is not as powerful as the child made it to be. In its attempt to fulfil its wish, the child then turns its attention towards a better site, the father (Freud) or the phallus (Lacan). It is this aspect of Freudian and Lacanian theory that Kristeva will challenge. While remaining loyal to the Freudian model, she reconsiders the logic of paternal supremacy in the process of subjectivation and rehabilitates the importance of the maternal. The subject's entry into language is marked by his/her access to a binary logic that was not 'present' on a pre-linguistic level. With Freud, the move from pre-Oedipal to Oedipal depended upon the presence of a paternal figure he termed 'father of individual pre-history'. Freud then sees the paternal as that which sets up subjectivation not only in the Oedipal moment but also before the onset of Oedipus. Furthermore, the move from maternal to paternal within the pre-Oedipal would be the active choice of the child. Kristeva believes that, while a dualism is present on a pre-linguistic level, its dynamics are regulated by the maternal function, not the child. The pre-linguistic subject does not actively operate within binary logic. Instead, that binary logic is passively 'imprinted' upon the child by maternal care (absence/presence, food is ingested/expelled, etc). With language, the child actively enacts the binary dynamic learnt in maternal care. Hence identification with the symbol means forsaking passivity and dependence upon the maternal in favour of autonomy offered by the social sphere. In other words, the identification with or existence of the subject within the symbol means the repression and forsaking of its pre-linguistic reality. The subject represses the maternal function and identifies with the paternal function, which has now become the new, symbolic guarantor of stability of the subject and their identity. No longer the loving agents of maternal protection, we find the paternal function is now represented in both religious and psychoanalytic

7 In the case of Freud, she does not possess a penis, in Lacan's, she does not possess the phallus. In more general terms, we could say that the mother is castrated twice, once by social law and a second time by the reality of patriarchal culture. Regarding Freud and Lacan's focus on the importance of the penis/phallus (and its lack in women) we can either consider that Freud and Lacan encourage the sexism of their time or merely read their theories as an attempt to explain the reality of the human subject in a patriarchal context.

narratives by more rigid figures such as 'the stern father, superego or God of Abraham' (Oliver, 1991: 55).

The term 'Genesis' is then appropriate in defining the symbolic subject who would be born out of a kind of paternal cult, as exemplified in its religious or psychoanalytic forms. We have introduced the idea of a paternal function in the early experience of the individual and suggested how religious and psychoanalytic discourses have participated in its portraying. We have further identified that the paternal function changes with the individual's entry into language with the move from a loving function of the paternal in the pre-symbolic to an arbitrating function in the symbolic. However, with Freud and Lacan and contrary to the religious discourse, psychoanalysis posits the death of the father as the premise for the birth of the subject. Although both discourses consider salvation in the paternal, religion's definition of the paternal function begins with the father's eternal life and immanence, the subject being but in the image of God. The psychoanalytic subject, Freudian in essence, requires the 'killing' of the father, in order to form a bond with his re-presentation as the symbolic father. If the terminology varies – the Name of the Father (Lacan), the metaphoric father (Kristeva) – all refer to the original Freudian concept of the dead father as the source of socialisation.

Kristeva believes that here lies the fundamental difference between religious and psychoanalytic discourse and ministration. If she agrees with the connecting of religious narratives with psychoanalytic ones, she also points out the independence of psychoanalysis in its understanding of the paternal function as the locus of revolt and of the subject's autonomy.

> With Freud as well as other theoreticians and philosophers, we find such an appropriation of [theology and art] traditions as a part of their revolution, their revolt. (Kristeva, 1998c: 9)

Psychoanalysis follows religious tradition, in particular Catholicism, in that confession inaugurates forgiveness, reconciliation and hope. However, in psychoanalysis, 'this hope is concomitant with the dissolution of the analytic contract' (Guberman, 1996: 11) while '[b]elievers belong to the name of the father, the community, the church, and an identifiable morality' (Guberman, 1996: 11). The psychoanalytic process requires that the paternal agent (the analyst, the father, God) be castrated ('killed') and ousted from His all powerful position, His Law questioned and transgressed so that the subject's relationship with the socio-symbolic can be renewed. Kristeva is aware of the difficulty this represents for the believer and in particular for the catholic believer. What is at stake is no less than challenging the religious construct that rests upon the belief in the existence of an all powerful God whose wrath will strike the unfaithful. Hence analytic 'confession' works towards the autonomy of the analysand and separation from the 'confessor' whereas religious confession binds the believer to God-the-Father, the priest and the community of believers. Although the beginning of analysis resembles the religious setting, with a supposedly omniscient analyst capable of curing the analysand of his/her suffering, psychoanalysis goes one step further from a purely punishing/rewarding function of the paternal.

Not all psychoanalytic practitioners and theorists agree with this. One of the most famous, Françoise Dolto, has analysed the differences between the New and Old Testaments (Dolto, 1991) and found no conflict between the christic and psychoanalytic messages. Dolto believes that the story of Christ exemplifies man‘s revolt against the stern God of the Old Testament and proposes a new covenant between the individual and the paternal function. The new covenant would promote a questioning of the Laws laid out in the Old Testament and the Passion of Christ would represent the path of subjectivation humans follow: sinning is transgression of the Father's Law (Jesus carries our sins); the subject's violation of the bond with the paternal function translates in the death of the subject (suffering and crucifixion), but also in their re-birth in the renewal of the bond with the paternal function (resurrection). Badinter (1981) also supports the Christic discourse as one of defiance of paternal authority. In her words: 'It was necessary to await Christ's word before there was any change, even theoretical. Guided by the revolutionary principle of love, Jesus proclaimed that the authority of the father is not established in the father's interest but in the child's [...]. In preaching love for one's neighbor, Christ established a limit to authority, no matter what its source' (Badinter, 1981: 7). However, the end of the Christic journey (ascension), that Kirschner described as 'redemption via reunion with God' (Kirschner, 1996: 4), is reminiscent of a return to the symbiotic state of the pre-linguistic child. Hence, Christ's reward in his search for a new covenant with the paternal function and a more autonomous identity is the antithesis of what Kristeva's psychoanalysis proposes.

The Paternal Function: from Freud to Kristeva

Kristeva clearly founds her work upon Freud's understanding of subject formation. This means that not only does she advocate the paternal function as the pivot of subjectivation, but also encourages the constant transgression of paternal law in the renewal of the relationship with the paternal function. Freud concentrated on defining the importance of the paternal function in the subject; his work focused mainly on mythical characters illustrating the relationship of the sons with the father: Oedipus (Freud, 1966), the sons and father of the totemic meal (Freud, 1996), Moses (Freud, 1986), etc. Juliet Mitchell explains this.

> The myth that Freud rewrote as the Oedipus complex and its dissolution epitomizes man's entry into culture itself. It reflects the original exogamous incest taboo, the role of the father, the exchange of women and the consequent difference between the sexes. It is *not* about the nuclear family, but about the institution of culture with the kinship structure of exchange relationship of exogamy. It is thus about what Freud regarded as the order of all human culture. It is specific to nothing but patriarchy which is itself, according to Freud, specific to all human civilization. (Mitchell, 1990: 377)

Freud's subject is first and foremost an Oedipal subject, constituted by and constituting patriarchal culture. It is limited to an experienced Oedipality (a thematic Freud finds in Oedipus's tragedy and others such as those mentioned above) and bears the question on the definition of a 'pre-subjectivity' preceding this constitutive Oedipus. Freud was aware of his bias and the difficulty in defining the reality of the pre-Oedipal person. He first construed this difficulty as an effect of the patient's memories or 'individual History' acting like a screen between actual Oedipal conflicts and pre-linguistic experience. The patient's transferential attachment to the father, projected onto the male analyst Freud, hindered the recognition of the earlier attachment to the mother. Second, Freud seemed incapable of grasping this pre-Oedipal attachment to the maternal space, 'so grey with age and shadowy and almost impossible to revivify [...] an inexorable *repression*' (Mitchell, 1990: 109; my italics). Freud's limitations in his theoretical understanding of the maternal were attributed to patients' repression and to Freud's own biology. Contrasting with this early view of resistance in analytic setting, contemporary practitioners are more inclined to attribute resistance to practitioner limitation (see Arnold Lazarus: 'at least 90 per cent of resistance is due to therapist ignorance'. (Dryden, 1997: 164). Kristeva also tends to agree with this. Resistance to symbolisation 'proves' the presence and accessibility of semiotic material in patients:

> I have questioned the archaic untold in language, that is to say the pre-Oedipal phases dealing with the child's relationship with its mother, this imprint of the maternal upon the psyche and upon language that I call the "semiotic" (distinct from the "symbolic" which is the proper of language, of its signs and its syntax). (Kristeva, 1998a: 26)

Thus the repression of the maternal and its revival within the confines of psychoanalysis depends not so much on the patient but on the ability of analysts to overcome their own ignorance of the maternal semiotic.[8]

From a historical perspective, Freud and Kristeva make a parallel between individual history (lifetime) and History. They suggest that on a Historical level, patriarchy was born from the destruction of a previous social order they term the Minoan-Mycenaean civilisation. Freud in particular describes the struggle and authority of the paternal function over the maternal.[9]

> It is in his study of female sexuality that Freud recognises that the archaic mother-daughter relationship, like the Minoan-Mycenaean civilisation beneath the civilisation of Greece, is a hidden layer of femininity and is of particular difficult access because subject to powerful repression. (Smith, 1998: 62)

---

8 Following Klein, Kristeva will show that this ignorance is in fact a form of resistance on the psychoanalyst's part; see chapter five.

9 Kristeva will emphasise Freud's suggestion that the overtaking of Minoan-Mycenaean civilisations by paternal cults is acted out in language production. See: Kristeva, 1996a: 188 and 210.

The positioning of pre-Oedipal (maternal) experience would be subjected to the logics of the Oedipus (paternal) complex. On an individual level, to be a speaking subject is to re-tell the monumental History of the paternal mastery of maternal contents. In other words, the genesis of subject formation as suggested by Freud, read as a historical text, describes the struggle, inscribed on the body of the speaking subject, between maternal space and paternal suprematism. The symbolic father and his Law emerge triumphant and the Mother and her semiotic body are abjected and repressed. Subjectivation is then an '*interiorisation of the founding separation of the socio-symbolic contract*' (Kristeva in Belsey and Moore, 1990: 215). Kristeva now believes the paternal function is failing in the process of subjectivation and that this failure is modifying both the subject and psychoanalytic perspectives on subjectivity. Because the paternal function is failing, we are witnessing the return of the subject to maternal time and a return of pre-Oedipal contents into symbolic production. Kristeva is calling for further research into the function played by the maternal in subjectivation.

> Nevertheless, it is interesting to wonder, regarding the prevalence of the phallus, what other logics could be, that would differ from the binary logic the phallus organises. In between, is it possible to conceive of the semiotic, the pre-verbal, along with other forms of fluid, sensorial organisations: from pictograms to other pre- or trans-linguistic representations. Research in the *types* of representations or psychical acts, which would not be that of the signifier or language, could have extremely important anthropological implications, since we would be dealing with, not only the maternal and the pre-Oedipal as thought, but also other forms of sacred which would not be exclusively the phallic sacred. (Kristeva, 1996a: 188)

Kristeva's work bridges two histories: on the one hand, she analyses the process of subjectivation within the individual, that is the interiorisation of the process of repression of the maternal and identification with the paternal; on the other hand, her interest in the maternal as thought is becoming increasingly manifest over recent years.

Freud believed that the theorising of maternal contents 'could still be explained without necessarily having recourse to a frame of reference other than the Oedipal one' (Laplanche and Pontalis, 1988: 285). He coined the paternal function which he described as the Oedipus complex and tentatively introduced concepts touching on the pre-maternal: the presence of a 'father of individual pre-history', anticipating the importance of the paternal function within a pre-Oedipal economy; the existence of the transference of the patient's bond to the maternal which he believed would be better achieved by female analysts.[10] Kristeva's work is then

---

10 Although the work of women like Melanie Klein, Anna Freud, Julia Kristeva confirms Freud's suspicion, the proliferation of recent texts on the femininity of men exemplifies the move away from biological categories and towards a positioning of the human subject within the maternal/paternal dichotomy. The maternal disposition of male

both a revisiting and a revision of Freud's Oedipal dynamic: within Oedipus, she is actively seeking a framework from which to grasp Minoan-Mycenaean pre-Oedipality.

> What interested me was, by way of the semiotic, to further elaborate a level of psychic representation that for Freud remains extremely primitive and imprecise, which is the representation of affects that are psychic inscriptions, hence very primitive and very fragile: drives and affects that are in fact already psychic. (Guberman, 1996: 22)

Laplanche and Pontalis delimit two schools of thought differentiated by their interpretation of Freud's Oedipal thesis and from which Freud's 'father of individual pre-history' can be analysed:

> […] one may either accentuate the exclusiveness of the dual relationship [mother/child] or else identify signs of the Oedipus complex so early on that it becomes impossible to isolate a strictly pre-Oedipal phase. (Laplanche and Pontalis, 1973: 239)

The former interpretation was furthered by Ruth Mack Brunswick who 'holds that the father, though certainly present in the psychological field, is not perceived as a rival' (Laplanche and Pontalis, 1973: 239). The latter encompasses researchers such as Melanie Klein, Jacques Lacan and Julia Kristeva. Their interpretations put forward a pre-Oedipal triangulation whereby a third term enters the dynamic of the mother/child equation: as the father's 'penis' inside the body of the mother in the infant's fantasy (Klein), as 'phallus' in the mother's fantasised desire (Lacan) and as 'loving father' in the mother's fantasy (Kristeva). In Kleinian interpretation, the pre-Oedipal phase is in fact an earlier Oedipal phase. Laplanche and Pontalis rightly point out that 'It may be asked, however, whether the presence of a third term (phallus) in the primitive mother/child relationship is enough to warrant the description of this period as an 'early Oedipal stage'. The father is not in fact present at this point as an agent of prohibition' (Laplanche and Pontalis, 1973: 239). Hence Laplanche and Pontalis prefer to classify Klein's understanding of the mother/child dyad as pre-Oedipal rather than Oedipal. There is however a distinction between Klein on the one hand and Lacan and Kristeva on the other in that Klein's third term refers to the infant's fantasy whereas Lacan and Kristeva's refers to a fantasy of the mother's desire. Although the presence of a third term in Kleinian terminology is not strong enough to justify classifying her work under the Oedipal model, the very capability of the infant to fantasise a part of the paternal function (the penis) in the mother is, arguably a key accomplishment of an Oedipal process within pre-Oedipality. Hence it could be argued that Klein's theories take after both schools: a pre-Oedipal not yet castrating figure of the Oedipal father and a primitive Oedipal father whose presence threatens the child's unity with the mother. From Freud to Kristeva, the commonality amongst these theorists is the

---

analysts will not be discussed here, but is increasingly being assumed a part of psychoanalytic case studies.

recognition of the early presence of a third term, an early paternal function, announcing the arrival of the Oedipal father proper and his authority. These theorists were then in a position to question and further develop the Freudian model and reconsider the mother-father-child triad and its dynamic. Although the research they carried out shows differences amongst themselves, as Laplanche and Pontalis point out, it can nevertheless be considered globally inasmuch as it contrasts with Freud's emphasis on the Oedipal scene. The contrast enables a reading of 'the Freudian subject' and provides an answer to the problematic of defining such a subject.

In her study of Anglo-American psychoanalytic cultural genealogy, Suzanne Kirschner defines contemporary Anglo-American psychoanalytic theories as 'three interrelated psychoanalytic schools or loosely affiliated groups of theorists under the broader umbrella of 'psychoanalysis'. These are ego psychology, object-relations theory, and self psychology' (Kirschner, 1996: 23).[11] She finds that, in spite of their current differences, these three groups are born of a common cultural genealogy:

> Transplanted to America and Britain, psychoanalysis came more and more to prioritize and elaborate upon the preoedipal narrative. In these culture areas, psychoanalysts have focused almost entirely on the difficult developmental path to autonomy's attainment, and on individuation's never-ending dialectical interplay with wishes for dependency and oneness. (Kirschner, 1996: 14)

We can add to Kirschner's analysis of the Anglo-American psychoanalytic scene, Kristeva's comment on the more classical psychoanalytic scene in France that 'those modern characters [analysands] testify that today we do not know how to elaborate primary narcissism' (Kristeva, 1983: 464). Narcissism refers to the subject's loving of their own image and inability to take an other than themself as object of love. In his later work, Freud defined narcissism as two moments in subjectivation he termed primary and secondary. Difficulties in secondary narcissism (when the subject does not relate to others) point to the subject's earlier difficulties in elaborating primary narcissism (when the child refuses to take an other than itself as love object). Both Kirschner and Kristeva are suggesting that, in dealing with the contemporary pathologies of secondary narcissism, psychoanalysis is increasingly looking for causes in the subject's pre-history and in particular primary narcissism. A 'sliding' of the Freudian model towards a time anterior to that marked by Freud as constitutive of the subject, the Oedipal phase, denotes the

---

11 Ego psychology: inaugurated by Freud and furthered by Heinz Hartmen and Anna Freud in the 1930s and then by Spitz, Jacobson, Mahler, Kernberg; Object Relation Theory (ORT): from Melanie Klein's work and taken in a different direction by the British School, Fairbairn, Winnicott, Guntrip; 'Heinz Kohut was the founder and leading proponent of self-psychology, which has been very influential in American psychoanalysis since the 1970s.' (Kirschner, 1996: 23).

concept of 'crisis'. The Oedipal phase is that which delineates the Freudian subject. This subject is in the image of the father, that is a paternal construct whose entry into the father's realm establishes his subjectivity: in Freud, if the mother procreates a human being, the father creates the subject. This recalls Catherine Clément's earlier suggestion that patriarchal cultures are organised around initiation rites during which the child is symbolically passed over, or re-born, into paternal law. In this context, Freud's efforts to grasp the maternal function in the process of subjectivation, in particular within himself, remained unsurprisingly on a tentative level. Perhaps his efforts were met with the cultural resistance of early century Europe, perhaps Freud resisted this 'maternalising' of his position. We can consequently speak of (Freudian) psychoanalysis as part of the reproduction of the paternal function and of its subject, re-actively defining the primacy of the paternal function (the Father) over the maternal function (the Mother). Freud's efforts at transcending paternal law and considering the pre-Oedipal time of the subject was reinforced by Lacan.

John Lechte (1991) compares and contrasts a Lacanian and a Kristevan approach to subjectivity. In his view, the pivotal difference between the two theorists revolves around their understanding of the dynamic unconscious/symbolic. For Lacan, 'the unconscious would be the quintessentially symbolic within the symbolic – the essence of the symbolic, as it were' (Lechte, 1991: 44-5). The unconscious, or phallus (Lechte, 1991: 44), stands 'for the loss of the mother as the subject's first object and for the mother's difference as one who does not have a penis' (Lechte, 1991: 50). Symbolicity essentially rests on an emptiness, an absence, a loss of the maternal evocative of death. When 'I' speak, Lacan suggests that it is in fact an 'Other' who speaks in the subject. This 'Other' Lechte describes as 'the Father, the phallus, the symbolic, desire, language, the unconscious [...], culture (Lechte, 1991: 45). What speaks in the subject is a symbolic reality that preceded individual existence and to which the subject collaborates to ensure its continuation. Kristeva will insist that the psychical health of the symbolic subject rests on the existence a priori and stability of the symbolic, before birth. In fact, the crisis in contemporary subjectivity partly stems out of a crisis in what Lacan would term the symbolic order, symptomatised in social phenomena (such as the breakdown of the family unit, the increase in psychotic acts, etc.). Lacanian logic gives a more prominent role to the maternal than Freud's when it suggests that subjectivity is founded upon a lack generated by maternal loss. However, Lacan, like Freud, privileges the paternal function as the sole guarantor of subjectivity. If we follow Lechte's reading of Lacan, subjectivity is born out of the individual's desire to be reunited with the maternal moderated by paternal law. Lacan equates the maternal with psychosis and death. Paternal law on the other hand dictates and ensures the continuation of symbolic life. In Lacan's eyes, the paternal, or symbolic order, is the pre-requisite and guarantor of individual and collective social existence without which subjectivity would collapse into psychosis. He then puts the paternal on a par with subjective life, the means by which the subject can defeat the deadly pull of the maternal. However, the symbolic order alone does not suffice to constitute a social subject. Lacanian logic also insists that the unconscious is another precondition to identity and thus differs from ego-psychology which 'is caught in the domain of self-identity constitutive of the ego and so is oblivious to the unconscious as a virtuality and the precondition of the (symbolic) ego' (Lechte, 1991: 46). A Lacanian approach suggests the interaction between unconscious and symbolic within the subject, with the eventual dominance of the former by the latter. This is where Kristevan theory differs.

Kristeva also suggests the interaction between unconscious and symbolic as the source of subjectivity. However, she does not envision symbolic life as the subject's definite triumph over the (deadly) unconscious. Rather, the boundary that separates the two is more permeable than in Lacan's. For her, if the symbolic is constituted of the interaction unconscious/symbolic, then signs of this interaction are present within or alongside the purer Lacanian symbolic. She finds for instance that any disruption of the symbolic chain (pitch, intonation, silences) 'proves' the presence of unconscious contents within the symbolic. So 'the issue of the relationship between logic, formalization, and the 'music' in language, constitutes the point of departure for the Kristevan *oeuvre*' (Lechte, 1991: 60). Indeed, in the 1970s she concentrated on setting a framework explaining the dynamics of language production, which would become the foundation of her future work. Today, she still evokes this early research into the symbolic/semiotic to explicate her later work on subjectivity. In the 1980s she produced more focused, introspective and specialised texts, with an increasing interest in deciphering how unconscious contents are coded within the symbolic. That time was also when she introduced the idea of a crisis of subjectivity in western culture. Lately, her work has tended to turn to reading women's symbolic production and the coding of the sacred. Yet, even if her work appears to tackle eclectic material, the spirit of Kristevan analysis remains close to its original intentions: to bring to symbolic light that which disrupts the symbolic order and constitutes the untheorised areas of subjectivity.

Given the history and contemporary understanding of subjectivity, we can conclude by noting how central the paternal function is in assessing subjectivity within psychoanalysis as a whole and Kristevan analysis in particular. This paternal function can take many cultural guises: religious groups, a career, political leaders, the analyst, the actual father, etc. The increase in extreme cultural manifestations, such as the attraction of sects or the increase in racist groups and racist acts, testify to the contemporary subject's need to find strong paternal images enabling the capture of their symbolic identity. We will see in the following chapter how Julia Kristeva has been arguing that the paternal function is now failing causing the revival of such fundamentalisms.

Conclusion

A traditional understanding of the family puts forward a clear separation between mother and father and identifies maternal and paternal roles respectively according to their biological and socio-symbolic connections. Clément (Kristeva and Clément, 1998b) and Badinter (1981) show that contemporary society attributes without question maternal identity to a biological reality and in reverse, that the biological mother's claim to motherhood is not disputed. Badinter (1981) challenges this view by considering birth giving and child care as two separate events. Through a historical study of motherhood, she demonstrates that although biology defines the mother, it does not follow that the mother naturally takes up her social role as maternal caregiver. Rather, she proposes that biology and social functions be considered separately, and that the maternal function be analysed in relation to the socio-political demands made upon the natural parent. In a traditional sense, the individual's claim to maternal identity is then anchored in a naturalness whereby biology is on a par with social function, birth-giving means maternal instinct, an equation Badinter sees as the legacy of early nineteenth century social conditions and governmental policies.

Clément (Kristeva and Clément, 1998b) suggests that if this equation nature/social function is not disputed for the mother, paternity claims upon the child do not follow the same logic. She shows that the paternal function is born of two factors: the mother asserting the father's natural link to the child and socio-symbolic rites aimed at reassuring the father of his paternal identity. In both cases, the father's paternal right is not so much the effect of his participation in a biological event, but rather the consequence of a symbolic enactment by which he is proclaimed father. The traditional contemporary apprehension of fatherhood is then rooted in the socio-symbolic sphere whereby, beyond biology, the child must participate in a 'second birth' to enable the existence of the paternal function.

We should keep this context in mind when approaching Julia Kristeva's work on subjectivity. Some researchers (Doane and Hodges, 1992) have described her work on parental categories while neglecting to question those categories. This omission has led them to a misreading of Kristeva's texts, which, in the extreme led to the construction of the Kristevan logic as a form of biological determinism. Smith (1996) and Lechte (1991) pointed out that most misreadings of Kristeva's work can be brought down to a difference in culture of her readership. They delineate two 'schools' of thought, namely Anglo-American and French, whose intellectual frameworks differ enough to create irreconcilable points of contention and also a space for fertile argumentation. Lechte points out that an Anglo-American audience clearly defines and separates categories such as mother, father, the individual and textual productions (in the postmodern sense of text) and consider those categories as pertaining solely of the order of the symbolic. To synthesise, an Anglo-American framework assumes the autonomy of the subject vis-à-vis their surrounding and vice-versa. Indebted to the work of Freud and Lacan, French thinkers like Kristeva assume the opposite. They see instead a permeability between the subject and their surrounding, an osmosis between the individual and their representations. They analyse categories such as society or art inasmuch as those categories carry within themselves the expression of a history pertaining to a particular individual or group. This history, for Kristeva, necessarily brings this individual or this group back to an analysis of what constituted them, that is the maternal and paternal functions. In other words, the French framework assumes some form of dependence upon collective and individual histories where the Anglo-American one seeks autonomy. In describing the crisis of subjectivity in contemporary society, Kristeva in particular interprets this crisis as the breakdown of the paternal function on a collective and individual level. In analysing the paternal function, she is then not analysing 'father', but a function understood in its metaphoric sense. This permits her to transcend cultural categories of paternal (the father, the State, etc.) while demonstrating how those categories can be interpreted as symptoms of the paternal metaphor. A similar framework will be used for the maternal function.

The paternal function is then the departing point from which 'crisis' should be apprehended. Kirschner's work (1996) proposed to analyse the relationship between two master narratives that propose the paternal function as central to individual and social organisation. Kirschner's work finds both an osmosis and tension between the two narratives. Both proceed of the same logic by which the subject gains subjectivity through the paternal function and to the exclusion of any other entity. Kirschner traces contemporary concerns such as subjective salvation, self-idealisation and individual autonomy back to Christian culture: the Christic journey epitomises the Son's search for the Father and final reunion with Him. Thinkers like Freud and Kristeva go further back and historically attribute the central place given to the paternal function in the process of subjectivation to the rise of monotheism: Man's Genesis begins through God the Father. A further marker that the paternal function occupies central stage in the making of the subject is found in contemporary culture. Kristeva believes that the difficulties encountered by the contemporary subject have provoked a return of fundamentalism, (sects, terrorisms, etc.). In their search for salvation, the subject in disarray seeks in an all-powerful father figure an answer to their predicament.

However, Kristeva (1985) also claims the autonomy of the psychoanalytic discourse vis-à-vis the religious discourse. Where the paternal function inaugurates the subject in both discourses, the (monotheistic) religious discourse sees the questioning of God's Law as damnation whereas psychoanalysis proposes subjective cure in the subject's autonomy from the all-powerful Father and their appropriation of paternal discourse. Yet, such traditional proposition still posits the father at the centre of the puzzle, even if his image is that which should be transcended. Kristeva's work proposes still a further dimension.

Psychoanalytic discourse posits the centrality of the paternal function in subject formation. While this function pertains to the symbolic dimension of the subject, the varied approaches, from Freud to Kristeva, testify today to a paternal function that can no longer be viewed as a monolithic structure. From a historical viewpoint,

Freud concentrated his study on the role played by the paternal figure during the Oedipal phase. He did allude to a pre-Oedipal function of the paternal which he termed 'the father of individual pre-history', but that part of research will be more fully apprehended by three of his successors: Klein, Lacan and Kristeva. Klein suggests the existence of an Oedipal dynamic by analysing the child's symbolic productions (Kleinian 'phantasy') before language is learnt. She thus challenges the previous belief that no symbolisation was possible before the onset of the Freudian Oedipal phase. Her recording of those child 'phantasies' testify to the presence of some form of paternal (symbolic) function alongside the maternal from birth. Lacan on the other hand proposes that the paternal function (the Symbolic Order) rests on the irredeemable loss of the maternal. Whether we call it weaning or castration, the individual must leave the maternal realm to take social membership. As a defence against this lack, against the maternal/child dyad then, subjectivity is founded by identifying with that which represents the Other than lack, the Other than maternal, that is the third term of the Oedipal scene, the paternal function. Although Lacan separates the subject from the maternal at the outset of the paternal function (symbolisation), he nevertheless posits the function of the maternal as founding symbolicity. In spite of their differences, the successors of Freud have in common an understanding of subjectivity that posits the subject at one point of a triangular dynamic with the maternal and the paternal at the other two. Since Freud, this understanding has come to be known as the Oedipal triangle, a relational dynamic forming the essence of the Freudian scene. In this Freudian discourse, the subject encounters the paternal function after it has established a dyadic relationship with the maternal. This third term is then an addition. Second, it is always experienced as a threat to the maternal/child dyad. Where the Oedipal triangle defined Freudian discourse, the introduction of the third term 'paternal function' on a pre-Oedipal level questions the Freudian definition of Oedipal and thus of subjectivity. It questions its onset, now envisioned much earlier. It also questions its boundaries: from Freud's mother/father, it proposes to theorise the subject's family triangle in terms of their metaphoric functions instead of their biology.

Chapter 3

The Failure of the Paternal Function

The Failure of the Paternal Function: A Modernist Crisis?

From the publications of *Les nouvelles maladies*, Kristeva consistently posits the crisis of the Paternal Function as the turning point in her own interpretation of the psychoanalytic project. Although she does not analyse the historicity of this crisis, she often explains that:

> [...] the fundamental crisis in which the contemporary world is living [...] began to unfold at the time of the French Revolution. [...] I would say, together with certain historians, that the French Revolution is now coming to an end. This can be seen clearly by taking account of the phenomena of the problems of authority, of democracy, of religion, and of language in its relationship to sexual identity. I think that the crisis has opened and there will be a succession of crises. (Guberman, 1996: 36-7)

The French Revolution represents the rupture of an equilibrium which paved the way for new forms of representations (new forms of democracies, new moral questions such as that of reproduction). This break with the old system rendered the crisis not only explicit but also made of crisis the new organising force. 'We can think of it this way: previous social forms counted on a certain calm, and crisis came periodically; but now an epoch has opened when we live in permanent crisis. What is provisional now are the moments of status quo' (Guberman, 1996: 37). What Kristeva is suggesting is then a stalling of the modernist project at the point of crisis, that is modernism now equals crisis. She also proposes a way out of crisis. Against a defensive rejection of the achievements of modernism, she believes that to move beyond the narratives of modernism will entail a 'passing through' (Guberman, 1996: 225) those narratives. In other words, to transcend the modernist deadlock is to work through its narratives, and more importantly its points of resistance with the aim of finding new modes of representations that would permit to move the project beyond obstruction.

The modernist narrative Kristeva chooses to 'pass through' is the psychoanalytic narrative. The overall body of work that Freud proposed takes its place amongst the prominent early twentieth century discourses. From the beginning, Freud attempts to find and map one universal structure that would represent and explain the human subject. His 1895 'Project' of neuronal systems φ, ψ and Ω (Elliott, 1998: 182-3) described the path from organic to symbol. Around the same time, Freud studies hysteria and concentrates on finding a unique causality to neurosis. He hypothesises that neurosis would be caused by a sexual trauma experienced before puberty and re-activated later on (Chartier, 1993), giving rise to the 'seduction theory' as a universal phenomenon. The first topic (the unconscious/preconscious/conscious model), the 'pleasure principle' and 'reality principle', the 'Oedipus complex' are all attempts at framing the subject once and for all in a systemic and universal order that would defy contradictions. That Freud later gave up on the Project, on seduction theory and on the pleasure/reality principles, that he refined his first topic with the addition of a second less inflexible one (the id/ego/super-ego model) and that he questioned the validity of the Oedipus complex with respect to the girl's development towards the end of his life characterises his work as modern. The key in Freudian thought is the move from the primacy of experience to the primacy of its representation.

Freud: A Modernist

'Freud was a committed modernist' Ferguson states in his *Freud and the Dynamics of Modernity* (Elliott, 1998: 169).[1] Freud had an impact on the understanding of subjectivity. 'Against the ontology of determinacy which has pervaded the history of Western social thought, Freud uncovers what is essential to the psychical world: namely, that this world is not predetermined but is actively created, in and through the production of psychical representations and significations. The psyche is the launching pad from which people *make meaning*' (Elliott, 1998: 7). Because psychical activity is founded upon a split between what is consciously known and what has been repressed into the unconscious, Elliott views the Freudian world as 'overdetermined': 'people make more meaning than they can psychically process at any one time' (Elliott, 1998: 7). The abandonment of the 'seduction theory' can be regarded as the turning point in Freud's work, the point when he himself begins to abandon the belief that the sum of the parts of someone's past determines them.

> In the autumn of 1897, Freud abandoned the 'seduction theory'; but crucially, he replaced it with a more critical interpretation of the relation of psychic life to the outer world. Central to this shift in Freud's approach was a radical revaluation of the internal processing of external reality, and especially of how individuals interpret, frame, and fantasize experience. (Elliott, 1998: 5)

What is important is not the actual experience, the reality of event but its representation. The event, be it real or not (as in the case of hallucination, dream and fantasy), should be apprehended as text. Text is what the individual apprehends as reality. Indeed, text is reality. Freud realised that it was not so much the event that is traumatic but the manner in which the individual internalises it. Hence the

---

1 At the turn of the century, Elliott edited a collection of essays reassessing the impact and relevance of Freud to today's world. Elliott's work is an example of contemporary readings of Freud.

value of truth drastically changed: 'Once Freud granted fantasy an active and subjective dimension, therefore, the psychic realm no longer functioned as a mirror to objective reality' (Elliott, 1998: 6). Psychic representation or text, would now be the material psychoanalysis would be built upon. '[F]or Freud the social recognition of trauma is only the beginning of the matter' (Elliott, 1998: 6). More precisely, the social recognition of trauma (social unrest, being tried for crime, etc) is outside the psychoanalysis, material to be dealt with by social organisation, legal, political, etc. Psychic representations underpin the experience of trauma. They are 'the imaginary components of experienced traumatic contradictions' (Elliott, 1998: 6) where the analyst will find 'the ways in which the event has been invested with, or drained of, meaning' (Elliott, 1998: 6). So, there is first the lived event, which comes to existence only through individual representation, and second this text which retrospectively endows the event with presence. Event per se remains outside, irrelevant shall we say to the definition of individual reality (and to psychoanalysis), while psychical imprint determines 'reality' (or realities).

Through a complex range of representations, influences worked over to produce 'reality' as a sub-set of possibilities, Elliott defines the individual as overdetermined rather than determined in linear fashion as the causal outcome of the singular stream of experienced events. Elliott seems to suggest the unconscious as some storage space from which the individual could, if desired, draw meaning at will and ad infinitum. This is not exactly what Freud imagined, but Elliott is right in noticing that because of such a set-up, Freud makes of the ego an agent with limited agency: the individual has little mastery over his/her psychical heritage. Some like Lacan and theorists of a post-structuralist tradition have emphasised this aspect of the subject, a subject forever alien or de-centred from ever knowing itself. Laplanche argues that '[t]here are two facets to the Freudian revolution in the radical decentering it offers. The first is classical: the discovery of the unconscious, in so far as it is precisely *not* our center, as it is an 'excentric' centre; the other facet, the seduction theory, is hidden but indispensable to the first for it maintains the unconscious in its alien-ness' (Laplanche, 1999: 61-2). Others like Kristeva have attempted to re-insert some form of human agency at the heart of subjectivity. 'In Kristeva's discussion of the semiotic dimension of human experience it is primarily a set of psychoanalytic observations about the formation and structuration of psychic space' (Elliott, 1998: 8), that we are dealing with. Freud initiated a split in the modernist drive towards the possibility to 'know thyself', a split we find in his construction of the subject between what can be known (text) and what cannot (unconscious), in other words a painful wound blown at the ego of the unified subject, what Freud will call a 'narcissistic wound'. Although at the time of Freud narcissism was ultimately defeated by the Oedipus complex, the coining of narcissism as moment of reckoning is today at the heart of the psychoanalytic crisis.

Post-Freudian thinking suggests a division along the following lines: one group, following Lacan emphasise what cannot be known or rather the process by which what cannot be known is what we know and can be likened to a postmodern 'tradition'. A second group, predominantly British or known as the British School

(Winnicott, Bion or Klein, but also in many ways Kristeva), is interested in a return to the symbol and the potential it offers to unlock the modernist dead-end society is supposed to be in. Those theorists are interested, as Kristeva explained, in 'rehabilitating pre-Oedipal and psychotic latences of the unconscious' (Kristeva, 1998a: 27). But there is a difference between the British and French Schools of thought: 'The English emphasise the catastrophic or psychotic dimensions of the unconscious whereas the French favour the erotic or Oedipal dimension' (Kristeva, 1998: 27). Put simply, British theorists focus on pre-Oedipality per se while the aim of French theorists is the re-insertion of pre-Oedipality in Oedipus. Elliott points to the existence of a third group. A certain understanding of modernity, pre-Lacanian and led by adepts of the Frankfurt School, Horkheimer, Adorno and Marcuse, has emphasised 'a conception of psychoanalysis as a negative theory: an account of self-divided, alienated individuals, which was understood as the subjective correlate of the capitalist economic order' (Elliott, 1998: 8). This group focuses 'on the rise of consumer society, the seductive imagery of mass media and the pervasiveness of narcissism' (Elliott, 1998: 9). This group's position is thus in between the Lacanian subject of lack and the British School subject of the pre-Oedipal. The former sees a void in the place of origin (event is lost, all we have is text), the latter asserts that some of our archaism is in part recoverable (we need to theorise the pre-Oedipal). This third group asserts 'the triumph of modern society over society' (Elliott, 1998: 8), that is the self is no longer the defining agent of its existence and the 'psychologisation' of the subject defunct. If we now consider the Freudian project and its current predicament, we find that they may have a point.

Truly, the issue of narcissism in both Freud and post-Freudian work suggests the end of the psychoanalytic narrative. Freud positioned his own 'Freudianism' in the continuum of great discoveries that he termed, along with those of Copernicus and Darwin, the 'narcissistic wounds inflicted to mankind'. These discoveries were damage to the vanities of historically located understandings of the self. There is no doubt that Freud began his enterprise with the intention to reveal a truth so far hidden from human understanding and that would revolutionise the individual's beliefs vis-à-vis the personal and the collective. Moreover, Freudian theory and psychoanalytic practice unsurprisingly develop at a time when individual concerns take precedent over collective ones. The Industrial Revolution and the rise of a bourgeois capitalist group were characterised by the move from a rigid feudal model of life-long allegiance to a God, a master and a social position to the possibility of personal achievement and promotion within society. This change of focus from social to individual can be charted, at least in France, over a period of about a hundred years from the Revolution of 1789 to the Third Republic (1870). During this time, a society formally reliant on eighteenth century values of rational, logical thought faced in quick succession empires, monarchies, republics and consulates punctuated by several wars, revolutions and coups. However, other writers see the Revolution as the outcome of a situation that had begun well before 1789. According to Denommé, conflicts between nature and society and the inadequacy of eighteenth century values to account for man's status in the community were already questioned by both philosophers and writers:

> Both the rationalist thinkers of the Enlightenment and the preromantic writers of the latter part of the century advocated a drastic change in the status quo. The former believed that an adequate definition of man could be achieved through controlled reason and logic; the latter suggested that reason alone was incapable of arriving at a comprehensive understanding of man in the universe. Both the rationalists and the preromanticists looked hopefully to the French Revolution which they had prepared for the solutions which they thought. (Denommé, 1969: 7).

The time of the Revolution and its political, social and technological aftermath were indeed a turning point in the individual's apprehension of themselves within societal organisation. Through his work, Freud takes part in emphasising the shift from collective to individual and in particular, to finding justification for the individual's tricky position against the collective body. Freudian theory partakes in questioning if not defying the paternalistic voice of the head of the State or the household so that the individual can become a self-determined agent of his social destiny rather than the mere compliant actor of a pre-set social game. But, as Weber pointed out, Freud also repetitively returns to the paternal voice when 'the narcissistic wound' (Weber, 1982: 134) he was so proud to have uncovered threatened his own theoretical edifice. To be clear, the clash between multiple representation and the unconscious defies the attempts of any 'know thyself' rational enterprise, such as psychoanalysis, to proceed towards scientific status. One is repeatedly forced back to questions of power.

The Repetitive Subject

> Freud was, of course, much concerned with the emotional problems generated by repetition, the actions people cannot stop repeating or the narratives people cannot stop recounting. He understood such repetitions as symptomatic of a failure to remember, the closing down of creative imagination. (Elliott, 1998: 9)

Repetition of narrative is at the heart of the postmodern critique of modernism. But while a postmodern practice cites the dull repetition of old narratives, the aim of the Freudian project was always to rescue this modernist crisis. 'For many social critics, the autonomy of the imagination is inescapably situated within the project of modernity' (Elliott, 1998: 9). It would appear then that the crisis of modernity rests with the crisis of imagination. The path out of repetition compulsions would then be located in rescuing the subject from the stalled programme of subjectivity and towards a renewed autonomy. This implies that such an autonomous subject exists in the first place.

In his 'Citation and Subjectivity', Boyne (1999) addresses such a question.

> Both phenomenological and Freudian frameworks allow a strong role for the forces of social reproduction, but both also concede the possibility of a minimally autonomous core self: in Freud this is the territory of the *id* ('the ego is that part of the *id* which has been modified by direct influence of the external world' [Freud, 1923: 363]). (Boyne, 1999: 210)

He proceeds to describe how '[r]ecent work within cultural analysis and sociology has rejected such a residue' (Boyne, 1999: Abstract). Reading the works of Judith Butler and Pierre Bourdieu, he first argues that 'we have now moved, it might appear, to a culture of citation, to the verification of identity through, and to the exhaustion of identity in, the citation of sources, rather than through some form of depth hermeneutical revelation of self' (Boyne, 1999: 211). The self would no longer refer to the individual's innate interiority moderated by the experiences learned from their environment. Instead, the self would be an amalgamate of identities collected like grocery in our cultural environment (advertisements, films, etc.), and kept alive through more cultural stimuli. However, the 'citational self' that replaces the autonomous core self exists insofar as citation is correct. Indeed, for the citational self to be true, the individual must respect the codes of citation, codes that Boyne finds were manipulated in the example of sex reassignment cases. Candidates to sex reassignment deceived their audience, the medical profession, by dissimulating the true 'nature' of their project, in order to satisfy the medical requirements and secure the sexual transformation they coveted. 'The culture of open citation is shown to be dependent upon external certitudes which duplicate, in potentially stronger terms, the very essentialism which the rejection of residual selfhood was first meant to defeat' (Boyne, 1999: Abstract). The manipulation of citation then would imply the return of a deviant, negative deceitful inner force intent on asserting its autonomy from environmental pressure: the old concept of subjectivity as the negotiating between inner core and environmental frustration is repeated.

The Failure of the Paternal Function

It is then not surprising that in the psychoanalytic narrative, crisis, the corner stone of late modernity according to Kristeva, is located precisely at that point of repetition. It is the point where symbolicity risks collapse before what Slavoj Zizek has termed 'the maternal superego' (Zizek, 1991: 99). Behind this apparent contradiction in terms, Zizek observes the consequences of a paternal function in retreat 'and the vacuum is filled by the 'irrational' maternal superego' (Zizek, 1991: 99) that he describes as regressive, ferocious, wicked, devouring, blocking 'normality', etc., in short the expression of aggressive impulses. Kristeva will emphasise, as Zizek does that, although it brings about a 'regime' of terror to social organisation, 'the disintegration of the ego-ideal [and] the installation of the 'maternal' superego [...] usually goes unoticed' (Zizek, 1991: 103). It may be explained by the fact that, when it does not lead to violence, the retreat of the paternal function is moderated by a new form of libidinal organisation, that of the pathological narcissist.[2]

Zizek (1999) proposes that the Freudian discovery and enunciation of the modalities of the Oedipus complex we described in chapter two marks the starting point of a reflection on the modernist crisis. Through his reading of Lacan, Zizek equates crisis with a crisis of Oedipus (or investiture of authority), that is a crisis of the father in psychoanalytic representation. Through Freud's work, Zizek defines the paternal function as three-fold: the 'father-jouisseur' (pleasure seeking), the symbolic father (or 'the big Other') and the tyrannical father (or 'Willing father'). The father-jouisseur and the symbolic father Freud described in *Totem and Taboo* (1912- 3), the former as the father who has sole enjoyment of the women, the latter as the ghostly figure who returns to haunt the sons after they have murdered and eaten the father-jouisseur. The symbolic father will later be described further by Lacan as the void found in the place of the father and filled with symbolic representation. Finally, the tyrannical father described in *Moses and Monotheism* (1967) represents the father whose Will rules and strikes the disobedient with his vengeance. His Will is absolute and needs no justification.

Zizek sees in the late nineteenth century bourgeois nuclear family a crisis of the paternal function offset by a reversal of the father's role. Historically, the real father and the symbolic father used to be separate entities endowed with separate functions. The father-jouisseur (the genitor) would inseminate the mother while a totem or spirit would be regarded as the real father of the individual (in aborigines cultures for example). With the rise of the bourgeoisie, both functions are performed by one man, the child's actual father. Freud (and Lacan) posit several conditions to the good functioning of the role of this 'combined father', conditions which form the corner stones of the Oedipal tragedy. First, the two functions jouisseur/symbolic must be separated again. This is the outcome of parricide, played out at the level of fantasy: the father-jouisseur is killed off and the empty place he left invested with what the father now symbolically stands for. Second, paternal prohibition must take place through the fear that the dead vengeful father will return to punish the child; Zizek notices that from *Totem and Taboo* to *Moses and Monotheism*, the symbolic father is no longer enough, in Freud's writing, to ward off parricide and guarantee that the prohibition of incest is respected. Freud thus imagines this other absolute and tyrannical instance of the paternal function who becomes the prime figure of the super-ego and the agent of castration in the Oedipus complex. Third, the individual must not only hide the parricide from the father but also forget that the father has been killed. Zizek explains that the separation and killing of the father-jouisseur leaves the symbolic father deprived of his virility. Consequently, the representative figures of the symbolic father (the leader, the head of the household) need to ignore their impotence to carry out their paternal function without a sense of ridicule. This also goes for the child who must

2 It is then no coincidence that Zizek's favoured field of investigation has been the cinema, the realm of pathological narcissism *par excellence*.

forget that the potent father-jouisseur is in fact already dead in order to preserve Oedipal efficiency.

These last two conditions, the ignorance of both the child and the father, is where Zizek locates crisis. Today's children would know the father-jouisseur is already dead and we might add, that they are not. 'So when, today, one speaks of the decline of paternal authority, it is *this* father, the father of the uncompromising 'No!' who is effectively in retreat' (Zizek, 1999: 322). The death of the father-jouisseur has knock on effects on the other two aspects of the paternal function. Zizek continues, 'in the absence of his prohibitory 'No!', new forms of the phantasmatic harmony between the symbolic order and *jouissance* can thrive again' (Zizek, 1999: 322). The absolute father and his Will can no longer impact the child with his threat of vengeance and is disempowered. This opens a new space for unregulated transactions between the father-jouisseur and the symbolic father, in other words, between transgression and narrative. But Zizek continues further in true Lacanian fashion that the discovery of the non-existence of the father-jouisseur (always already dead) not only leads to the demise of the tyrannical father but also amounts to the non-existence of the symbolic father. For if the symbolic father replaces the dead father-jouisseur, and if the father-jouisseur never existed, then neither does its symbolic representative: 'the nonexistence of the big Other is ultimately equivalent to the fact that the big Other is the *symbolic* order, the order of symbolic fictions which operate on a level different from that of direct material causality' (Zizek, 1999: 322).

In material causality humans' understanding of themselves and their environment was founded on a phenomenological approach to the material world. Today's society, dominated by the culture of the virtual, the fake, of the simulacrum of the real, is more inclined to *believe* symbolic fictions (words, images, etc.) than rely on the veracity of sensory information. This is the era of the 'believe what I say, not what you see' as Zizek puts it. Belief is the key to understanding how symbolic organisation was restructured around the knowledge of the father's death. '[T]he 'nonexistence of the big Other' is strictly correlative to the notion of belief, of symbolic trust, of credence, of taking what others say 'at face value'' (Zizek, 1999: 323). Without belief, Zizek thinks that symbolic efficiency would fail:

> [...] it concerns the minimum of 'reification' on account of which it is enough for us, all concerned individuals, to know some fact in order to be operative – 'it', the symbolic institution, must also know/'register' this fact if the performative consequences of stating it are to ensue. Ultimately this 'it', of course, can be embodied in the gaze of the absolute big Other [...] (Zizek, 1999: 326-7)

In other words, after the father's death, society behaves *as if* the father was still out there. Individuals know that the death of the father (God, the paternal function) means the end of his immanence and transcendental function, but by an act of faith, the symbolic contract is preserved. The fact that '[t]he big Other is thus the order of the lie, of lying sincerely' (Zizek, 1999: 329) is echoed by Boyne's suggestion that 'we have now moved [...] to a culture of citation, to the verification of identity through, and to the exhaustion of identity in, the citation of sources, rather than through some form of depth hermeneutical revelation of self' (Boyne, 1999: 211). And we saw that in this new order of 'sincere deception', the self of citation then, is far from being a reliable structure for a new form of subjectivity.

Conclusion

The crisis of modernity identified in the crisis of one of its narratives, psychoanalysis, suggests we have now reached a dead end. As far as the psychoanalytic narrative is concerned narcissism is the outcome. Over the past hundred years or so, the death of the father has not meant the re-organisation of the social around a different pivotal entity. On the contrary, the system restructured 'its rules in order to accommodate itself to new conditions by incorporating the originally subversive moment (Zizek, 1999: 328). Effectively this clinging on to the paternal function has meant that individuals had to find ways of adapting their very social being to changing structures increasingly regulated by capitalism. Zizek (1991: 102) enumerates three stages of libidinal organisation: 'the 'autonomous' individual of the Prostestant ethic' we described in chapter two; 'the heteronomous 'organization man'' who gains social status through his allegiance to a group, and 'the type gaining predominance today, the 'pathological narcissist'' . Narcissus is the heir to a fatherless system, a perversion according to psychoanalysis. If theorists are in agreement over the rise of Narcissus, their readings of narcissism vary. From the postmodern stance of the subject as a free floating, dispersed or dis-unified being, to the hard-core psychoanalytic position on narcissism as the incapacity to relate socially, interpretations are multiple. Two of those stand out: Narcissus, the dispersed identity lost in the multiplicity of false selves (Kristeva) and Narcissus in relation to a changing symbolic function (the 'big Other') that regulates his social performance and determines his fluid but nevertheless contained identity (Zizek). Yet, the issue of the 'maternal superego' (Zizek) or the 'abject mother' (Kristeva) is a reminder that crisis is also the outcome of a failing paternal function which remains the organising force. So, narcissism is the way individuals have found to adapt to the failure of the paternal function and the rise of the 'maternal superego'. But this, ironically, could also be the way social members have found to keep the social contract alive, in spite of the death of the father: carrying on *as if* the paternal function were still present and avoiding the violence correlative to such a loss.

The Crisis of Subjectivity in Contemporary Society: An Illustration[3]

In 1991, Kristeva published a novel, *Le vieil homme et les loups*, which, as Bernard Sichère put it 'brings to the fore a dark, negative dimension, an outlook on the

3 An earlier version appeared in Fendler and Wittlinger (1999).

world that is more pessimistic' (Guberman, 1996: 163). In this novel, Kristeva shows a more pessimistic view of society and depicts the crisis she believes the subject is going through:

> The thrust of my new book stems from the conjunction of the personal shock of mourning [...] and a public unease – the acknowledgement, which was barely present in my first novel, of a general disarray in a society - to begin with, our own. As a psychoanalyst (that is one of my frames of reference), I am sensitive to the collapse of minimal values and the rejection of elementary principles. (Guberman, 1996: 163)

Guberman describes her pessimism as 'a world tainted with pain, disorder, mourning, violence, apathy, depression, barbarity, and banality' (Guberman, 1996: 162). Although the novel (and interviews of the time) confirm Guberman and Sichère's views, *Le vieil homme et les loups* is also a eulogy of subjectivity: against the deadened characters of the novel, Kristeva opposes more vibrant 'heroes', whose capacity for subjective survival, give the novel a more positive note.

Synopsis

Le vieil homme et les loups could be described as a murder mystery. Its opening section 'the invasion' is set in 'Santa Barbara', a town paralysed by the tyranny of an unknown entity, 'the wolves', who have invaded the town and commit murders at random, keeping the inhabitants in a state of permanent terror. Three characters are prominent in this first part: Sceptisius Clarus, the old man, a paternal and philosophical figure who refuses to bow to the wolves' might, Alba Ram, the old man's pupil and a hazy character whose persona, thoughts and actions appear unclear (to the reader and to herself) and Vespasian, Alba's condescending husband, whose relationship with the old man seems to be one of contained courteousness. Vespasian is having an affair with 'la collègue du lifting', 'the face lift colleague', a seemingly happy-go-lucky character whose purpose in life is to lift other people's spirits and bodies. The first part of the story is told in the third person and conveys a feeling of confusion, of being in a twilight zone closer to the atmosphere of dreams than reality.

The second section, 'série noire' sees the arrival of Stéphanie Delacour, ex-inhabitant of Santa Barbara and a journalist enquiring about one of the murders. Her enquiry, conducted in the first person, leads her to remember childhood traumas, to consider the identity of the other protagonists, to re-define her own identity as an exile, and after the death of the old man in the third section 'Capricio', to re-live and mourn the death of her own father and seek the true face of the wolves.

Le vieil homme et les loups is based on much of Kristeva's personal experience as a Bulgarian native. Santa Barbara, a name reminiscent of 'Sainte Barbarie', Saint Barbarity, could be any town, anywhere. It presents aspects of many cities, with markers which identify Santa Barbara as both western and eastern: readers from the

East recognise the invasion of the wolves as emblematic of the Red Armies invading Eastern Europe, while readers in the West will remember Santa Barbara as an American television series. The narrator thus implies on the one hand a globalisation of the difficulties human subjects are experiencing and on the other a crisis pertaining to late 20th century society.

The Paternal Function: Between Disillusion and Illusion

Kristeva is concerned about the disillusionment of the people of the East, who, after encountering the failure of socialist ideals, are left in a state of distress and turn to the West to provide them with the democratic answers that will help them rebuild their social space. The 'new nomenklatura' is presented to us as a masquerade of the old, a new wolf/'loup'[4] to disguise the fact that the old regime is not entirely dead, but operating under a more pervasive disguise. Indeed, Kristeva sympathises with the predicament of former dissidents from the East who, in a context where wheeling and dealing, political passivity and incompetence are de rigueur, are at a loss to define what they now might be dissenting against.

The author is critical of the two models presently available for the shaping of post-cold-war society. These two models, eastern and western, rest on the role played by authority figures (the guarantors of the paternal function) in the process of identity formation. If authority is exercised too rigidly, as was the case in eastern Europe, the paternal function does not permit any deviation from the norm set by that authority; the existence of difference within the individual's identity is negated and its expression forbidden and punishable, be it politically or artistically. On the contrary, if authority is not exercised, and Kristeva suggests that it is the case in western Europe, the paternal function is not performed, that is to say the individual is unable to position theirself in relation to paternal authority; here again, the sense of identity is negated since there is no paternal entity to identify with or against.

Kristeva is indeed pessimistic about the state of democratic societies in western Europe. She is very critical of the political arena in democracies which she defines as a 'technocratic setup' within which the political leaders are:

> […] responsible but not guilty - and this means that all subjective and moral dimensions have been reabsorbed, eliminated, by the inexorable march of bureaucracy that is more and more anonymous and responsible to itself alone. There are no more culprit [...] : since good and evil don't exist, total bureaucracy, another version of totalitarianism, has trivialized and animalized the human. (Guberman, 1996: 174)

In the absence of a clearly defined positioning of authority, the place of power is being left vacant. Instead, we are being offered a moralising euphoric discourse, a consensual ideology which erases problems rather than addresses them and around

4 In French, 'un loup' is also a black velvet mask, worn at masked balls to disguise one's identity.

which we rally. As no one seems to be in charge, an increasing and alarming number of individuals are losing interest in political issues.

Santa Barbara is representative of both eastern and western realities. It stands at the junction between two opposite processes, a place where inhabitants seem to have lost their identity and the desire to reconstruct themselves. They operate collectively, the one identical to the other, a town of nobody's in a world of illusions. In Santa Barbara, people sense that crimes[5] are being committed, but there are no bodies to be identified as victims and nobody can be identified as the criminal(s). The inhabitants know of crimes because of rumours heard behind closed doors but these are never addressed openly. Even the character of Stephanie, from whom the reader expects some kind of logic and organisation of the plot, ends up identifying the dead body of Alba, only to meet Alba alive again later, and as a self-proclaimed criminal. No one is willing to take a position of knowledge either on the victims' or on the criminals' parts, and those who do either mistake appearances for the truth (Stephanie) or die (the old man). Yet, even the death of the old philosopher, which would have proven that Santa Barbara is hiding its crimes, is inconclusive as the reader does not find out whether he dies murdered (victim of someone else's crime) or as a reaction to the shock of seeing the truth in a deadly vision of crime (victim of his own crime). Everyone is, at some point in the story, a victim and a criminal, with a blurring of the frontier that separates the two identities. In the absence of a clear definition of 'crime', be it in the evilness of the criminal or the innocence of the victim, the very notion of 'crime' disappears, and the official knowledge is that there is no crime in Santa Barbara. It is also, for Kristeva, an absence of the sense of what is good and bad, that is to say a vacancy of the voice of authority (the State, the author-narrator, the reader, the inhabitants of Santa Barbara) which disables us from taking a position for or against that authority.

The impression left by Santa Barbara is that of a town built on illusions, with everybody being excited about the spectacle of crime they heard of, but that no one seems to care about as a real life event, as if the inhabitants had become bored with or blasé in the face of the banality of reality. As in the American series of the same name, Santa Barbara is a place where life occurs on the surface and the surface has been modified, disguised, lifted to a state of ever lasting excitement: not only excitement for the body-beautiful, as for the fans of the television series 'Santa Barbara', but also excitement for the illusory spectacle of life and death as presented by the media. Behind that fabricated surface, there is nothing to be found of the human subject; it is this vulgarisation of subjectivity, of human life, mainly but not solely by the media, that Kristeva sees as criminal, because illusion has become the norm and because we revere those mirages like sacred images of true life.

5 literally (reminiscent of the Red Army) and figuratively (the withering away of human identity).

The Impoverishement of Psychical Activity

For Kristeva, this situation is barbarous and it is precisely this combination of East/West issues, totalitarianism, collapse of idealistic values, malaise, banality, which converge in Santa Barbara under the guise of Wolves. Moreover, as a psychoanalyst, Kristeva sees a parallel between the socio-economic situation and the disquieting loss of interest in psychical life. Three solutions to the impoverishment of psychical activity are presented to us: pharmaceutical answers, in the character of Alba who resolves her depression through the personal use of drugs, and later through administering a concoction of drugs and poison to Vespasian, as an answer to the anxiety caused by their relational problems; media answers, with soporific ready-made images of trivia; religious answers, with the resurgence of fundamentalism, be it religious or nationalistic.

This impoverishment also has repercussions on a linguistic level with the 'withering away of language just as there is a withering away of culture' (Guberman, 1996: 169). Languages, like cultures, display a general laziness which can be perceived in the tendency to copy and recreate the structures of the American English language, with a particular predilection for the phrases recurring in media productions (video games, film industry, television series, etc.), often but not necessarily American. Kristeva envisions two possibilities to protect the diversity of languages and cultures from being homogenised on the American model, a protection vital in a Europe rich of its linguistic diversity: either a reactive turning back to tradition, to an idealised past we are nostalgic for precisely because it is lost (this is the domain of the purists and the conservatives), or the open grafting of aspects of other cultures and mentalities onto the language under threat, in order to insert within that language, the seeds of awareness and awakening.

In *Le vieil homme et les loups*, Kristeva grafts onto French the Latin language, which carries a sense of loss, sorrow and mourning as Latin is a dead language to us. Hence, Kristeva privileges subversing (sub-verse, like an under current breaking the course of the linguistic and cultural flow) over the implementation of drastic linguistic measures in which no one takes responsibility since responsibility is projected onto the linguistic imperialism of the invasive 'other'.

These three cultural phenomena (pharmaceutical, media and fundamentalism), combined with the levelling of languages and identities on the American model, are symptomatic of the impoverishment of western culture and the vacancy of the psyche which seeks elsewhere for its answers: a culture of illusion, running on empty images of false hopes which draw the contours of our 'psychic laziness, fleeting narcissistic mirages' (Guberman, 1996: 173) that rest on 'the careful shunting aside of the reality of suffering and the necessity to confront such suffering with a full knowledge of the facts' (Guberman, 1996: 173).

'Ecriture': Recapturing Subjectivity

Faced with the knowledge of these facts, Kristeva then addresses the question of whether there might be different solutions from those mentioned above. Her work revolves round three issues which all deal with aspects of language: psychoanalysis and literature which are epitomised in the process of writing, in the French sense of 'écriture'. 'Ecriture' can be defined as a literary practice that defies discursive pretensions, on the writer's part, to omniscience and neutrality. Theoretical discourse is an obvious example, but we can also consider most discourses pretending to hold the truth, by removing the fallible narrator from the text, hence endowing him (the masculine is appropriate, as 'her' would imply a questioning of the 'gendered truth") with special powers of insight, beyond the text itself.

To the contrary, 'écriture' carries within its own discourse the heterogeneity particular to human experience. In her understanding of 'human experience', Kristeva[6] takes up Freud's concept of 'heimlich/unheimlich. Freud suggested that the subject's entry into the symbolic sphere is marked by the repression of what threatens the integrity of their ego, that is to say, symbolisation stems from a process of estrangement from the pre-linguistic sphere. The subject must become an other, a stranger in order to become a subject; the symbolic subject is a foreigner in exile from their pre-linguistic territory: the maternal. What was part of the baby's experience of its pre-linguistic time (the here-and-now experience of being without language, without separation) has now become strange and this strangeness the subject must repress in order to be represented. However, repression is never perfect and the human subject experiences over and over again this process of repression (Freud's 'return of the repressed'). With repetition, repression itself becomes familiar or the process of estrangement is familiar territory. Kristeva argues that, in the first process of estrangement, what is repressed is 'the processes and the representative contents no longer necessary for pleasure, self-preservation and for the adaptive growth of the individual as a speaking subject and a living organism' (Kristeva, 1988: 272-3). These processes and representative contents deal with the questions of death, of origin (the feminine, birth: the maternal) and possibly the drives acting as a frontier between the organic and the psyche. It is precisely those drives that the process of 'écriture' pretends to symbolise: 'to put the neutral surface of abstract words into contact with a whole dynamic of recollection that leads us at once to recall traumas, the pains or the pleasures, and the most archaic sensations' (Guberman, 1996: 55). Style, 'one possibility of being in contact with our unconscious [...] our sensations' (Guberman, 1996: 55), occurs when the memory of these pains and sensations are translated into language. Writing is a journey of reconciliation between the subject's body and his/her memory, which appears to the reader as changing style. 'Ecriture' then deals with the symbolisation of the archaic memory of the pre-linguistic bond with the maternal space, in brief, re-enacts the move from the maternal to the paternal

---

6 See *Etrangers à nous-mêmes* (Kristeva, 1988), especially chapters one and eight.

function. This movement is precisely what Kristeva attempts to illustrate in the novel.

Kristeva's style in *Le vieil homme et les loups* displays this process/trial the narrator goes through by displacing any fixed position the subject appears to be in to start with. On the one hand, the murder mystery genre enables the narrator, especially in section two, to break the linearity of the story, as the fragments of evidence that she finds on the way trigger several stories that the narrator imagines are related to the murder. On the other hand, the atmosphere of the novel is, overall, disturbing, as the scrambling of voices and genres prevents the reader from taking position: clipped dialogues, the abundance of allegory and metaphors, the narrator's voice being displaced from first to third person, etc., block the reader's effort to settle comfortably into one fixed reading identity. These shifts confer a multiplicity of identities, on both the narrator and the reader's parts.

Moreover, the heroes of Santa Barbara are from nowhere specific; they are created/born foreigners, with no origin à priori. Yet they are from somewhere since they exist and belong in the continuum of human history. The reader's identification with any of the characters thus challenge the meaning of their own existence, questioning the relationship between origin and social belonging: from organic to psychical to social subject. Santa Barbara is a town built out of real life details, gathered together as the product of the narrator's imagination and calling the readers' memories and fantasies about their own place of origin. Hence, the narrative path followed by Stéphanie, from order to disorder and finally to subjective truths is also that of the reader: what began as a comfortable reading activity turns into a disrupting journey, at the end of which the reader is left alone to gather the scattered pieces of their reading experience and through the process of 'écriture' renew their definition of their own image.

The narrator's journey is a reminiscence of her foreignness re-lived with its affects though 'écriture' and enabling a renewal of identity. This journey is also shared by the reader through a process of transference effected in the use of metaphors. Metaphor 'operates, giving form to infantile psychic inscription that are located on the border of the unnameable' (Kristeva in Guberman, 1996: 163-4). Hence, through metaphors, the narrator addresses, beyond the realm of consciousness (and resistance), the reader's own psychical imprints. 'Ecriture' is not a totalising mode of writing pretending to arrest its progression at perfect meaning; rather, it is an endless process in which homogeneity and heterogeneity interact in the production of a renewed identity that is to say an identity of multiplicity rather than sameness.

In *Le vieil homme et les loups*, this dynamic is exemplified in Stephanie, a character who stands out at the end of the novel, as a positive identificatory figure. Stephanie embodies the foreigner. She is both from Santa Barbara and an outsider, an exile from the place. From the moment of her arrival, she positions herself as an exile from her past in the town and lists what she recognises as familiar in the same town ('heimlich'/'unheimlich'). As a foreigner,[7] she has a privileged relationship and understanding of the move from maternal to paternal, that is of the process of subjectivation. In a novel where all attempts at escaping crisis have failed, she takes on the image of saviour, the one whose knowledge of 'where we come from' might allow a renewal of identity. However, this 'knowledgeable saviour' image soon vanishes with her failure to provide the reader with a coherent interpretation of the crisis that beholds the town. Her journey as a character proceeds from this reminiscence which leads her, not only to investigate crimes, but also to reflect on the other protagonists' relationship with the wolves, to finally question her own psychical space. Stephanie's arrival breaks the fragmented course of the first section; she steps into a situation of crisis and chaos and brings, to begin with, a sense of hope for order through the detached and non-committal attitude she displays. In this sense, Stephanie endows the story with a psychoanalytic tone, as she exemplifies the same positioning as an analyst at work, in both her postures and her thinking processes. However, she soon turns the analysis on herself as the event of death calls for a deeper reminiscence of her past. Especially in the third part, Stephanie faces the unconscious upheaval that her encounter with her own foreignness and death have opened; she then begins to address her relationship with mortality and origin. The message is clear: if there is salvation (the novel ends ambiguously), the subject will not find it in omniscient others, the gurus to lost souls, but within themself, by engaging in an act of re-collection and interpretations of their past. In short, the renewal of the subject in crisis is about symbolising the maternal.

If Stephanie represents the only positive (even if inconclusive) character in the novel, her path is contrasted by Alba and Vespasian's closing of psychical activity; Alba, in her depressed state, remains untouched and untouchable, a truly repressed

---

7 The foreigner has long held a privileged place in people's imaginary and the media have been exploiting the gold mine that foreignness is. Foreignness and its associated emotional charge is being recuperated and marketed in various productions precisely because the foreigner's strangeness induces a dualistic re-action: they can be both attractive and repulsive. Their differences confer to them powers and knowledge that the natives, in their sameness, do not possess and are both attracted to and threatened by. Present representations of the foreigner, in a time of globalisation and loss of a clearly defined enemy, are moving away from the 'Kung Fu' image - that is the other as an enigmatic traveller, with exotic customs, a 'sexy' accent or look, etc., whose image we can define, control and buy/sell. We now look for 'our' foreigners beyond the realm of human consciousness in the proliferation of cyborgs and aliens who are now invading our lives, X-entities we cannot even name, but which fascinate us and which we must ultimately destroy. In the light of the issues of origin and death mentioned above, it is interesting to note the success of a series such as *The X-files*, which clearly transcends the boundaries of origin and death; viewers are attracted and repulsed by the prospect of an origin which transcends the limits of human reproduction and the questioning of a death which might offer something other than the utter destruction of the subject.

character whose capacity to question her psychical space is being made impossible by the fact that she chooses hatred and crime without guilt and without responsibility. Similarly, Vespasian portrays the caricature of male violence, destructive, murderous, a monstrous character who does not appear to have any kind of inner depth to his personality. Both Alba and Vespasian embody the death of psychical life; they are more like automatons than human beings and therefore their subjectivity has become meaningless, a series of unquestioned and unquestionable automated tasks.

In relation to racial crimes, Kristeva stated that: 'Should we condemn, be indignant, punish? Necessarily. Absolutely. I am afraid, however, that [...] in simply pointing out evil, we run the risk of authentifying and fixing it' (Kristeva, 1990a: 10). In Santa Barbara, crime is not authentified, not fixed, which enables the novel to move beyond a mere detective story. At the end of a detective story, order is restored when the culprit is brought to justice and given a cross to carry; that cross is both a punishment for disrupting our social peace and in some way a projection of our own guilt for secretly experiencing the erotic pleasure (in abjection or attraction) the spectacle of crime triggers.[8] The eroticism of crime brings out, in the human subject, a form of bestiality of which the wolves of the novel are reminiscent. Stephanie, realises that '[s]ociety is founded on a crime committed together' (Kristeva, 1990a: 18). Santa Barbara's social order is a reversed sense of order; as representative of a society, Santa Barbara's existence rests on a fantasy of crime and the assurance that crime as a fantasy goes on, as the pulling force that gathers members of its society. Chaos is the norm, order (finding culprit, denouncing good and evil) would bring this social edifice down.

Two questions support the novel's intrigue: what crime is being committed? And who commits those crimes? Stephanie moves from investigating the crime of others (the inhabitants) to questioning the possibility of another, more invisible crime, the crime of the other within the self and which concerns and threatens an entire social organism. It is a movement away from scapegoating and towards identifying scapegoating as the crime. Targetting the other, the different, the foreigner as the recipient of my shortcomings means that the 'I' does not take any responsibility or guilt for the crime committed. As an innocent party, this 'I' can denounce and clearly fix crime in the other's subjectivity and therefore reinforce the dynamic of 'xenophobia' which cements the social. *In Le vieil homme et les loups*, 'crime' is identified not as an event but as a generic term bearing a function of control of the inhabitants who then reproduce the same dynamic of control onto

---

8 Apart from the obvious success of the 'mediasation' of crime (OJ Simpson, Louise Woodward, the proliferation of serial killers' representations in films, etc), there are numerous accounts that the spectacle of criminals being hanged, in Great Britain, provoked in the crowd of spectators erotic feelings ranging from orgasms (death as sexual excitement) to vomiting (abjection of the death drive). Kristeva recounts in 'Pourquoi?' (Kristeva, 1990a: 9) how 'Hitler cynically asserted that antisemitism was the only authorised form of pornography' at the time of the Third Reich.

the next social layer (the wolves-Vespasian-Alba for instance). The wolves, the ones who commit the crimes, symbolise this invisible dynamic; it is the entire society which is responsible in closing up the psychical potential of its members and rejecting the responsibility onto an invisible other, the wolves themselves.

The only characters who do not fall prey to the wolves are Stephanie and the old man who both turn the dynamic onto themselves, thus breaking the contagion. The old man, in all his wisdom, dies of too much awareness, murdered by the wolves: whether the wolves are others', who could not bear to be exposed, or his own, having had the unbearable vision of his own and others' otherness and of a social space reduced to the acting of a spectacle of murder, the question remains open at the end of the novel. Stephanie 'dies' symbolically in the psychical experience of her encounter with the reminiscence of her father's death. This experience put her in contact with the turmoil of sensations and affects reminiscent of the pre-linguistic, maternal experience. However, Stephanie's 'écriture' enables her to support this reminiscence of the maternal with the symbolic (paternal) function. She then emerges from the ashes of her inner journey renewed and prepared for another investigatory challenge.[9]

The Failure of the Paternal Function

Freud defined his patients' illnesses as the result of unresolved Oedipal conflicts, that is a failed encounter with the Oedipal father. Today's psychoanalysts 'have expanded [their] definitions of psychological structures and introduced new categories such as the 'borderline' personality or the 'false-self'. [...They] now place a greater emphasis on the pre-oedipal stage and on the relationship between the psyche and soma' (Kristeva, 1996a: 10). Contemporary understandings in human pathology suggest that a changed cultural scene means a change in the characteristic forms of human personality. Social membership rests on the individual's understanding and adaptation, 'by means of which the individual reconciles himself to instinctual deprivation and submits to the requirement of social existence' (Lasch, 1979: 76). For the individual, socialisation means coming to terms with the loss of the pre-social or instinctive world of infant experience and consenting to socio-cultural demands. These demands are dependent upon a given history and society: social membership today rests on a different social contract than in medieval society for instance. It then follows that characteristic forms of psychological deformation are an expression of the culture that fostered them. Freud had already insisted 'on the continuity between psychic health and psychic sickness' (Lasch, 1979: 76), conceiving of both health and sickness as metaphors of individual or collective psychical life. Analysing the paternal function, Oedipal and pre-Oedipal, as the locus of a failed subjectivity is to construe the failure of the paternal function as a cultural pathology pertaining only to the current cultural

9 See Kristeva's third novel *Possessions* (1996d).

climate. Yet, some also believe that the Oedipal model might in itself be failing the representation of all subjectivities, present and past,[10] suggesting the 'failure of the paternal function' as a modernist expression of current cultural concerns. The efforts to construe the human solely as a monolithic structure (in the neurosciences for instance), could be understood as an attempt to by-pass the limitations of such psychoanalytic meta-narratives. However, those efforts are themselves part of the problematic of subjectivation, recreating the idiosyncrasies of the human subject, rather than creating an understanding of subjectivity from another base.

The Two Moments of Failure of the Paternal Function

Kristeva suggests two ways in which the paternal function is failing. In 1983, she stated that:

> There has been too much stress on the crisis in paternity as cause of psychotic discontent. Beyond the often fierce but artificial and incredible tyranny of the Law and the Superego, the crisis in the paternal function that led to the deficiency of psychic space is in fact an erosion of the loving father. (Oliver, 1991: 55)

In a first stage, Kristeva suggests a flaw in analysing 'psychotic discontent' as symptomatising solely a crisis in the Oedipal paternal function. Instead of casting blame on one corner of the Freudian triangle, she prefers to argue for an earlier triangulation, preceding and preparing the Oedipal one. Yet, in the 1990s, Kristeva has increasingly been raising the alarm against the crisis in/of authority, pointing out the increasing absence of the Oedipal paternal function. 'No one any longer respects authority; no one any longer occupies the seat of power, [...]; and no one is in charge' (Guberman, 1996: 167).

In 1980, she forecast a shift in psychical disorder away from the 'traditional' Oedipal neuroses and towards an increase in the production of borderline children. She conjectured that the increase in 'the number of helping institutions for early childhood' (Guberman, 1996: 119) were an attempt to 'replace the failed mother, as is remarked only too often, but it is above all to replace the non existent father: to play the role of separator' (Guberman, 1996: 119). Behind these compensatory measures, testifying to a society's attempt at counteracting the absence of a paternal figure, is hiding the 'underestimation of the paternal function' (Guberman, 1996: 119): an anonymous social collective re-places absent authority with coping measures. The prognosis was confirmed later with the emergence of 'new maladies of the soul'. 'Today's patients are different from the ones Freud saw. They do not correspond to the traditional classification systems consisting of three or four categories (hysterical, obsessional, paranoid, and so forth)' (Guberman, 1996: 10).

10 Blanck and Blanck (1986) suggest the failure of subjectivation on a pre-oedipal level not only in contemporary subjects but also in Freud's early 19th century subjects. See: Blanck and Blanck (1986).

Many psychoanalysts today note the growing number of post-Freudian psychic organisations (borderline, false self and schizoid especially).

The failure of the paternal function is then theorised at two moments of the individual's history. There would be first a failure of the paternal function within the pre-linguistic maternal function, a failure of the 'loving father' of the primary Oedipal triangle. This failure would later be reinforced during the Oedipal phase proper, by a crisis of that function on a symbolic level. If we follow Kristeva's logic, the failure of the Oedipal paternal function is simultaneous with the failure of the pre-Oedipal paternal function. Although she does not specify the relationship between the two aspects of the paternal function, the infant's pre-Oedipal paternal function and the mother's Oedipal paternal function can be conceived as two aspects of the same function. For example, the mother's love for her work functions as a separating agency (from her child), rewarding the mother's process of socialisation and structuring her symbolic self. This love for an other than the child is perceived by the infant both as a threat to its desire to keep the mother all for itself and as maternal protection: the paternal function protects the mother from de-structuring and therefore protects the child in need of maternal care. Moreover, the child desirous to keep maternal love endeavours to occupy the place of this threatening other-than-itself, to replace the Oedipal paternal function in the mother's heart. It then identifies itself with the Oedipal paternal function and by doing so becomes a symbolic subject itself.

We are dealing with two aspects of the same function separated by the advent of speech (symbolisation) in the individual's life. The leap into symbolisation inaugurates a history of the paternal function and its failure. Considered from the subject's individual history, this failure, although present from the beginning, is identified only when they reach subject 'status': a difficult relationship with the symbol signifies the earlier failure to access symbolicity. From a historical perspective of psychoanalytic theory, this failure is noticed as a resistance to symbolic activity, or analytic failure, directing psychoanalytic research towards pre-symbolic experience. Cooper and Maxwell (1995) sum up the view of many contemporary analysts when they state:

> In any event, the prognosis of these [narcissistic] patients is poor. If it does come, change comes about very slowly. Freud (1914) was not wrong when he claimed that their resistance was 'unconquerable'. Whether they clamour for insight or not, the 'how', 'what' and 'why' is rarely understood by them [...] given that the idealised primary object is untouchable. [...] it may well turn out to be an analysis that goes nowhere as a result of the patient's early childhood experience of non-containment. (Cooper and Maxwell, 1995: 124)

In spite of these negative views, the resistance of these new types of patients has stimulated some theorists and practitioners like Kristeva, into reconsidering the psychoanalytic field, its aims and prospect. The survival of psychoanalysis, and its psychotherapeutic derivatives, as a viable method of cure of contemporary psychical impasses, rests on understanding and overcoming contemporary resistance. Analysts are dealing with 'early childhood experience of non-containment', as Maxwell and Cooper put it, that is the construction of a subjectivity in the absence of a protective pre-Oedipal paternal function. Early non-containment results in the subject's inability to reproduce containment on a linguistic (Oedipal) level: 'I' am not contained in the symbol, 'I' do not connect what 'I' am with its representation. What is perceived in psychoanalytic terms as 'resistance' is, on the one hand the analysand's failure at connecting with the actualisation of unconscious contents in the person of the analyst, that is the transference on the Oedipal paternal agent (the analyst) of the pre-Oedipal; on the other hand the analysts' failure at connecting with the 'idealised primary object' (Cooper and Maxwell, 1995: 124), that is the counter-transference of the analyst (Oedipal paternal agent) of pre-Oedipal contents. If we imagine the individual histories of both analyst and patient as constituted of two moments, pre-Oedipal and Oedipal, the disconnection for Kristeva or resistance for Freud occurs when the analyst fails to hear the patient's pre-Oedipal tale or when the patient fails to tell their pre-Oedipal experience. Laplanche and Pontalis define 'resistance' as 'everything which, in the acts and words of the analysand, is opposed to his accessing unconscious contents' (Laplanche and Pontalis, 1991: 420). The term 'resistance' would then be inappropriate, and should be substituted it for 'absence'. The new subjects are not so much presenting unconscious resistance to the analyst's interpretative work but encountering a void in the place of early identification, translated as an 'absenteeism' of the subject in their relationship with the symbol. In reverse, the analysts' frustration in analysing the subject results from encountering a void in the place where they traditionally expected to interpret a narrative of subjectivity: words and affects are disconnected, rendering interpretation of unconscious desire void. Cooper and Maxwell (1995) point out that 'today, there is a growing trend which explains impasse in terms of treatment error and puts the responsibility on the analyst' (Cooper and Maxwell, 1995: 122). They are referring to a psychoanalytic group named 'the Independents' who emphasise the importance of the environment in contributing to the subject's health as opposed to Kleinians who focus on the infant's part. Taken to the extreme, such a shift of responsibility from the individual to the environment is itself part of what Kristeva sees as a symptom of the failure of the paternal function: individuals are blameless in their difficulties and relinquish their authority upon their own subjectivation process to environmental failure (and cure).

The Independents' views can be paralleled with Freud's views regarding pre-Oedipality. Freud failed at articulating the importance of pre-Oedipality due to his own resistance to the maternal. We are today witnessing a similar resistance of the psychoanalytic field, hesitating between hanging on to its old Oedipal model and tempted by the prospects of uncharted pre-Oedipal territory; this division is itself symptomatic of the failure of the paternal function, with a subjectivity split between a repairing of the subject's relationship with the Oedipal (and a resistance/absence of pre-Oedipality) and a return to pre-Oedipal contents in order to verbalise it again.

The New Maladies of the Soul

Kristeva's latest work (1990s) suggests that society yearns for an absolute Oedipal paternal function capable of erasing the uncertainties of the pre-Oedipal paternal function. In an interview for 'L'Humanité' (Kristeva, 1997b), she describes how this yearning for the absolute is symptomatised under various cultural guises. The cultural tendency to reduce the psyche to a monolithic structure, opposed to the Freudian model of heterogeneity, is one such guise. Freud imagined the psyche as a multi-layered structure enabling the processing of information from sensory system to abstract thought. As part of his vision, Freud recognised the existence of 'filtering' processes that translate raw data into psychical imprints. These imprints, the human subject can translate into an infinite combination of symbolic representations, making the (Freudian) human psyche the locus of endless and unmeasurable processes. In contrast, certain scientific and media efforts are geared towards a genetic determination of psychical activity and aim at a biological definition of the human subject whereby body and psyche are totally symbolisable into a spectacular vision: the human subject can be totally seen and known.

> The "new maladies of the soul" are characterised notably by a slowing down, if not a destruction of the faculty to fantasise. We are swamped with images, some of which sound like our own fantasies and appease us, but which, due to a lack of interpretative discourse, do not liberate us. Moreover, the stereotypy of those images deprives us of the possibility to create our own imagery, our own imaginary scenarios. (Kristeva, 1997a: 125)

Such a change in patients has called for the refining of both theoretical models and psychoanalytic practice. In the new types of illnesses noticed in psychoanalytic practices, the common denominator is an increasingly poor relationship between the body (soma) and the word (psychical activity), with on the one hand a disinvestment of speech by bodily drives and on the other, a disempowerment of the subject in their ability to represent the body. Kristeva describes how patients speak a technical discourse where dreams and fantasies have been replaced by 'operative fantasies' (Kristeva, 1997a: 126), which indeed 'operate' and typify the subject rather than testify about the subject's interiority. There is a parallel between the withering away of imaginary activity on the one hand, and the absence of authority and the growing place given to media images on the other. The cultural profusion of ready-made images is diminishing and even replacing the human need and ability to create those images.[11] Moreover, the absence of a separating agency, the paternal function, has generated a human subject more and more incapable of

11 Philip K. Dick had imagined a society where emotions, no longer human-made, are generated by pre-programmed technical devices. See: Dick (1997).

separating itself from its image. The subject, unable to create significations, adopts substitute images which 'operate meanings' in its place, define subjectivity according to a type, but in which little is found of the plurality of individuals. The subject's images remain unformulated on a pre-psychical level and the non-verbalised body is mutated into somatic discharge and acting-out.

> [...] the "new maladies of the soul", that contemporary psychoanalysis encounters, testify of a lack in the elaboration of psychical conflicts: to the extent that not only are our contemporaries unable to judge good and evil and sink in its trivialization [...], but that many do not manage to represent their conflicts psychically (in sensations, words, images, thoughts), and consequently expose themselves to vandalisms, psychosomatic disorders, drugs. (Kristeva, 1998a: 69)

The 'new maladies of the soul' then testify to a clash between psychoanalytic definitions of the subject and a changed apprehension of the human. On the one hand, western culture apprehends psychical activity like software activity: 'maladies' can be measured and dysfunctions corrected with the help of technology. On the other hand, Kristeva is interpreting 'maladies' as symptomatic of a robotised subjectivity: psychical activity cannot be measured but interpreted and transformed into a more sociable outcome.

The attempt at totally representing the psyche is not a new idea. Freud himself had, in his earlier research, presumed the possibility of knowing and mapping the unconscious, by positing language activity as mediator between unconscious and conscious (figure 1): 'language constitutes an intermediary zone, interfaced with unconscious and conscious, and enables us to posit the former under the domination of the latter' (Kristeva, 1996a: 85). This led Freud, and psychoanalysts in general, to the enthusiastic belief that the unknowable in the subject could at last be known. Kristeva points out that because psychoanalysis partly rests on such a theoretical construct, the unconscious is also 'the 'promised land' of analysis' (Kristeva, 1996a: 88). This aspect of Freud's work, Kristeva prefers to distance herself from:

> My major disagreement with Freud in this field lies in the attention that I pay to language. In certain cases, the discourse of the melancholic is so impoverished that one wonders on what could one base an analysis. The depressive feels that it is not worth talking for the connection between the subject and the other has been virtually severed. The depressive feels that one can only weep and fall silent. [...] The language of the depressed person is not psychotic. But it rests upon a denial of the signifier which results from the dissociation of the affect from language. It speaks, but it does not touch me. (Kristeva, 1998c: 16)

The Freudian optimism of 1910 is today paralleled with a certain technological optimism regarding the cure of that which troubles the human. Lasch (1979) terms 'blind optimism' the manner in which western society 'surrounds the individual with manufactured fantasies of total gratification' (Lasch 1979: 389). He believes contemporary society is pathologically narcissistic, that is defensive 'against feelings of helpless dependency in early life' (Lasch, 1979: 389) and working towards countering the effects of such helplessness in adulthood. 'The new paternalism preaches not self-denial but self-fulfilment. It sides with narcissistic impulses and discourages their modification by the pleasure of becoming self-reliant, even in a limited domain, which under favourable conditions accompanies maturity' (Lasch, 1979: 390). In other words, a new form of Oedipal paternal function has emerged, to counter the failure of pre-Oedipal experience. Rather than functioning as a frustrating agent of the subject's needs, the Oedipal paternal function promotes itself as the fulfilment of needs. Hence, instead of acting as separator of the subject from their archaic impulse for reunion with the maternal, the new paternal function advertises the fulfilment of those impulses as desirable. The site of desire is not the mother but symbolic agents of the paternal in its function. Advertised as absolute answer to frustrated desire, the sites supported by the paternal function are never absolute enough to prevent further displacement onto others. The constant is the maintaining of a dualism: on the one hand the subject's unresolved pre-Oedipal experience predisposes them to dependence; on the other a society's pathological defence against dependence erects symbols of its maturity and control over itself. Following Lasch's argument, the Oedipal paternal function offers itself as reparation for a failed pre-Oedipality, by first reproducing the failure of separation from the pre-Oedipal on a symbolic level; second, a whole social edifice capitalises on the failure to separate, by offering the cure to discomforts in the form of tablets, software, slogans, images, etc. From anti-depressant consumerism to the mapping of human genetic encoding, contemporary 'discoveries' are the optimistic if not utopian message of human salvation. Behind it is the dynamic of the contemporary subject's link to this contemporary form of paternal function encouraging the disease while selling the cure.

Against utopian discourses of perfectionism and salvation, Kristeva remains adamant that psychical activity is not knowable because it is irreducible to language. We can 'discover' different linguistic combinations that are different expressions of the subject, carrying within their narratives the dynamic of identification with the paternal function. Contemporary narratives tell of a superseding of the relationship body/psyche by a relationship image/psyche. Kristeva is suggesting a replacing of bodily processes by the absorption of technological stimuli. In the first instance, fantasy is generated by a quantitative stimulation of the biological body, located at the point where the body and the outside world meet (sensory system). Stimuli are translated unconsciously into a qualitative charge and imprinted in the psyche as mnesic traces. Not yet objects, these traces are the transitory data between body and world. On the one side of the process, they retain the psychical, pre-objectified qualitative imprint of the body's points of contact with the outside; on the other, mnesic traces are the reserves of material from which the subject can draw and formulate their images. In the second instance, where images are formulated by another agency than the speaker, there is a reduction and quasi-suppression of both the necessity for the body to know the outside world and the processing of quantity into quality. Instead, we are witnessing a reduction of the 'subject' to visual stimulus, where human psychical processes are increasingly described in terms of computer software and the connection subject/world is a connection eye/screen.[12]

Moreover, where sight would be the sole point of contact between the body and the outside, this locus is itself a 'stereotypy' of the relationship body/world, an imagery reduced to a classifying of the body/world experience into a standard, homogenising the human into a ready-made fantasy shared by the collective.

> I see this transmission [of information] as if by a TV with fifty to a hundred stations, each different, transmitting very different information - although they cancel each other out - since one often has the impression they all participate in the same ideology or, in any case, in something held in common and not easily discernible but that is perhaps a form of resistance to anything surprising or to anything that could undermine the norm. (Guberman, 1996: 130)

Fields such as genetics and televisual technologies seek to simplify identity, or the conglomerate body/psyche, to a material image based on calculations. The psyche is either absolute or absent: banalised into a monolithic structure, reducible to technological certainty (degree 0 or 1), ready made and custom made (media, neurosciences), always reprogrammable and modifiable (pharmaceutical solutions, drugs, genetic manipulations), totally meaningful (nationalistic and religious fundamentalism, popular psychology). The cultural trend is to reduce the human subject to an intelligible symbol and in this equation, to erase the existence of the unconscious and of its endemic complications in the transformation of the body/psyche activity into symbols. In short, contemporary culture seeks to transform the (Freudian) subject into a robotised subject.

The robotisation of the subject is exemplified, not only in its technologisation (neurosciences, media), but also in the social sphere. Kristeva suggests that society has filled the space left vacant by the paternal function (actual father figures) with an absolute paternal function even more powerful that it is nameless, blameless and without clearly defined boundaries. The absolute of the paternal function can remain absolute (stable and fixed) because the actual functioning of paternal

---

12 Contemporary cinematographic productions testify of both a competition and an over-loading of visual narratives. In Ridley Scott's *Blade Runner* (1991), human society is presented in flattened narratives contrasted by the 'sensoriality' of android narratives. The quasi absence of a story line and the monotone delivery of the voice-over narrator suggest the doom of human narratives, conflicting with the extraordinary richness of androids' visual narratives. In a hyper technologised world where humans have survived by relinquishing the ability to sense and feel, Ridley Scott hints at an android identity exceeding that of humans' and so over-charged with sensory information that humans could not access it within the constraint of their schizoid 'nature'. The film closes on a potential android future, only visible to non-human eyes and understanding. See also: Dick (1997).

authority has been displaced onto the social arena itself and rendered absent. In the void hence created, the paternal function is without a symbol or 'represented' by the absence of a symbol. This symbol of paternal authority, once provided by human figures, has become a concept, a function controlled by the different parties that contribute to it their mechanisms of social enhancement: Science will provide its true formula, the media will market its image, politicians will translate it into a euphoric slogan, citizens will buy its promise of permission and potency, etc. In other words, the locus of authority, once physically occupied by a paternal figure is being disembodied and replaced by Absolute paternal 'sites': medical, political and religious discourses have replaced the 'I' of the former leaders' speeches. Paternal sites offer an exact narrative of the subject's dilemmas, from which uncertainties regarding the body/world experience have been removed. These narratives by-pass the question of a shaky or missing link between the individual and his/her world. Instead of verbalising the body, this link is displaced onto the site of paternal Absolutism. From this site, social members are gratified in their hindrance, The body is indeed the enemy. Paternal sites provide ready-made solutions that relocate the individual's discomfort in paternal care to provide a re-pairing of the link individual/world. The failure of the paternal function is first a failure to separate the subject from pre-Oedipal time, and second capitalises on pre-Oedipal need in order to re-create dependence of the subject on the Oedipal level. This failure is what binds the social together as it becomes the site where the subject and the paternal function, dependent upon one another are reconciled.

However, we might also suggest that the reproduction of pre-Oedipal time on a socio-symbolic level is also an attempt at controlling maternal time: the return of the maternal semiotic ('vandalisms') in the subject cannot be severed and is instead manipulated into an object of social enhancement. Lasch points out that modern day psychoanalysis has shifted its focus from primary narcissism (pre-Oedipal) to secondary narcissism (Oedipal). This 'shift from a psychology of instincts to ego psychology itself grew partly out of a recognition that the patients who began to present themselves in the 1940s and 1950s 'very seldom resembled the classical neuroses Freud described so thoroughly'' (Lasch, 1979: 80). Although Lasch's findings confirm the move from Oedipal (paternal) to narcissistic (maternal) concerns, Kristeva argues that the shift from primary to secondary narcissism is an attempt to repair the paternal function while by-passing resurging maternal experience.

New Maladies: New Transference

Kristeva is concerned with the increasingly pronounced presence of narcissistic depression, a form of depressive melancholia she interprets as the child's failure to encounter the 'loving father' (or the mother's failure to provide such a figure). The endeavour to 'isolate *The* modern disease, the one that colours the end of the 20th century and transfers it into the third millennium' (Kristeva, 1983: 463) calls for a 'softening' of the psychoanalytic tool, that is for a lessening of the analyst's (absolute) distance/silence. The change in subject pathology poses a new challenge to the psychoanalytic field.

Since her debut in the 1960s, Kristeva has increasingly relied upon the psychoanalytic model to articulate her ideas while increasingly complaining that the place of authority is being left vacant. Psychoanalysis is thus faced with an apparent contradiction in terms: a growing crisis of the paternal function nullifies the prospect of 'salvation' by traditional Freudian thought. If indeed the psychoanalytic (Freudian) model is to function, it needs the subject's link to the paternal function to exist in the first place. Freudian theory, but also Lacanian theory, rests on the primacy of the paternal function in the process of subjectivation. If that function is withering away to the point of vacancy, how can psychoanalysis be articulated as a theory and practice? Since the psychoanalytic model rests upon symbolic castration, traditional psychoanalysis might prove to be increasingly at a loss to understand a changing link between the subject and the paternal function. Psychoanalysis is today faced with an increasing resistance of patients to analysis. This endemic phenomenon is symptomatic of an absence, on the patient's part, of representations of affect that renders the analyst's interpretative work void. Analysts are then disempowered in their use of a methodology founded upon the Oedipal, castrating function of the analyst: as the 'new maladies' present them with a subject already disconnected from their symbols, castration would befall on a void. For this reason, Freud saw the analysis of the disconnection subject/paternal function as impossible.

Today, Kristeva is putting forward the possibility of cure beginning with the re-education of the subject to speech:

> The first task of the cure, therefore, is to re-establish the bond with language [...] healing the narcissistic wound in order to restore confidence in the self and in the other sufficiently to reinvest in language. [...] The work of the analyst is to reconnect language and affect. (Kristeva, 1998c: 16)

The initial step to analysis is now the re-connecting of language and affects. It means that analysts must reconsider their role as guarantors of the paternal function, or more precisely they must re-assess the definition of 'paternal function'. The 'softening' of the analyst's distance and their more invested connectedness with the patient suggests a different kind of transference/counter-transference in analytic setting. Instead of transference onto the separating (castrating) figure of the paternal function, Kristeva is suggesting the possibility of transference onto the holding aspect of the paternal function. In other words, the analyst's position is shifted from Oedipal (castrating) to pre-Oedipal (containing) paternal agency. Once the connection symbol-affect has been re-established, the psychoanalytic scene is also reinstated and a more traditional methodology restituted to the analyst, enabling the process from pre-Oedipal to Oedipal.

Arguably, Kristeva is promoting the reconstruction of the subject in order to meet the demands (and survival) of psychoanalytic methodology and she questions herself the ethics of such a practice.

> The stake of psychoanalysis - but also the crisis of psychoanalysis - is there. Should we build a psychical space, a certain mastery of the One, at the heart of the psychical upheavals of anguished, suicidal and impotent people? Or on the contrary should we follow, thrust, facilitate escapes, driftings? Is it about rebuilding a proper space, a "home" for contemporary Narcissi: repair the father, appease the mother, and allow to build a rich introspective inside, master of its losses and wanderings, assuming that such a goal is attainable? Or is it that the recurring of suffering which finds release, relaxation and satisfaction only in intoxication [...] indicates that a psychical era has come to a close? (Kristeva, 1983: 470)

Kristeva is putting forward a practice that rehabilitates the subject's relationship with the paternal function. Ironically, her aims are not dissimilar to the aims of other practices she has been decrying. When neurosciences aim at perfecting the representation of the human, they are effectively attempting the perfect mirroring human-symbol, that is the adhesion of the subject to an absolute paternal function. Hence, although diametrically opposed in methodology, it appears that different practices share a common interest in the rehabilitation of a paternal function in disarray. Assuming, as Kristeva puts it, that psychoanalysis can repair and appease patients' parental functions, should it do so? In the affirmative, psychoanalysis would create a dependency of the patient upon psychoanalysis and could become no more than a 'psychical fix', on a par with pharmaceutical or genetic solutions. In the negative, psychoanalysis would be participating in the ending of a psychical era, and the end of psychoanalytic narratives. Beyond this dilemma, Kristeva is advocating a medium term solution: the patient's psychical activity would first be restored in order to enable analytic work to take place; second, she is calling for intensified research in the elaboration of pre-Oedipal experience.

In this, Kristevan practice distances itself from others in its interpretation of failure of the paternal function. The failure of the paternal function is a symptom of the subject's pre-history. Cure is envisioned only in the re-actualisation of the subject's past in order to investigate the earlier site of failure, the pre-subject and its relationship with pre-symbolic time. The suggestion is then the re-assignment of the paternal function to maternal time, an enquiry that has so far interested the psychoanalytic field only and that remains limited to a proportion of that field. The investigation of maternal contents means the investigation of an a-symbolic reality symbolically described as madness (psychosis). To investigate such reality requires the investigator's willingness and ability to relate to psychotic contents. This is where Kristeva remains doubtful of the value of exact sciences, as the translation of the human into abstraction misses out on the reality of pre-Oedipality. Moreover this longing for the abstract (formulations, images, slogans, etc.) epitomises the contemporary subject's craving for a strong paternal protection against resurging maternal contents. Psychoanalysis would for now remain the privileged tool of investigation of such pre-history. In effect, relating to pre-Oedipality amounts to an intensified 'countertransferential mode of listening' (Guberman, 1996: 88), while maintaining the reality of symbolic constraints. The analyst's ability to maintain their connection with the symbolic while investigating pre-Oedipality is crucial in operating the 'move" from pre-Oedipal to Oedipal contents. Short of this ability to sublimate, the analyst can either resist the counter-transference of maternal contents and fail in their analytic work, or fail to keep the link with the paternal function and enter psychosis.

> Is it possible to go to the frontier of original repression, where the symbolic character of the human collapses into chaos? The extreme anxiety of the analyst him/herself is so strongly required, in the journey towards this strangeness, that few of us are capable of bearing it: the number of analysts who have the necessary sublimatory capacities to "go there" without "staying there" is minute. (Kristeva, 2000: 340- 1)

If psychoanalysis is to disappear as a theory and a practice, it will be through a failure to investigate contemporary 'new maladies', either through a dogmatic loyalty to Freudian methods or through the trivialisation of psychoanalysis. The development of new research into the uncharted frontier of original repression is then called for, a field of research that constitutes the biggest part of Kristeva's oeuvre. The 'salvation' of human subjectivity rests in analysing the departure of the subject from a failed relationship with the paternal function, a process only psychoanalysis attempts to interpret. 'It is about making of a crisis a 'work in progress'' (Kristeva, 1983: 471). The reassignment of the paternal function to the maternal disposition entails the elaboration of different transferential processes and represents the place where the 'new maladies' can be defined and understood.

Conclusion

The crisis of subjectivity constitutes a key narrative of contemporary psychoanalysis and should be positioned in relation with the stalling of the modernist project. Put shortly, the crisis in late modernity is illustrated in the crisis of psychoanalytic theory. More precisely, the crisis of the psychoanalytic narrative can be narrowed down to a crisis in the paternal function. Socio-political changes, the French Revolution, industrial advancements, the rise of the bourgeois state and of capitalism, have brought about the questioning and for some, the end of master narratives, the paternal function being but one of those narratives. In turn, the death of the father has meant a change of perspective on the subject but has also impacted individuals in their identities. Indeed, theorists now believe that we are witnessing the rise of the narcissist as the prevailing form of identity. Correlatively this has also meant the rise of maternal contents no longer kept at bay by the paternal function. The modernist project is at a critical end and, from a psychoanalytic perspective at least, the obstruction is a failing paternal function. Kristeva believes that the way out of crisis for the modernist project must be a revitalising of those dying narratives, a kind of like-cures-like cure. It means a revisiting of psychoanalysis in the place where it fails, that is the re-defining of the paternal function. For others, like Zizek, the demise of the paternal function has also meant the rise of narcissistic pathologies and the prevailing of the 'maternal superego'. However, Zizek's analysis of the paternal function may not be as pessimistic as Kristeva's. In fact, far from being the end of the father, narcissism may be a way for the father's progeny to claim him and his function in spite of his absence. But this deceitful trick of the subject would then also mean the repetition and continuation of modernist 'crisis', as Kristeva sees it, rather than its resolution.

In 1991 Kristeva attempted to illustrate cultural crisis in her second novel *Le vieil homme et les loups*. The interpretation of crisis is staged in a condensed format: within the frame of the narrative, the difficulties Kristeva has been describing in her analysis of contemporary society converge in the world of a fictitious town, Santa Barbara. She sees the collapse of the eastern bloc and eastern ideals as a significant event that enabled the encounter East/West and exposed the disarray western democracies find themselves in. Easterners in search of new values turned to a western democratic system which held much promise for the reconstruction of their lost identities. What some naively regarded as a Western 'El Dorado' proved equally corrupted, although under a different form. Kristeva's strategy is not so much to describe eastern and western socio-political organisations but to describe under the guise of a murder mystery, the crisis common to both sides. In her novel, the location could be either (or both) eastern or/and western. In this setting with ill defined boundaries, the narrator tells of the protagonists' common fate in their relationship with the paternal function: the latter is represented by sinister figures (the absent leaders, the devouring wolves), or tragic characters whose 'goodness' is rewarded with death (the old man). The narrative implies that the paternal function is either too rigid (forbidding subjective differences), or too evasive (forbidding subjective stability). The combination of both aspects results in a vision of the paternal function that encourages the confusion between the good and the bad and facilitates perversion. Subjective development is arrested in a state of apathy where protagonists have lost the ability to question the status quo and therefore the desire to change it. In other words, inasmuch as *Le vieil homme et les loups* is representative of contemporary social reality, it proposes that society is faced with the impoverishment of psychical activity. Social members are rewarded for presenting a deadened aspect of themselves and punished for proposing a semblance of inner life. Kristeva finds proof of the subject's decreasing psychical activity in the proliferation of compensatory measures taken by contemporary society. First, the promoting of bio-genetic and pharmaceutical research as cures to the individual's discomfort puts forward a message of salvation privileging the manipulation of biology over the analysis of psychic and socio-psychic processes. Second, the manufacturing of media images enables the replacement of the individual's weakening power of imagination with standardised images causing the homogenisation of the human imaginary. Finally, the resurgence of fundamentalism enables the subject to form strong identifications with an authoritative voice that requires no questioning from the subject. These symptoms of the subject's psychical impoverishment form the three recurring complaints in Kristeva's recent work.

Faced with such symptoms, Kristeva remains adamant that a certain practice of symbolisation she calls 'écriture' offers a way out of the crisis. Ecriture is based on an understanding of Freudian 'heimlich/unheimlich', that is the process of estrangement from the maternal that founds the social subject. Succinctly, the individual must leave the 'mother' to join the 'father's' society. In this process, the necessity to repress maternal contents means that the individual necessarily represses their own existence within the maternal to become a stranger within paternal reality. The process of repression and estrangement is never perfect and is repeated each time the individual positions themself as a symbolic subject. Hence Kristeva argues that symbolisation requires that the subject be returned to the point of contact between maternal and paternal. Ecriture is a form of symbolisation that welcomes and exposes this moment of transition between nature (maternal) and culture (paternal), thus carrying over elements of the subject's estranged archaism. Ecriture then demands a more invested psychical activity in its translation of the individual's pre-history. For if it can testify to the subject's pre-symbolic memory, then there is some form of subjectivity, albeit an archaic form, before the onset of (Freudian or Lacanian) symbolicity. For this reason, Kristeva deplores the impoverishment of psychical activity, suggesting not only the continuation of crisis in the individual but also the impoverishment of 'human'. A Kristevan understanding of 'human' is founded upon the belief that there exists an inexhaustible number of combinations translating the archaic memory of individual and collective experience. This source of plurality, of human richness, is today threatened by the belief (media, neurosciences, genetics, etc.) that human experience can be reduced to a set of pre-fabricated images, or types, to which methods of enhancement or cure can be applied. In response, Kristeva makes herself the defender of the psyche and in her novel *Le vieil hommes et les loups*, proposes her own écriture founded upon personal and psychoanalytic experience.

Kristeva believes that a rehabilitation of psychical activity, and the way beyond societal crisis, means a reassessment of the paternal and maternal functions. Noticing a change of pathology in contemporary subjects, she, along with other researchers (Lasch, 1979; Blanck and Blanck, 1986; Cooper and Maxwell, 1995; Sterne, 1998; etc.) has turned her attention to a re-evaluation of traditional psychoanalysis. Where Freud's theories were based on observation and analysis of neurosis, these are too limiting for today's borderline or false-self for instance. The limitation rests with the Freudian assumption that the Oedipal phase inaugurates the subject. Instead, contemporary researchers suggest that there is a need to consider an earlier onset of subjectivity, without precluding the key role played by the Oedipal model in explaining the individual's later experience.

Kristeva explains this shift in human pathology by postulating that the crisis in contemporary subjectivity stems from a failure in the paternal function. More precisely, it is the weakening, even absence, of the separating function within the paternal that she sees as the root of the subject's transition into a different psychical organisation. Because she envisions the role played by the paternal function as double, pre-Oedipal (maternal) and Oedipal (paternal), she also believes that its failure on the Oedipal level is a repeat of the earlier failure on a pre-Oedipal level. Psychoanalysis points to the failure of the paternal function because it notices an increasing resistance to psychoanalytic cure. As the paternal function supports the psychoanalytic model, its failure translates in the failure of psychoanalysis. Crisis is then that of the subject but also that of psychoanalysis as a theory and a resolution of crisis. Psychoanalytic failure occurs when the subject enters analysis with unresolved issues pertaining to their pre-Oedipal history. If the analyst is working within the Freudian framework only, they will fail to 'hear' the elements constitutive of the patient's crisis. Instead, the analyst encounters a void or absence of the subject that they cannot analyse. In other words, the analyst as guarantor of the paternal function is disempowered. In reverse, the patient's failure at symbolically re-presenting pre-symbolic contents is reinforced by the analyst's silence. They encounter a familiar void in the place of the paternal function. The diagnosis of failure is currently limited by the framework available to its identification and analysis: symbolic language. If crisis is to be remedied, it must be identified at its onset, and if psychoanalysis is to maintain its claim upon psychical cure, then the framework of analysis needs revisiting. This means a re-assignment of the very notion of 'symbolic language' to its onset: the pre-linguistic maternal. The question of whether or not to re-assign the Freudian model to an earlier part of the subject's history constitutes a big part of contemporary debates in the psychoanalytic community. On the one side are the defenders of traditional analysis, resisting change in the manner in which subjectivation is apprehended, and proposing a repairing of the subject's relationship with the Oedipal father. On the other a more pioneering spirit animates those who, like Kristeva, believe that the chartering of pre-Oedipality holds the key to the superseding of crisis and a renewal of subjectivity.

During the past twenty years, Kristeva's work shows in shift from theoretical texts, and often cryptic to the non-initiated reader, to more approachable writing describing what crisis entails. Her novel, *Le vieil homme et les loups*, partakes in this loosening of style and can be understood as a more accessible illustration of crisis. Other texts such as *Les nouvelles maladies de l'âme* (1993), her two volumes *Pouvoirs et limites de la psychanalyse* (*Sens et non-sens de la révolte*, 1996 and *La révolte intime*, 1997) and recent interviews (part collected in Guberman, 1996) describe the symptoms of crisis in contemporary, western subjectivity. The subject's difficulty to produce their own fantasies and the counterbalancing of such psychical impoverishment by the production of ready-made media or scientific images, are symptoms of crisis. The replacing of individual fantasy by outside prefabricated ones is a marker that the human subject's experience of theirr world is closer to a hallucinated reality than to a reality constructed from within. To put it bluntly, the human is being robotised, imprinted with images that may resemble but are not individual experience. These 'operative fantasies', as Kristeva puts it, constitute profiles of 'human' according to pre-set types.

Kristeva's research does not aim at identifying and listing those types but rather at showing how the typifying of human fantasy aims at totally representing human processes, psychical and otherwise, hence leaving out the question of the elusive Freudian drive. The advantage is the total objectification of human processes and the possibility to modify unwanted parts of the human profile, hence maximising individual and collective potential. Freudian theory, on the other hand, envisions human production as a series of processes beginning with the relationship body/mind. From the individual's apprehension of the world though the sensory system to its linguistic symbolisation, information is filtered, suppressed, repressed, displaced, condensed, etc. to become speech. Speech is then the symptom of a subject invested on the one hand in a bodily reality and committed on the other to social belonging. Kristeva believes that the suppression of one side of the equation results in the prevention to symbolically represent bodily processes and the somatisation of those processes into what she terms 'vandalisms': disorders of the self, increase in violence and drug use, etc. Those undesirable side effects are countered by the availability of fantasised solutions. Lasch (1979) adds to Kristeva's views that those images are a form of paternalism that increases the subject's neediness while promoting itself as fulfilment of those needs. Psychoanalytic theory views the journey to autonomy as one of separation from the maternal and identification with the paternal. In other words, subjective maturity means the frustration of needs in exchange for social membership. Through Lasch's work, we see the opposite: the total fulfilment of needs is promoted as desirable. Hence, the 'new' or failed paternal function encourages dependence upon the maternal instead of separation and offers itself as absolute reparation for a failed process of subjectivation.

This failure of the paternal function to symbolically 'castrate' the subject from the maternal is objectionable within Kristevan analysis. However, Kristeva is also aware that the increase in narcissistic pathologies poses a new challenge to the traditional psychoanalytic tool. The analyst traditionally positions themself as a castrating figure against whom the patient can resolve their ambivalence vis-à-vis paternal authority. If paternal authority is now weakened, perverted, even non-existent, Kristeva is proposing that too strong an authority figure in the person of the analyst's part will defeat cure. Both protagonists will resist the analytic scene. But where Freud, and traditional psychoanalysts, believe that a void connection subject/paternal function renders analysis impossible, Kristeva is promoting new methods of cure, starting with the re-education or re-connection of the subject with the symbol. Paradoxically, she is then advocating what she is also critical of, as an initial step towards analysis: the re-pairing subject/paternal whereby the paternal agency supplies to the subject the fulfilment of their need. However, unlike the social setting suggested by Lasch, the aim of reconnecting is to facilitate analysis proper, that is challenging paternal authority towards a more autonomous mode of symbolisation. To explain this new analytic method Kristeva proposes that, beyond the separating function of the paternal, there exists another function of the paternal, a function of containment permitting the reconstruction of the subject before its questioning. This other function, containing, constructing, holding, loving, is associated with the pre-Oedipal maternal. Indeed, the argument is that the maternal function is that which teaches the pre-linguistic child to move from a scattered reality to a unified apprehension of itself. Rather than adopting a castrating position at the start of analysis, a re-pairing of the subject with the pre-Oedipal paternal is advocated, with the temporary relocating of paternal in the person of the analyst. This may explain the resistance of certain analysts who equate such a method to a maternalising of their position. On the one hand they would remain strongly connected to the symbol while on the other connecting with the patient's world of pre-objects, archaisms and scatterings. In other words, such analysts would need an anchoring of their symbolic self so strong as not to be drawn, in the counter-transference, in the psychotic world of the pre-symbol. Given the reality of new pathologies and of a changed socio-symbolic contract, Kristeva firmly believes that the future of the subject and of psychoanalysis rests in developing new counter-transferential modes of listening, and that this necessarily entails the re-visiting of the maternal function.

Chapter 4

Reassignment of the Paternal Function to the Maternal

Between Paternal and Maternal: A New Terrain of Investigation

In *The Myth of Motherhood*, Elisabeth Badinter (1981) notes: 'Whoever controls the child and has him in his camp can expect to win out whenever society's interests are identified with the child's' (Badinter, 1981: 4). In a patriarchy, this control rests with the father, which as Clément noted, is symptomatised in strong rites of passage. In Clément's views, rituals aim to reassure the father as to the child's true paternal lineage, giving the name of the father to the child for example. But other rituals also assert the father's claim upon the child. Schooling for instance rests upon a value system rewarding and punishing the child for mastering, or failing to master, paternal discourse. If, for Clément, a patriarchal society asserts the child's paternal lineage through ritual, for Badinter parental claim to the child goes further than mere genetic reassurance. If society is defined as the sum of its parts, investing in the child's existence and welfare equates with investing in the existence and welfare of society in general. The parent claiming the child is then investing in social belonging. Parental roles serve a system founded upon economic and political needs: 'In all fairness, it must be admitted that the man was stripped of his fatherhood. In granting him (and him alone) an economic role only, society was gradually removing him, literally and figuratively, from his child' (Badinter, 1981: 258). If the parent 'increases' their social membership through the child, then the social can also ensure social membership by reinforcing the link parent/child. The parent's social performance is established through the politico-economic construction of biology: the father's function is to facilitate the production of 'child' and guarantee its maintenance, the mother's function is to carry the child in and out of the womb to social maturity (hence child custody is awarded to the mother in divorce settlements while the father finances the arrangement). Through the control and modification of parental functions, contemporary society uses the child as the social commodity through which it can serve its own needs.

Badinter demonstrates that parental care and in particular maternal love, or maternal instinct, are not constants through time. She argues that, in fact, contemporary cultural understanding of the natural parent (naturally loving, caring, etc.) was inherited from late eighteenth century values. In western Europe, the state shifted its interest from wanting 'docile subjects for His Majesty' (Badinter, 1981: 118) to wanting to avoid 'the waste of human beings that characterised the Old Regime' (Badinter, 1981: 118). Writers, administrators, doctors were recruited to shift cultural values from authority to love. Badinter argues that this translated in a shift from paternal authority to maternal love, initiating the move from the paternal to the maternal function. Nineteenth and twentieth century literature reinforced the move from authority to love (and from paternal to maternal) as their interpretation of pre-eighteenth century accounts were tinted by the new parental ideology.[1] The effect was a new organisation of parental roles: 'the mother and the state had usurped, each in their own way, the essentials of the father's role [...]. His qualities as a father were measured more by his ability to support his family than by any other criterion' (Badinter, 1981: 258). With 'the replacement of the patriarchal family by a 'patriarchy of the state' (Badinter, 1981: 253), the paternal function is now performed by the state, in partnership with the mother.

From a psychoanalytic viewpoint, the father has then moved from the actual father of the Freudian family triangle to the symbolic father of Lacan. Badinter (1981) explains that recently, 'some psychoanalysts have reconsidered the question of the father, dissociating the symbolic father from the flesh-and-blood father' (Badinter, 1981: 281). With the work of psychoanalytic theorists such as Lacan and Dolto, the involvement of the actual father has become less important than the function played by his name, his law or his word. In fact, the efficacy of the paternal function is at its best when the actual father remains distant, even absent, permitting his replacement by a more potent figure, the symbolic father, guarantor of the law of prohibition against incest. Freud believed that social organisation rests on an historical event where the sons, jealous of the father's exclusive sexual intimacy with the women, murdered the father and ate him. Riddled with guilt, they then forbade themselves any sexual encounter with the father's women (the mothers) and thus avoided further parricide. Freud insisted that the father became more powerful by virtue of being dead, giving rise to the idea of the 'dead father complex'. Badinter's description of the psychoanalytic construction of the symbolic father is founded upon the same logic as Freud's dead father complex. Psychoanalytic theory advocates the actual father's distance, in order to enable the symbolic father to play its powerful role in the process of subjectivation. The

---

1 They interpret past accounts of maternal indifference (even cruelty) as an effect of the socio-economic difficulties of the period, while maintaining that maternal instinct is a human constant: 'some have drawn the conclusion that mother love may vary in intensity depending on the external difficulties, but that it always exists. Mother love thus becomes a constant in history' (Badinter, 1981: 59). For instance, Badinter argues that maternal indifference was not the result of high child mortality rates whereby the mother would protect herself from constant mourning through indifference; rather, the high mortality rate amongst children was a direct cause of maternal indifference and negligence, which was itself caused by the State encouraging parents to produce docile subjects (Badinter, 1981: 60).

father's quasi absence has consequences for the actual parents. The father is relegated to a secondary role, supporting the mother-child dyad without much scope for a close father-child relationship. More importantly, if the father is made less important than the mother, the responsibility for any shortcomings in the child's development falls onto the mother. '[T]he pathogenic father has been discussed far less often than the pathogenic mother, the bad father less often than the bad mother' (Badinter, 1981: 288). 'Those who demand an accounting equal to the mother's are few indeed' (Badinter, 1981: 288).[2] Indeed, the crisis in subjectivity still remains often linked with the mother's right and wrong doings, while the father is either not mentioned or not involved.

Within the context described by Badinter, Kristeva's 1980s work adheres to traditional psychoanalytic views. Her writings on the metaphoric father, Oedipal or loving father, also show complacency towards the actual father's responsibility and place much emphasis on the mother's role in the health of the future subject. However, her more recent work breaks new grounds with the refinement of the term 'paternal function', now reassigned to the maternal realm, and the introduction of a more metaphoric maternal function which, if not equally available to women and men, is nevertheless dissociated from biological determinism. Furthermore, in analysing the crisis of the contemporary subject, Kristeva is now clearly pointing the finger at a breakdown of the paternal function, not at the actual mother, and explaining how this paternal function affects and is effected by actual men and women but also symbolic entities (state, school, etc.). This is where Kristeva still remains at the forefront of contemporary research on subjectivation.

Today, theorists of different psychoanalytic orientations seem to be harmonising their differences in the belief that 'preoedipal pathology is pandemic to our contemporary situation' (Kirschner, 1996: 41) and moving towards a common understanding of what their profession needs. Psychoanalytic theorists, whether practicing analysts or not, promote the necessity to research further the causes of psychological illnesses, with a particular suspicion that the Freudian model, the Oedipus Complex, might today be too limiting to fully explain contemporary diseases. Where borderline and narcissistic conditions constitute a trademark of the modern man or woman, a failed resolution of Oedipality or the failure of the paternal function seems inadequate to elucidate fully these existential difficulties. Some (Blanck and Blanck, 1986) go further and suggest that the Oedipal analysis of Freud's patients, and recorded by Freud as illustrations of the validity of his model, fails by today's psychoanalytic standards to convincingly account for the pathology of those early twentieth century subjects. Post-Freudian theorists are overall agreeing that the myth of Oedipus, as representative of a universal tragedy of humankind, conveys an incomplete image of the human and is

---

2 Badinter puts forward the work of Francine Fredet (1979) *Mais, Madame, vous êtes la mère*. We can also mention Christiane Olivier (1980, 1988 and 1990) who, against psychoanalytic tradition, goes further and advocates the more pronounced presence of the father, especially for the girl.

thus not entirely adequate in analysing the subject.

In her study *Narcissus and Oedipus* (Hamilton, 1993), Hamilton exposes the Freudian model as inadequate. Post-Freudian research (Klein, Bowlby, Winnicott, Stern amongst others), has challenged Freud's views on primary narcissism: instead of an early objectless stage of development upon which the presence of a frustrating paternal function will impose separation from the maternal and enable the subject's relation with objects, the baby would on the contrary actively relate to objects around it from birth.

> The problem of development is reformulated. It is no longer a question of how the other, the 'object' as it is called in psychoanalytic literature, is to be added on to an original unit [...], but how difference interposes itself in the original, synchronous, mother-child relationship. In my view, primary narcissism theories lead to a misidentification of the central problem of human development. In an original, divided world, a problem arises about linking and object-relating. (Hamilton, 1993: 4).

If the pre-verbal is already the domain of some form of subjectivity, the question of Oedipus as representative of subjectivity must be reconsidered.

Reviewing Hamilton's work, Eric Rayner believes that Freud's Oedipal model for understanding human drama 'is not simply about a boy's sexual desire for his mother and wish to kill his father. It is also about knowledge and ignorance of reality, the lengths to which people will go to hide uncomfortable truths, and how tragedy is born of such deceits.' (Hamilton, 1993: xiv). In the Oedipal myth,[3] the hero, abandoned by his birth parents and subsequently adopted, commits parricide and incest because he does not know of his origins. Having consulted an oracle who prophesied that he would kill his father and marry his mother, Oedipus believes he is escaping the prophecy by running away from his adoptive place. Oedipus's effort is geared towards respecting the law against parricide and incest, which constitute him as a social subject. Read metaphorically, the myth is first an effort at evading his desire for maternal symbiosis (narcissism) and choosing the social (Oedipal) over instinctive impulses. Second, the hero's social standing entails that he should remain ignorant of his desire. For most part of the play, Oedipus ignores the role that parricide and incest have played in shaping him. Indeed, while searching for the identity of the culprit, Oedipus vehemently resists and denies the tragic truth. This battle between the reality of his origin and the denial of it constitutes the character 'Oedipus'. To return to Rayner's argument, Oedipus is seen as a consequence of Narcissus, an effort to 'forget' the active early experience of the infant imprinted within the subject's psyche, by disconnecting this subject from that knowledge. It is only at the cost of this amnesia, and the conflicts it constitutes, that the subject can be a social subject. Although Rayner proposes a more inclusive image of the pre-Oedipal within the Oedipal dynamic, his statement still suggests a classically Freudian interpretation of subjectivity

---

3 See: Sophocles (1959).

because it locates reality within the mother-father-subject (Oedipal) triangle. In other words, subjectivity is envisaged from the moment the paternal function appears in the child's reality, corresponding to this child's ability to express its otherness (symbolisation, language).

Other researchers like Christopher Bollas (1987) insist on the importance of non-verbal contents when working with patients whose development is seemingly arrested at the pre-verbal stage of infancy (autism for instance). In these instances, Bollas finds that 'neither the classical nor the Lacanian view addresses the play of the subject and other in the transference and the character of that part of the psyche that lives in a wordless world' (Bollas, 1987: 3). Complementing Rayner, Bollas also suggests amnesia in respect of the time anterior to the child's acquisition of language. In what he terms 'the unthought known', Bollas attempts to convey both the subject's knowledge of pre-verbal experience and the impossibility for that subject to articulate this knowledge within language: this amnesia reflects a disconnection between being and thought which is a disconnection between narcissism and Oedipality.

Hence, we find two 'schools' of thought within the psychoanalytic field: on the one hand, classical analysis sees pathologies of a narcissistic type as the regression of a patient into narcissism and a resistance to Oedipal truths proposed by classical analysis. On the other hand, analysts like Bollas or Kristeva construe the seeming regression of patients into narcissistic territories, or the overall societal increase in pre-oedipal pathologies, as the marker of a society's mimetic 'expression' of a breakdown between narcissism and Oedipality. Those contemporary psychoanalysts have thus increasingly turned their focus to an earlier origin of subjectivity and its illnesses. This means relocating the advent of the subject and considering forms of subjectivity prior to the traditional Oedipal genesis. Theorists like Klein or Kristeva analyse a much earlier Oedipal dynamic and thus an earlier manifestation of subjectivity than Freud had anticipated. Such work calls for new methods of research to enable access and theorising of a time anterior to the symbol. Proposing to stretch back the birth of the subject means seeking new modalities regulating this early subject, and this includes a changed investment of the analyst vis-à-vis their patients. The paternal was the function permitting the subject to 'perform' the representation of their self in the symbol with which they identify. In extending the possibility of subjectivity before the full acquisition of language, Kristeva, like Klein and unlike Freud, now emphasises the function of the maternal. But unlike Klein, Kristeva also re-assesses the function of the paternal on a pre-Oedipal level and suggests extending the role of the paternal function as guarantor of some form of 'symbolic' performance. In other words, Kristeva reforms Freud's early Oedipal theory by counterbalancing the over presence of the Freudian paternal function with her own maternal function. She also relativises Klein's strong maternal figure by relocating the paternal function alongside the Kleinian maternal.

The psychoanalytic argument for an earlier paternal function is not new. Concerning pre-Oedipality, Freud had belatedly introduced the idea of a 'father of individual pre-history', a kind of transcendental entity who, beyond the mother/child dyad, embodies the containment of all things symbolic and enables the child to transcend the loss of the maternal in its identification with the paternal. However, Freud remained convinced that the Oedipal structure he had created was sufficient to explain subjectivity and its shortcomings. More precisely, Freud saw the Oedipal link between the subject and the paternal function as overriding any primitive link and prevailing when theorising the subject. In the latter part of his life, Freud put forward the opposition between the life drive and the death drive as a new structuring of the human psyche. Although he viewed the death drive (Thanatos) as the most radical or instinctual of the two drives, he insisted that the life drive (Eros) ultimately dominated psychic life. With reference to depression, Kristeva exemplifies the two terms as follows: 'While *Eros* means the creation of bonds, *Thanatos*, the death drive, signifies the disintegration of bonds and the ceasing of circulation, communication, and social relationships' (Guberman, 1996: 79). If we follow Freud, the life drive, or that which enables the creation of social bonds, 'normally' overrides the death drive or the disintegration of socialisation. Effectively, Freud's theorising of such domination of Eros over Thanatos is paralleled in Kristeva's work with the subject's departure from the maternal and entry into paternal society (Oedipus). Yet, Kristeva is today positing the failing of the bond subject-paternal and the return of maternal contents, interpreted in the disintegration of the social fabric and its mode of exchange. She is now questioning the Freudian interpretation of domination of the death drive by the life drive. In this, the influence of Melanie Klein must be acknowledged.

Klein (1988a and 1988b) emphasises the dualism between the life drive and the death drive and modifies Freud's thought by positing this dualism from birth rather than from the Freudian Oedipal phase:

> We may assume that the struggle between life and death instincts already operates during birth and accentuates the persecutory anxiety aroused by this painful experience. (Klein, 1988b: 31)

Klein is in fact proposing a re-assignment of the paternal function, in the sense of a function separating the individual from its maternal objects and constitutive of subjectivity, to the realm of the maternal. Klein's work has opened the door to new ways of considering subjectivity (British School of Object Relation Theory or ORT): a lengthened 'Oedipal' moment beginning with birth, a dualistic 'subject' present from the start and a new methodology to articulate human archaic experience and its difficulties. Julia Kristeva will subsequently stress this part of Kleinian theory to which she will add her own notion of 'abjection'.

> After having made of eroticism our God and of the phallus the guarantor of identity, with Freud and Lacan, we are invited, with Klein, to replenish our ambitions for freedom in the more rugged and more archaic regions of the psyche, where the *one* (identity) cannot *be*. (Kristeva 2000: 393)

Kristeva sees in Melanie Klein's focus on a return to archaic maternal contents a school of thought offering insight into the subject's contemporary difficulties. She understands for instance a certain form of art, montage of bodily fluids upon which fantasmatic words and images are placed or the violence of the televisual discourse (video games, cartoons) upon which children project themselves, as an 'inversion of the process of symbolisation' (Kristeva, 2000: 394). In both cases, maternal contents and symbols are superimposed to the point where the subject can no longer distinguish image from reality. The 'possession' of the symbolic subject by imaginary maternal contents translates in a regression to what Klein terms the 'paranoid-schizoid position' (Klein, 1988a/b). Kristeva adds that in the absence of a symbolic instance to represent such position through speech, the symbolic subject is engulfed in the maternal and towards the acting out of archaic fantasy. For instance, she proposes the recurring killings in American schools as resulting from a subjectivity with 'only the televisual screen for *baby-sitter* and, with no word at all to dispossess them from imaginary hold' (Kristeva, 2000: 394).

Is the answer then to reinstate the paternal function in the hope of recuperating a subject now possessed by maternal contents?

> To repair the father and restore knowledge of reality [...] are secondary objectives, of little interest because potentially tyrannical, and besides, unrealisable without the creation of a psychical life. (Kristeva, 2000: 392-3)

The indiscriminate restoration of the paternal function would lead to an impasse. The paternal function can work only in the condition that the subject has already mastered the representation of psychical activity into the expression of symbol and affect. What partly characterises the contemporary subject is a disconnection between symbol and affect, nullifying transferential processes into transference to a void (schizoid). In psychoanalytic practice, the traditional 'playing dead' method of the analyst translates in the patient's resistance to transference, a resistance experienced by the analyst in their counter-transference as a void in the place of symbolic exchange. The expression (if any) on the patient's part of pre-Oedipal material is met by the silence of the analyst. Where the analyst expected to encourage the patient to leave the pre-Oedipal continent and fill the symbolic silence offered, instead, too limited an investment on the analyst's part is experienced as paternal rejection of the patient's pre-Oedipality. In this sense, a subject already suffering from an absence of identification with the symbolic function would perceive the symbolic or castrating function of the paternal as persecutory.

If to repair the paternal function is secondary, Kristeva insists on the importance for the health of the subject and of society, to access this secondary objective in the subjectivation process.

> Crimes and other more or less aggressive acting outs are only failings of the symbol,

> they testify to a failure of imaginary matricide which, alone, opens the path of thought. (Kristeva, 2000: 218)

The paternal function permits the murder of the maternal on a symbolic level, that is the speaking subject can linguistically 'act out' the murder of the maternal instead of actually murdering maternal entities (the mother, children in the case of American schools, etc.). In equating symbolic matricide with the preservation of socio-symbolic life, Kristeva is first repeating Freud's conviction of the life drive dominating the death drive: the survival of the symbolic rests upon 'the irrevocable loss of the beloved object which at the time is secretly hated, a loss that is never worked through' (Guberman, 1996: 79). Second, a correspondence between death drive and maternal on the one hand, and life drive and paternal function on the other can be established. Freud envisioned the life drive as 'a drive of connection' (Kristeva, 1996a: 103) enabling the creation of a bond subject/object typified in social relationships. On the contrary, the death drive would be a 'drive of disconnection' (Kristeva, 1996a: 103), cutting the subject from their objects, exemplified in instances of murder, of the other or of the self. Moreover, Freud posited the death drive as the most radical or fundamental of the two while 'the life drive is only a kind of calming off process, a cohesion of the former' (Kristeva, 1996a: 104). In analysing the crisis of the contemporary subject, Kristeva is not only highlighting Freud's findings but also identifying the failure of the subject in the passage from death drive (maternal) to life drive (paternal): a failure to impose coherence to the radical instincts of primal contents. So unlike Freud, Kristeva points out that the failure of the paternal function arches back to a failure in the subject's imaginary to leave the maternal realm. Against paternal castration of the maternal, a 'neither forbid it nor repress it' methodology is advocated (Kristeva, 2000: 394) to better investigate the subject's archaic contents.

The Maternal Realm: Kleinian Phantasy or Representation Before the Symbol

> A disparate entity, made of verbal and non-verbal representations, of sensations, affects, emotions, movements and actions, even concrete objects, Kleinian fantasy is a true theoretical impurity defying purists, precisely, as much as it enchants clinicians, especially those dealing with childhood, psychosis or psychosomatic disorders. (Kristeva, 2000: 225)

Susan Isaacs proposed the use of 'phantasy' to differentiate the Kleinian concept of fantasy from others (Mitchell, 1991). Fantasy refers to the subject's conscious or repressed diurnal dream-like state whereas phantasy designates the psychical activity that precedes repression or consciousness. By positing the existence of phantasmatic representation before the formation of consciousness, Klein is effectively positing a form of representation before the unconscious and challenges the corner stone of Freudian theory:

> Analytic work has shown that babies of a few months of age certainly indulge in phantasy-building. I believe that this is the most primitive mental activity and that phantasies are in the mind of the infant almost from birth. (Klein, 1988a: 290)

Freud based his research on the understanding that subjectivity originates from a process of repression generating both conscious/preconscious (secondary process) and unconscious (primary process).

> For Klein, what is unconscious is the biological and affectual condition of the human being. In essence, by the time of her later writings, the unconscious is equivalent to the instincts: to the life drive and death drive and their affects. (Mitchell, 1991: 24)

Klein is not concerned with the division conscious/unconscious as constitutive of the symbolic subject but focuses on an archaic symbolic subject before the function of primary/secondary processes. The symbolic subject is not a symptom of the unconscious. Instead, symbolism is already manifest before the onset of unconscious processes in the form of 'phantasy'. Phantasies then precede and hold, virtually from birth, the essence of later unconscious processes:

> As Klein's friend and colleague Susan Isaacs wrote: 'The primary *content* of all mental processes are unconscious phantasies. Such phantasies are the basis of all unconscious and conscious thought processes.' (Mitchell, 1991: 24)

Referring to figure 1.1 of chapter 1, phantasy would be a psychical representation positioned between drive activity and symbol and not yet subjected to censorship, that is in the top zone of the diagram in system PSY and just before language processes. Phantasy is then 'the representer before representation' (Kristeva, 2000: 225), before fantasy. Kleinian theory proposes the existence of psychical representation before the subject's entry into the symbolic sphere proper (language). The pre-linguistic subject, the baby, would already possess an archaic type of symbolisation, regulated by its relationship with the maternal. In Klein's work, the mother's breast represents for the infant the whole of the mother and is invested with gratifying/frustrating powers.

> Now, what one might call the 'good' breasts become the prototype of what is felt throughout life to be good and beneficent, while the 'bad' breasts stand for everything evil and persecuting. (Klein, 1988a: 291)

Hence, the maternal breast is the pre-verbal locus upon which the infant already projects its own conflictual reality. In Klein's words: 'The relation to the gratifying breast in some measure restores, if things go well, the lost prenatal unity with the mother.' (Mitchell, 1991: 211); it 'is instinctively felt to be not only the source of nourishment but of life itself' (Mitchell, 1991: 211). The good breast represents inclusion, continuity from containment to connection and protection against the outside while the bad breast symbolises exclusion, the interruption of the maternal-child symbiosis and is experienced as death-bearing. These conflicts are later replayed in processes of repression and suppression already described by Freud.

Klein's proposition confronts contemporary psychoanalytic theory with a new challenge:

> In other words, Kleinian phantasy includes elements pre- or without representations, that Klein's successors will try to conceptualise. [...] The entire psychoanalytic actuality is played out in this clinical and conceptual exploration of the trans-verbal archaic highlighted by Melanie, and which defies the representation of ideas and visual representation. (Kristeva, 2000: 232)

Kleinian theory defies the findings of Jacques Lacan. Succinctly, Lacan insisted on the 'visual aspect of phantasy and develops, with the mirror stage, an optical model to support his own theory on fantasy [...]' (Kristeva, 2000: 227). Lacan analyses the pre-linguistic subject as possessing language but not speech: the child understands utterances but cannot formulate their own. Lacan is putting forward a theory by which the acquisition of language, or the establishing of a connection subject/paternal function, would equate to a changing of that connection from identical to similar. The pre-linguistic child forms a connection between two items based on the fact that they are visibly identical. For instance as in the case of Little Dick, a train can be the father because they share the identical trait of penile visibility (Kristeva, 2000: 228). With language, the subject moves to forming a connection of similitude between items and their symbols: the train is not the father but is similar to him and so represents him. In this, Lacan confirms what Klein and Kristeva's works suggest: first the 'representer' precedes representation. Second, the 'representer' follows a metonymic logic, the part (penile shape) represents the whole (father). Representation, on the other hand, is based on a metaphoric logic whereby the symbol is always other than what it represents but stands for it; the word 'father' for instance, is the representation of the paternal agent.

In Kleinian interpretation, any object similar to the penis can represent the paternal image, whatever the linguistic background. The word 'father' on the other hand represents him only in societies of English-speaking culture. In the instance of metonymy, the importance is on a similitude already present as sense (visual, tactile, etc.) between two objects, while in the instance of metaphor, the subject must learn to connect two previously unconnected items according to the pre-defined linguistic conventions of their socio-cultural background. Hence, the move from metonymy to metaphor is also a move from senses (inside, affective) to thought (outside, social). Kristeva objects to Lacanian logic that it considers only the visual similitude between two objects. To reduce the senses to vision is for her closer to metaphor than metonymy because to see an object is to see the space separating the individual from that object. In other words, to recognise the object as separate from itself, the child must already possess some ability to recognise itself as other than the object seen. By giving too much emphasis on visibility while excluding other senses of drive activity and by insisting on the visual, Lacan already positions the pre-subject in a relationship with an outside idea/vision of itself and the world. His work thus does not elucidate the relationship between inside (sensation/affect) and outside (object) but reduces subjectivity to an irredeemable loss of the maternal and identification with the paternal. In other words, subjectivity would be the relinquishing of the pre-subject's affective link to its apprehension of the world as sense replaced by the subject's connection with their socio-cultural framework. Kristeva is more interested in the step preceding Lacan's interpretation, that is the relationship between senses/affects and the outside world before they are identified as other.

Klein is more radical in her understanding of child phantasy and Kleinian research offers itself as a better authenticating method of the pre-subject's experience of drive activity. The radicalism (and sometimes crudeness) of Klein's work need emphasising. For instance, the Kleinian idea of the child's desire for the penis inside the mother (combined parent) is interpreted by Lacan as desire for the 'Name of the Father'. But Klein suggests more crudely the child's desire to destroy the intruder between him/herself and the mother. Hence, in Lacan, desire is for the paternal metaphor: desire for the penis is the visual fantasy of the child's desire for the representation of the penis or phallus, that is the father and his paternal function. In Klein, phantasies of destroying and being destroyed by the penis translate the child's desire for the mother: phantasies illustrate an aggressive act to exclude the paternal function (phantasised penis) from the maternal/child equation.

In proposing symbolic representation as a metaphoric equivalent, on the paternal level, of a pre-symbolic, maternal dynamic, Kristeva finds Freud's representation of drive activity 'much too 'diplomatic'' (Kristeva, 2000: 231) and Lacan's focus on 'the appearance, the visibility of *eidos*' (Kristeva, 2000: 232) too restrictive. Klein's understanding of psychical representations, 'sensations, affects, motions, acts, verbal and non-verbal representations, even concrete objects' (Kristeva, 2000: 231), suggests there exists another modality of 'representation', exceeding (or preceding) the subject's relationship with the paternal function, and embedded in the pre-subject's relationship with the maternal.

> I have repeatedly put forward the hypothesis that the primal good object, the mother's breast, forms the core of the ego and vitally contributes to its growth, and have often described how the infant feels that he concretely internalizes the breast and the milk it gives. Also there is in his mind already some indefinite connection between the breast and other parts and aspects of the mother.
>
> I would not assume that the breast is to him merely a physical object. The whole of his instinctual desires and his unconscious phantasies imbue the breast with qualities going far beyond the actual nourishment it affords. (Klein, 1988a: 180)

Against the traditional understanding of language production as a succession of processes acquired from birth to psychical maturity and upon which our understanding of subjectivity rests, Klein proposes instead the existence of an innate competence to narration: 'The 'pre-narrative envelopes' would be accompanied by 'analogical representations', neither pure lived experience nor pure abstraction, but intermediary. Phantasy would be one such analogical representation of the pre-narrative envelope, experienced in virtual time' (Kristeva, 2000: 238).

Contemporary research has confirmed Klein's pioneering work as to the innate ability of the subject for narration. Amongst others, Daniel Stern demonstrates why those 'pre-narrative envelopes' are believed to exist from birth (Stern, 1998). Kristeva will speak of 'event representations', 'event arrangements' or '*cognitive affective models*' (Kristeva, 2000: 236) as forms taken by pre-narrative envelopes and witnessed in babies under one year of age. These would constitute 'a fundamental unit of experience enabling the exploration of the baby's psychical reality' (Kristeva, 2000: 236, fn.1). From a non-psychoanalytic base, generative grammar is focusing its attention on defining 'a basic narrative structure' present from birth and proposes 'an innate linguistic competence' of the subject based on 'a minimal matrix for all enunciation: subject-verb-object' which would later translate into 'grammatical *performances* according to the rules of different languages' (Kristeva, 2000: 237). Klein herself preferred to record more crudely the reality of phantasy and interpret it as an expression of very early anxieties. One of her most famous case study, the analysis of Little Dick, illustrates this (in Mitchell, 1991: 100- 3). She shows how her play technique 'follows the child's symbolic representations and gives access to his anxiety and sense of guilt' (Mitchell, 1991: 102). Over several analytic sessions, Klein observes how the child's phantasy of fear of and attack on the maternal are illustrated in play. Dick playing with a train repeatedly makes the train enter the station and cuts off parts of the coal cart's load of coal. Klein suggests Dick's phantasy play is an expression of his desire to enter the mother's womb and attack her from the inside (destroying intestinal matter). She also suggests, in a not fully autonomous child, that the attack is also on himself, an analysis reinforced by Klein's knowledge of Dick's difficulty over toilet training, his suffering with indigestion, a prolapsed anus and haemorrhoids, suggesting the pain associated with the rejection of what is inside (the maternal and him). In his play, Dick expresses his primal anxiety, fear and anger, over his separation from the maternal body (birth), explaining the arrested development of ego formation and his intolerance for socialisation.

Phantasy in Kleinian theory is not solely the multi-layered representation of reality but an imaginary narrative of the real in the Lacanian sense. Lacan understood human apprehension of reality as interplay amongst three registers he named real, symbolic and imaginary (RSI). The real corresponds to that which is not symbolised. As in Freud, symbolisation is a layered process; some 'aspects' of human experience are not symbolisable and are thus excluded from symbolisation. These 'aspects', the antithesis of the symbolic, constitute the real. The imaginary refers to the register of the specular image, which is constituted by the early subject's ability to see or recognise the object as other than itself; the imaginary is then an early form of symbolisation. Lacan is speculating that our understanding of reality is a combination of both symbolic and imaginary while the real is that which is excluded from reality. In this, Lacan went one step further than Freud did. The Freudian approach to consciousness rests upon an understanding of the subject as symbolic enactment of early experience (or pre-history). What the subject experiences as reality (or consciousness), is a metaphor of pre-verbal time, supported by the paternal function. Freud's work focuses mainly on a description of the relationship between the Oedipal subject and the paternal metaphor. Lacan subsequently conceived of a more precise description of 'pre-history', subdivided into real and imaginary, with the imaginary touching on both pre-history and conscious reality. However, Lacanian logic like Freudian logic is more interested in interpreting the subject's utterances as metaphor rather than metonymic. In other words, Lacan and Freud remain focused on articulating a framework explaining the (metaphoric) function of the paternal rather than the (metonymic) sense of the pre-verbal maternal.

In privileging interpretation of the paternal discourse, Kristeva is guarding against the tendency in traditional analysis to interpret the metaphorisation of the real as the metaphorisation of the imaginary. This misinterpretation of patient discourse equals to denying the subject's pre-history, when this pre-history is constituted by both real and imaginary experiences. In turn, the (mis)interpreted discourse of the analyst anchors the subject in a confusion between real and imaginary. For example, while the separation of the child from the maternal figure is real, the anxiety experienced by the child is imaginary. '[T]he *phantasmatic* fear and anxiety have more impact than the *real* separation' (Kristeva 2000: 234). The real experience and its imaginary analogy form the subject's pre-history, that symbolisation metaphorically reactualises. Kristeva reads the Kleinian subject as a series of transformations, the path of which basically follows Freud's understanding. Drive activity is a process by which the body experiences a charge of energy pushing it towards an aim; the charge is the cause of the drive while the aim is to find release from the drive in a chosen object. For instance, deprivation in the infant causes hunger and translates in the child seeking the breast (or any substitute) as object of release. Infant reality is one of separation from and deprivation of the maternal body and the biological survival it represents. Kristeva suggests birth as the prototype of this primal separation. Deprivation (external stimulus) is experienced as bodily tension (internal stimulus) and translated into drive activity which, in Klein, is described as anxiety. Anxiety causes the infant to seek an object to release its discomfort. In Klein, the breast comes to represent the whole of the mother and her power over the infant to be satisfied or frustrated. In other words, the maternal (in its metonymic representation, the breast) becomes identified with frustration/gratification, that is the maternal sets in motion a dualism at the heart of infant experience, well before the child's entry into the linguistic sphere. Klein suggests that these pre-linguistic modalities are evidenced in the phantasies reported by the child, as in the case of Little Dick: the infant forms imaginary phantasies as a means to compensate for the loss of the maternal. The bad breast is phantasised in narratives of attack and persecution. The good breast is phantasised in narratives of reparation where the infant, eager to save the breast from aggression attempts to recapture the bond with the maternal. These narratives are motivated by the dualism set in motion by maternal frustration/gratification and phantasies constitute a 'symbolisation degree zero', determined by the maternal function and before the subject's entry into the paternal realm.

From Phantasy to Symbol: The Paternal Function

The move from the maternal to the paternal function presents us with two paradoxes. A Freudian approach constructs the maternal as natural and opposes it to paternal authority, which regulates social law. The maternal thus becomes the antithesis of culture and what the child must leave in order to take social membership. With the work of Klein (and later Kristeva), the maternal is not only the site of nature but also becomes the locus of an early subjectivity, termed 'archaic' or pre-symbolic. The maternal is then not only pre-symbolic in the sense of an anti symbolic site but also an archaic form of the symbolic: it is both the site of nature and culture. As Kelly Oliver (2000) highlights '[t]he first relationship with the maternal body, then, is in the paradoxical position of both providing the prototype for all subsequent relations and threatening the very possibility of any social relation' (Oliver, 2000: 2-3). The paradox is in making of the maternal function both a natural function, birth and nurture being the enactment of maternal instinct, and what sets subjectivity in motion, anti-social (relation-breaking) behaviour resulting from the failure of maternal care (child 'abandonment'). Oliver points out that the construction of the paternal function is also paradoxical. As guarantor of culture the paternal function is founded, according to Oliver, 'on the father's natural authority because of his natural strength or aggressive impulses' (Oliver, 2000: 3). She further suggests that the association between paternal and culture rests on the disembodiment of the father: 'His body must be evacuated to maintain images of his association with culture against nature' (Oliver, 2000: 4). To maintain the paternal function solely as natural would put it on a par with the maternal function and threaten the social subject's fallback into nature and the disintegration of culture. Where Freud's views were of a maternal function anchored in its naturalness and a paternal function secured in the social,[4] current

---

4 See for instance Freud's analysis of Michelangelo's statue of Moses carrying the Tablets of the Law (10 Commandments): 'Discovering the Jews in adoration before the golden calf, Moses is about to express his rage but, realising that in pouncing to punish his people, he risks dropping the Tablets of The Law, he masters his anger. The statue by Michelangelo represents him in the third movement: that of contained anger.' (Babin, 1990: 92-3). Freud was particularly interested in what precedes containment and drew two other sketches: the first shows Moses holding the Tablets in a solemn fashion; the second shows Moses' instinctual response (rage) and the Tablets of The Law slipping from his grasp; the

research shows that both functions take part in the subject's move from natural to cultural being. In both Klein and Kristeva, the dynamics of early identification, interpreted as phantasy, are present in processes of incorporation and rejection of the maternal and affirm the maternal as cultural function. Kristeva goes one step further and also revisits Freud's early assumption of a loving function of the paternal. In explaining the move from nature to culture, the debate is then not so much on a division of parental tasks, according to a natural division of the mother-father conglomerate, but a questioning on how the child moves from an archaic form of symbolisation to symbolisation.

With language, phantasy gives way to fantasy: fantasy is the metaphoric incarnation of phantasy, a substitute where the combination sensation/affect associated with an object is now represented in the symbol. The object sought in the release of drive activity is no longer the metonymic breast but language itself. Language is the site *par excellence* where the child becomes represented as other than natural or instinctive, that is where the child becomes a social subject. In replacing phantasmatic activity with symbolic activity, the child effectively moves from the realm of the maternal to the realm of the paternal. Much of Kristeva's work has been to construct a framework explaining the move from maternal to paternal. She thus posited the existence of a form of paternal function already at work within the maternal at a much earlier stage than was traditionally imagined.

Klein saw the paternal function within the maternal as secondary. For her, the paternal is present inasmuch as it is a part of the maternal. With what she terms 'the combined parent figure' (Mitchell, 1991: 208), Klein attempts to convey the child's feeling 'that the parents are always getting sexual gratification from one another' (Mitchell, 1991: 218). In this phantasy of constant gratification, the infant feels excluded from ever satisfying the parent's need. The child's love/hate relations are construed as directed towards both parents. However, it is towards the prime object, the maternal, that the child directs its conflictual impulses. For Klein, subjectivity occurs first as a realisation that 'he [the child] cannot keep his mother to himself as his exclusive possession' (Mitchell, 1991: 218). This realisation is reinforced secondarily by 'the gain of new objects who can be loved - the father and siblings - and other compensations which the developing ego derives from the external world' (Mitchell, 1991: 218). Thus, the Kleinian maternal is the locus of the child's developing subjectivity. Kleinian theory posits the existence of an archaic form of symbolisation before the establishment of the Freudian split between unconscious and preconscious/conscious. She is then proposing symbolisation before the castrating function of the paternal founds the primary/secondary process. Primarily, the child desires the mother, or her phantasmatic representation the breast, and only secondarily desires what the mother possesses, the father or in infant phantasy, the penis. 'The father, or rather what he is reduced to, is only a possession of the mother' (Kristeva, 2000: 193).

---

third is a copy of Michelangelo's model, and has Moses holding the Tablets with one hand and his abdomen with the other.

Where Freud suggested an archaic paternal function, the 'father of individual prehistory', as containing the pre-subject in its endeavour to separate from the maternal, the Kleinian paternal is an '*appendage*' (Kristeva, 2000: 195) of the maternal, not an early function of the paternal.

Kristeva both criticises Klein's relegating of the paternal function to a secondary role and praises Klein's pioneering work in recognising the maternal function in the process of subjectivation. On the one hand Freud's idea of a supportive paternal function needs rehabilitating and developing. On the other, Klein's vision of an archaic capacity of the paternal function to separate the child from the maternal realm as an integral part of the maternal function must be maintained. In so bridging the Freudian and Kleinian models, Kristeva will develop her own framework explaining the mechanisms of socialisation and the subject's contemporary difficulties.

Following Klein, Kristeva will emphasise the theorising of drive activity linking the human on the one hand to biological activity (sensation and affect) and on the other to a nascent symbolic activity (the metonymic object of phantasy). Her work enables a deeper understanding of how symbolisation occurs in the subject. The move from real to phantasy is where the capacity for symbolisation is founded: 'Kleinian phantasy is the mechanism [...] of the drive's fate to be inside and outside: a drive 'in search of an object'' (Kristeva, 2000: 233). It is inside in its connection to sensations and affects regulated by the body; it is outside in its search for a representer of itself, a representer preceding representation or symbolisation proper. In this, Klein pinpointed the original moment of the socio-symbolic contract and by extension, the source of its failure. Her work has led Kristeva to believe that 'the imaginary is the terrain of truth, without which the true would be confused with repression' (Kristeva, 2000: 242). This makes of phantasy the object of analysis: the analyst's job is to interpret the analysand's imaginary contents, thus enabling the move from phantasy to the symbol. Although her suggestion appears anchored within the Freudian tradition, Kristeva is in fact critical of a 'hard-core' form of psychoanalytic practice which by-passes archaic material: either imaginary contents are mistaken for the real or they are disregarded through the analyst's dogmatic abiding to the paternal's forbidding/repressing function. In psychoanalytic setting, 'the risk would consist precisely in under-estimating the metaphoric sense of phantasy; to hear only the reality of named objects, without the metaphorised part; in short, in denying imaginary metaphorisation and settling for a form of psychological realism' (Kristeva, 2000: 239). This criticism posits a problem to psychoanalytic practice: traditional analysts are faced with an issue of methodology and the necessity to reassess their practices with regards to the analyst's distance and to interpretation. In order to elucidate the confusion between repression and the real, analysts are now faced with the co-presence of two symbolic modalities in the symbolic subject, demanding different listening and interpretative skills on the part of the analyst. A further difficulty pertains to the current climate more favourable to exact sciences than to a re-assessment of the psychoanalytic subject.

On the one hand, Freudian logic explains symbolic production as the condensation or displacement of repressed unconscious contents. In this instance, psychoanalytic practice follows the traditional methodology initiated by Freud. This tradition is today threatened by the cultural tendency to conceptualise subjective production not in terms of a symptomatology of repressed contents but in terms of replacing contents missing from conscious production with ready-made ones. For instance, the increase in cases of depression leads to an increase in the prescription of anti-depressants rather than to an increase in prescribing psychotherapies; genetic research strives to write an abstraction of 'human' (see for instance the decoding of the human genome); the capture of the subject's fantasies into media fantasmatic typographies can be construed as efforts to propose a ready-made objectification of human imaginary, suppressing the necessity for imaginary activity; finally, to some degree, the assimilation of the subject's unconscious contents to a lack of awareness, as is the case in a cognitivist or behaviourist understanding of the human, proposes a cure of human discomfort as the exposition of obsolete behavioural patterns subsequently replaced with healthier ones. Kristeva's work suggests that such cultural practice further condense/displace 'human' and that in consolidating the process of repression in the subject, we are also creating 'a time of great human distress' (Guberman, 1996: 269).

On the other hand, Kristevan theory proposes a somewhat different approach. Although critical of contemporary treatments of Freudian neuroses, she also criticises psychoanalytic practice, which does not address the new forms of distress of the contemporary subject. Following in Klein's footsteps, Kristeva uncovered the presence of other contents not subjected to repression, that abstraction does not explain and that she terms 'abject'. These new symbolic modalities, phantasies in Klein, abject in Kristeva, generated by the reassignment of the paternal function to the maternal realm, are the basis for a new challenge in psychoanalytic theory and practice.

Conclusion

A contemporary of Freud, Melanie Klein belonged to the Freudian tradition. But her work also generated its own school of thought. In spite of differences amongst post-Kleinian researchers, there is a common interest in furthering her pioneering ideas into the key role played by the maternal in the process of subjectivation. Freud and contemporary post-Freudians, on the other hand, although recognising the importance of the maternal, believe that the Oedipal model overrides any nascent subjective modalities that may have existed prior to its onset. The debate is thus narrowed to a discussion comparing the importance of the Oedipal phase and the narcissistic one. More precisely, knowing that Oedipal processes pertain to subjectivity, can narcissistic processes indicate the early or archaic presence of that subject? Rayner (in Hamilton, 1993) suggests that both myths are intricately related to the point that he sees Oedipal history as a consequence of Narcissistic 'choices' and Oedipus as inclusive of Narcissus. In other words, the symbolic subject would be a consequence of pre-linguistic existence and would carry within its economy the subject's pre-history. This is echoed by Kristeva, and her concept of poetic language, and by Bollas (1987) in his analysis of non-verbal modalities within symbolic production that he terms the subject's 'unthought known'. Others like Hamilton (1993) consider the Freudian model as basically flawed and believe that the pre-linguistic child, although deprived of linguistic symbols, nevertheless displays a propensity for non-verbal symbolisation. Pre-oedipal infants would then not be the objectless beings that Freud made them to be. Indeed, instead of the pre-Oedipal dyadic unit mother/child that the Oedipal father will later break, we are faced with a different pre-Oedipal reality. If symbolisation rests on the subject's repression of the maternal and identification with the paternal, it follows that pre-Oedipal symbolisation would also rely on some form of triadic dynamic. The triad maternal/paternal/child must be present on a pre-Oedipal level. The archaic subject should then be considered more closely, by considering the work of Melanie Klein who initiated such school of thought.

In association with the Kleinian model, Kristeva's vision of the maternal and what the absence of a paternal agency may initiate in the speaking subject adds a further dimension. The absence of separation between the subject and the maternal causes a confusion between fantasy and reality. The maternal is the place before symbolic organisation, a place of chaos, fragmentation, scattering of object and self, psychosis, etc. 'Successful' symbolisation equates with symbolic matricide ensuring the continuation of the socio-symbolic contract. Given Kristeva's understanding of 'maternal', social membership rests on the killing of the maternal in speech acts, marking the subject's separation from the maternal, and through identification with the paternal, enabling maternal contents to be organised in a socially acceptable fashion. In cases where the paternal function failed to play its role as separator, the subject is then faced with the impossibility to commit matricide symbolically and acts out this matricide instead. The non-differentiation between fantasy (symbolic) and reality (a-symbolic) means that the fantasy of murder of the maternal equals the reality of murder. Kristeva sees for instance, the murder of children in American schools, attacks on mother figures, a certain form of art (images of flesh, human waste, violence, etc.) as proof of this confusion. They act as carriers of the maternal, images or 'objects' fantasised as the maternal, again with no apprehension of the difference between the reality of the maternal and its fantasy, between the symbol and the real.

Melanie Klein's work further elucidates the importance of maternal matricide in the process of symbolisation. Differences between the Kleinian and Freudian models highlight how critical the differentiation maternal/paternal is to subjective health. Freud considered that the repression of pre-Oedipal wishes (incest with the mother and the murder of the father) constitutes the onset of the division conscious/unconscious. In effect, repressed contents are the unconscious while their symbolic expression (symptoms, condensations, displacements, etc.) are parts of the conscious. In other words, although generated by an original 'event', what is symbolisable is the antithesis of the unconscious. The Freudian subject is themself testimony to this, a symptom of their pre-history that is irredeemably lost and will remain for most part unconscious. While Freud subtly suggests that the recovery of some unconscious contents (and thus of the maternal) is possible in the context of analysis, others like Lacan will go as far as to suggest the loss of the maternal as the founding stone upon which subjectivation exists.

Klein, on the other hand, proves the existence of some form of symbolisation (phantasy) before the Oedipal stage and proposes birth as its starting point. Consequently, she believes that symbolisation is not the antithesis of the unconscious. Rather, phantasy or archaic symbolisation exist before the Freudian unconscious and will constitute part of it with the Oedipal phase. 'Successful' subjectivation depends not so much on paternal castration of the maternal/child dyad, but on the maternal function during the individual's pre-history. Klein proposes that the infant and pre-linguistic child experience the maternal as gratifying or death-bearing. In the first instance, the maternal function (or 'good breast') offers the infant nurture, life, containment and protection against the outside. In the second instance, the maternal withholds these from the infant and is cause of anxiety ('bad breast'). The psychical health of the future subject depends on how well the maternal will have negotiated its function, between the two extremes.

The Kleinian model opens two new paths in the understanding of the individual's history. First, the genesis of the subject is no longer initiated solely by the paternal function as in Freud and Lacan. Second, if subjectivation precedes Oedipus and some form of archaic symbolisation is conceivable from birth, then theorists like Klein, but also Stern (1993) and Kristeva (2000), are assuming narrative competence as innate rather than learnt. They are not suggesting the ability of the newborn to 'speak' but the existence a priori of a programming of the human mind for narration. They are however envisaging the process of subjectivation as the activation of this innate programme by other humans from birth to linguistic maturity. Successive forms of narration translate the individual's personal experience, phantasy and fantasy being but two aspects of them. This in turn has crucial consequences for the analysis of subjectivity, in particular in the context of psychoanalysis. Proposing that several forms of symbolisation, from archaic to fully mature, can co-exist in the subject's mind, bears the question of analytic methodology. Kristeva is indeed concerned that the confusion on some analysts' part between narrative registers will cause misinterpretation and misguide the analysand towards a false history. To avoid such pitfalls, Kristeva reiterates her belief in researching the modalities that constitute the maternal. The aim is on the one hand to re-present those aspects of the maternal that take part in the crisis of subjectivity, that is to support maternal contents with symbolic elements. On the other hand, the intentional bringing forth of the maternal to symbolic light will enable to re-instate the boundary that separates the maternal from its fantasy (symbolic). In other words, Kristeva is eager to re-establish the link and frontier between maternal and paternal in the hope of transcending contemporary subjective crisis.

In re-visiting the passage from maternal to paternal, the Kristevan model presents a paradox. The move from the one to the other is initiated much earlier than Freud had anticipated. Klein in particular sees this move from birth in infant phantasy. As the site of passage, the maternal then becomes the place where the early move from nature to culture is operated. The paradox lies in constructing the maternal function as both a natural and a cultural function. Klein had anticipated the lack of logic in pairing two mutually exclusive functions in what she termed 'the combined parent'. What appears to the adult as an impossibility within symbolic constraint, constitutes the infant and young child's experience of the pre-Oedipal. This experience confirms Klein's suspicion that the differentiation conscious/unconscious has not yet taken place and announces Kristeva's 'semiotic'. She constructs her theory of the semiotic as what partly constitutes the unconscious and more importantly as a modality autonomous from Freudian repression. As opposed to Freud's belief that linguistic production is subject to a process of repression (condensation/displacement), Kristeva will show how the subject's 'pre-repression' experience of the maternal bursts forth into symbolic expression virtually unmodified. The co-existence of two modalities within symbolic activity, the semiotic and the symbolic, thus proposes a re-play of the pre-Oedipal experience of the combined maternal/paternal. Kristeva's work emphasises this combination and will show particular insight in articulating a framework explaining the move between nature and culture, a framework she will term "abjection". Through abjection, she will further Kleinian research in infant reality and describe how this early experience of the maternal can be deciphered and analysed in the adult.

Chapter 5

The Maternal

Prior to the actual mother/father/child family dynamic, Kristeva sees a pre Oedipal triad, maternal/imaginary father/infant. In the Oedipal myth, the child must relinquish their wish for parricide and incest, leave the mother and choose the father's society. In what she terms 'Oedipus prime' (Kristeva, 1996a: 200), Kristeva follows both a Freudian and Kleinian dialectic: she maintains the dyadic unity mother/child that the presence of the father is going to separate. However, where Freud envisioned the triangulation with the actual figures of the mother, the father and the child, Kristeva's model slides towards a more Kleinian approach. Instead of relying on actual people, the subject is positioned in a more phantasmatic triangulation. With Klein, part objects (the breast, the penis) replaced the actual parents in an attempt to represent infant reality in a world without fully formed symbols. Early in her work (Kristeva, 1974a) Kristeva distinguishes 'two registers: the register of the symbolic and the register of the semiotic' (Guberman, 1996: 21). The symbolic would refer to the logic of language (grammar, syntax, etc.) while the semiotic would recall the early efforts of the infant towards the organisation of echolalic, vocalic, visual information into language. The semiotic utterances of the infant:

> [...] presuppose that the possibility of language exists either as a genetic program that allows the child to speak one day, so that the echolalias are stages before this possibility of speech, or as a social environment - the child is already in an environment where the parents speak, his desire to speak already exists in the discourse of the parents, and so the echolalias appear in this environment. In short, there is an already there of language. (Guberman, 1996: 21)

Whether biological or cultural, a pre-existing linguistic ability preceding the child's capacity for linguistic mastery is thus posited. While Melanie Klein was interested in the presence of early verbal and non-verbal productions, or phantasies, deciphered in child play, the focus is now on the co-presence symbol/semiotic in the speaking subject. While patient material, supporting both theorists' interpretative work is different, play for Klein and language for Kristeva, both come to a similar conclusion: children and adults alike present to the analyst material pertaining to a difficulty over the separation from the mother or the maternal. Klein's quintessential example is probably the case of Little Dick and his desire and aggression vis-à-vis the maternal. Kristeva for her part puts forward the increasingly fragmented discourse of contemporary individuals as the marker of an archaism that the subject so expresses. Contemporary illnesses, the 'new maladies of the soul' are a failure of the paternal function, not solely on the Oedipal front but more crucially on a pre-Oedipal maternal level. These 'new maladies' (borderline, false-self, etc) are the marker of a 'shattered narcissism' (Kristeva, 1998c: 11) that is interpreted at once as the new figure of the modern time subject and as a symptom of the subject's crisis:

> [I]t may be more interesting today to insist on the originality of the narcissistic figure, and the quite singular place it holds, first in the history of Western subjectivity and second, considering its morbidity, in examining the critical symptom of this subjectivity. (Kristeva, 1983: 134)

In her more recent work, Kristeva has tended to abandon a specifically psychoanalytic vocabulary in favour of a lexicon more palatable to the layperson and to discuss parental categories in terms of their functions. The spirit of her entire oeuvre is testimony to this effort to construct the maternal function as that which carries within itself an early form of paternal function, and to understand what enables the subject to move from maternal to paternal sites.

The Paternal as Maternal Desire

Returning to the earlier presupposition of 'an already there of language' (Guberman, 1996: 21), language acquisition can only happen within a dynamic of parental desire for the child to become a speaking/social subject. In most cases, the child complies with these pre-set parental/social requirements. In this sense, parental functions act as a kind of program, with the parents themselves responding to a generational program drawn under the terms 'society' or 'culture'. To be a member of the social sphere is to be a speaking subject. It may be, as some suggest, that the ability to symbolise is inherent to the human genetic make up, but this genetic disposition requires a second, cultural trigger in order to form a social subject. The case of humans who have developed away from human company is well documented.[1] These children show more than a remarkable adaptation to another species' environment; records illustrate the extent to which these human beings develop the metabolism, emotions, sensory responses and even physique of their adoptive species.[2] The success of their reinsertion into society remains mitigated by the length of separation from human society and of animal

---

1 Based on the work of Lucien Malson (1972), William D. Wylie's *The Basic Human Being: The Wild Child* (on line) gives a comprehensive list of cases of wild children and their limitations to adaptation to human society.

2 All cases report how the prime interest of these children was feeding. Children brought up by predators (leopards, bears, wolves, etc.) would fight on fours with teeth and claws; those cared for by harvesters would climb trees and feed off eggs and berries.

programming received: the 'failure' to learn to be human effectively marks the moment human subjectivity is arrested: erect locomotion, recognition of themselves in a mirror, learning sign language, etc., act as landmarks in human subjectivation: in reported cases of 'wild children', these landmarks are a gauge of the amount of human (or of 'wild') present in these children.

The examples of 'mal-association' of child with parental desire, resulting in non-human forms of subjectivity, does not stop at children subjected to non-human parenting. In a dramatic account, Victoria Hamilton (1993) recounts the story of baby Tanya, whose mother's prime attachment was for the family dog, which translated into the child imitating the animal's crawling, eating manners and barking. Hamilton concludes that her observations of baby Tanya illustrate her point on the importance of seeing the child 'as a developing centre of initiative' (Hamilton, 1993: 113) rather than wish it to please the parent. Failing to encourage the child to become an autonomous human subject means that they will develop abnormally.

Some caution is called for in identifying abnormality. What appears to adults as child desire to please may not be as selfless as it may seem. Indeed, the child does not so much please the parent as respond to survival instinct. In its attempt to obtain the best care for its needs, it will instinctively strive to occupy the place of maternal interest or desire. In Tanya's eyes, maternal desire was for the dog and being like the dog, in locomotion, feeding and vocalisation, would get her the same attention the dog was getting. In other words, Tanya's development follows a normal path; it is the ab-normal aspect of maternal desire for animal 'society' rather than human society which causes abnormal identification. It would then appear that no matter the form taken by maternal interest, provided this interest in something other than the child exists, the child will develop some form of identity.[3] Kristeva's suggestion of an innate programming of the future subject is then entirely adequate. When human subjects are born with the instinct to survive, the struggle to take a place in some form of human society is dependent upon the 'already there' of the socio-symbolic sphere. In the case of 'wild' children and baby Tanya, this already there is in the former case inexistent (or non-human) and the latter falsified. The already there is then determined (and for the neonate, predetermined) by the parental relationship with the socio-symbolic. For the infant, this relationship is in Kristevan terms construed as maternal desire for the paternal function. The child wishing to keep the bond with the mother, positions itself in the place of the mother's desire, that is the place of an other than itself.

There is an important difference between this Kristevan pre-Oedipal dynamics and the Freudian Oedipal model. With Freud, the child sacrifices its symbiotic relationship with the mother and sides with the threatening father; with Kristeva,

3 On the condition the form taken by maternal is human. Animal care results in animal 'identity'. Moreover, experiments in teaching infants via technology, television for instance, resulted in failure. Children respond only if another human being mediates the information conveyed to them.

the infant forsakes its unity with the mother in order to keep her. In the second instance, it is neither the mother (in Freud) nor the bond child/mother (in Lacan) which is forsaken but the link infant/maternal. Kristeva argues against Freud that the threat of paternal castration is not enough to justify the child choosing the paternal over the maternal. In contrast, the pain of separation would be a strong motivation for the child to remain fused in the maternal/child dyad and develop into a psychotic being. As psychotics[4] represent a minority in the vast majority of individuals who form society, the desire to move from maternal to paternal must have another origin than the one suggested by Freud. Kristeva believes that separation from the maternal occurs earlier. An integral aspect of the maternal function would be to push the child away from the maternal and towards the paternal.

> [...] maybe the good-enough mother is the mother who has something else to love besides her child; it could be her work, her husband, her lovers, etc. She has to have another meaning in her life. (Oliver, 1997: 334)

If the move from maternal to paternal is instigated from within the maternal function, the child's cooperation with maternal desire is conceivable. By occupying the place delimited by maternal desire, the child at once gains maternal interest and leaves the maternal for the place of an other than itself, that is a symbolic self. Hence, the child's effort to become a symbolic subject is motivated by its attempts to keep the maternal bond. The maternal function appears as a paradox that defies paternal (phallogocentric) logic: what is kept is what is lost. The maternal function thus consist at once of symbiosis and separation: first a corporeal separation (birth), then a psychical separation (desire).

Contemporary accounts suggest that the second aspect of the maternal function, its psychical separative function, is now failing. The failure of the paternal function within the maternal is intrinsically linked to the failure of the paternal function on a symbolic level. The lack or instability of paternal representation means that maternal desire for a symbolic instance is also lacking or unstable. The child then forms early identifications by positioning itself in the place of the vacant or precarious paternal image that the mother desires. In the failure of the maternal to provide a strong paternal site to support the child's move from maternal to

---

4 Psychotic is to be understood in the sense given by Freud in the last stages of his work and described by Laplanche and Pontalis as a rejection of the reality of castration (Laplanche and Pontalis, 1988: 372). Psychosis can be described as the rejection of the social or paternal constraints made upon the subject and which define them as social subject. Lacan will add that subjectivity rests on the realisation that the child cannot be the Phallus of maternal desire and thus cannot fulfil her. Hence, a Lacanian understanding reinforces a Freudian apprehension of subjectivity as castration. Psychosis is then about refusing to conceive of the paternal function as the locus of maternal desire.

paternal, the child is left to face what Kristeva terms the 'maternal abject' (Kristeva, 1980 and 1987a).

The Maternal as Abject

For Kristeva, the move from maternal to paternal signifies the move from nature to culture.

> For in order to become autonomous, it is necessary that one cut the instinctual dyad of the mother and the child and that one become something other. (Guberman, 1996: 118)

As the maternal represents the link between the subject and its naturalness (birth, nurture, survival instinct), abjection marks the moment the individual moves from nature (instinct) to culture (symbol). What is abject manifests itself in the symbolic subject as that which draws the boundary between nature and culture and which the subject finds disgusting. The work of Cindy Sherman is a good example of the attempt at representing the abject.

Angela Marie Smith (on line) argues that Cindy Sherman's 'disgust' pictures (Sherman, 1995) illustrate abject items and provoke in the reader a movement of abjection. On the two pictures reproduced above, we see first items scattered on gravel: a pool of vomit, a pair of sunglasses reflecting the face of a woman screaming (Sherman, 1995: 96); the second picture presents us with a table covered with dirty dishes and melted wax with on the foreground a plate of glistening worms (Sherman, 1995: 95). Both pictures engage the reader with images of bodily waste (vomit) or bodily decay (worms) associated with representations of the maternal (woman's face, feeding) and suggest the morselling of identity when it touches nature (scattered objects, leftovers, screaming face).

Figure 5.1 Cindy Sherman (1995), Untitled disgust pictures

For Kristeva, abjection 'is an extremely strong feeling that is at once somatic and symbolic' (Guberman 1996: 118). It is somatic in its visceral response of revolt against what might suggest the subject's biology: its origin (the maternal) or its death (waste, decay). The encounter with the abject exposes subjectivity as construct, and thus as evanescent and illusory, causing a violent response of denial (disgust, retching, etc.). It is then symbolic as a revolt against what signifies the anti-subject. As a revolt, it is a re-asserting of subjectivity. Kristeva's premise of abjection as a symbolic act is further supported by the fact that the form taken by the abject is defined by society. In her analysis of abjection (Kristeva, 1982), she puts forward abjection as a universal phenomenon, inherent to all human subjective development, while its coding takes different shapes according to different cultural systems. The abjection of food is but one of the numerous accounts analysed in *Pouvoir de l'horreur*. In the case of wild children mentioned earlier, one peculiarity is the absence of disgust for what society regards as abject (foul smell, animal carcasses, etc.). Similarly, in infants the smell of vomit or urine does not cause any reaction while bitter and acidic smells are strongly rejected (Atkinson et al., 1996). Hence the act of abjection is the marker that what society codes as abject has been internalised by the subject. Kristeva then views abjection as an early step towards symbolisation.

Abjection occurs at the level of the maternal function, when the child moves to the archaic triangulation infant/maternal/prehistoric father, that is a passage between the dyadic unity to the narcissistic (pre-Oedipal) position. But what is abjected is the space and time anterior to that triangulation. Hence, in adults, when the subject 'experiences' abjection, they are first pointing to a time before the Oedipal structure, a time when they moved from the maternal to the paternal, from nature to culture. Second, in abjection the symbolic subject is confronted with the knowledge of the abject maternal: abjection requires the recognition of the abject. What is abjected is the symbiosis maternal/child, the natural origin of the social subject. In abjecting the maternal, the subject also abjects itself as natural. Kristeva then posits the 'abject' and 'abjection' as two moments and two sites in the structuring of the subject. This is better apprehended diagrammatically:

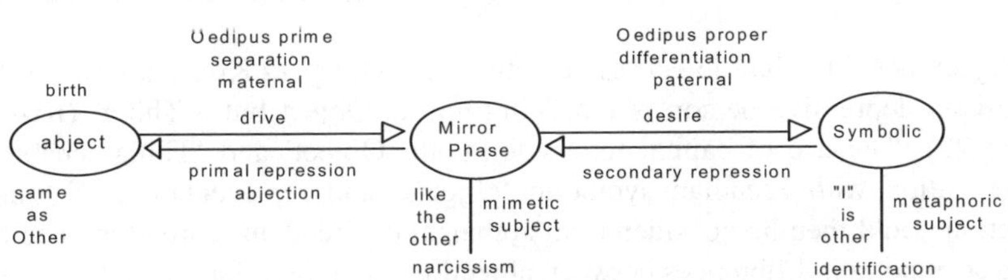

Figure 5.2: The two moments of subjectivation

Considering figure 5.2, Freud's former Oedipal phase has now become two moments of the Oedipal phase that Kristeva defines as 'Oedipus prime' and 'Oedipus proper'. The former refers to the pre-symbolic baby, before it can apprehend the specular image described by Lacan under the term 'Mirror phase'. Kristeva believes that the Lacanian logic of the specular already points to the baby's symbolic ability, rather than it explains imaginary 'logic'. The latter, 'Oedipus proper', refers to Freud's understanding of subjectivity. The identity of the Freudian subject is construed as other than the individual. Freudian subjectivity follows a metaphoric logic, upon which identity is constructed as other. The dynamics of desire and of secondary repression were proposed by Freud in his unconscious/pre-conscious/conscious model (first topic) to explicate the dualism inherent to the Oedipal subject. On the one hand, desire would point to the subject's unconscious wishes (for the maternal); on the other, secondary repression would be the subjective response to desire, a choosing of the paternal metaphor, of social membership. The theory of the unconscious depends then 'upon a dialectic of negativity' (Kristeva, 1982: 7): the subject, in its symbols, is always other than what it 'really' is, that is, the (conscious) subject is what it is not (unconscious). Both parts of this irreconcilable equation are being held within the subject's psyche. Freud proposed the first topic as a possible mapping of human psychical dialectic. In this mapping, affects and contents unacceptable to the conscious are repressed into the unconscious and return to the conscious realm under disguised forms (return of the repressed: parapraxis, symptoms, hallucinations, etc.). Hence Freud envisaged a system by which the subject is split within a dichotomy conscious/unconscious and this split is constitutive of both the unconscious and the conscious, and of the symbolic subject.

On a pre-Oedipal level, Kristeva problematises an earlier 'repression' she terms 'abjection' and describes as an archaic split between (archaic) subject and (archaic) object. As illustrated in figure 5.2, abjection is situated in time, before, and in place, beyond, the subject and their desire for an object, even partial.

> [Abjection] does not have, properly speaking, a definable *object* . [...] The abject has only one quality of the object - that of being opposed to *I* . [...] Not me. Not that. But not nothing, either. A 'something' I do not recognize as a thing. (Kristeva, 1982: 1-2)

The abject, acts like the 'object' of abjection, its 'Thing' as Kristeva terms it: 'The narcissistic depressive person is mourning not an Object but a Thing' (Kristeva, 1987a: 22). The use of capital letters for both 'Object' and 'Thing' enable the differentiation with Freudian symbolic 'objects' and representation of 'things'. Abjection could then be considered an archaism of Freudian repression. There are however important differences between abjection and repression.

First, in repression, Freud envisages a split within the subject's psychical structure. The psyche is the locus of both unconscious contents and their translation into symbols. In abjection, the abject is what the subject defends against, excludes[5]

5 Kristeva uses the term 'exclusion' to avoid confusion with Freudian 'repression'.

from the inside and throws outside. For instance, nausea can be construed as the abjection of food. Given the connotation between feeding and maternal desire, the abjection of food symbolises a rejection of maternal desire. It is a refusal by the *I* to assimilate the parent, a separation from that desire. Since the subject in abjection is neither subject, nor object, the 'object' of nausea "is not an 'other' for 'me', 'who am only in their [the parents] desire, I expel *myself*, I spit *myself* out, I abject *myself* within the same motion through which 'I' claim to establish *myself*' (Kristeva, 1982: 3). In other words, the becoming of the future symbolic subject is a constant movement inside/outside. The parent acts as 'programmer' of the child's subjectivity, in their desire for the child to become a social subject. In the desire of this other, subjectivity can be construed as a mere extension, dare we say 'application', of the parental figure (inside = outside). Nausea is a symbolic act establishing separateness of the subject from the other's desire, founding the new subject's autonomy from the parent (inside separate from and thrown outside). Yet, it is also a desire to be like the other, to be another desiring being like the desiring parent (inside = outside).

The process of subjectivation rests then upon the expelling of the pre-symbolic being: the maternal space and its correlative inside/outside movement. Abjection rests on a 'killing' of the archaic subject so that the symbolic subject can live. Nausea is also interpreted as the biological act by which the pre-symbolic subject inflicts death upon itself (starvation). In this, the destructive impulses of the baby towards both itself and the maternal are stirred. Kristeva sees a link between the maternal and the death drive: '*Thanatos*, the death drive, signifies the disintegration of bonds and the ceasing of circulation, communication, and social relationships' (Guberman, 1996: 79). In abjection, we are dealing with a not fully differentiated subject who cannot yet engage in social exchange. Rather, abjection marks the onset of an early, archaic subject, a subject in the making, whose autonomy from the maternal is not yet fully achieved. The attainment of social membership rests on a symbolic matricide, a 'killing' of maternal sites, a 'killing' of the not yet differentiated subject. In other words, although abjection is not a fully symbolic act founding subjectivity, Kristeva is also suggesting that it marks an early form of symbolisation.[6] Unlike Freud's conscious/unconscious which occurs within the psyche, abjection permits an archaic split between the inside and the outside of the body, but this split is not yet strong enough to permit the

---

6 Abjection permits separation through the exclusion of the bad 'object'. Melanie Klein and Object Relation Theory have focused on this aspect of the subject's archaic split. The terms 'separation' and 'differentiation' are often used interchangeably by theorists (see in particular Cooper and Maxwell, 1995). In figure 5.2, the two terms are used to indicate a difference in the problematic. Differentiation deals with the symbolic subject in relation to their objects (identity is 'other'). Separation refers to the inside/outside split described by Kristeva: the subject is in relation with an archaic object but that object is endowed with qualities projected by the subject upon this object (archaic identity is same as the archaic other).

exclusion of the archaic being for the distinction of the symbolic other: the archaic subject is located on both sides of the boundary (skin). Consequently, a second difference between repression and abjection arises: although the process of abjection resembles that of repression, Kristeva finds that exclusion is not strong enough to permit the differentiation I/Other. In other words, exclusion of the abject is not constitutive of symbolicity while repression of unconscious contents is.

Kristeva notes in the speech of borderline subjects a 'sublimating discourse ('aesthetic' or 'mystical', etc.), rather than a scientific one' (Kristeva, 1982: 7). Scientific discourse is equated with the ability to judge and differentiate. It can be read as metaphor of the Freudian model founded on a dialectic of negativity or repression. The sublimating discourse does not rely on negativity but on a 'representation' or coding of archaism (mimesis for instance). Kristeva believes that when we speak, the frontier of ideas corresponds to the frontiers of the body. Expression is difficult in the place where nature resists symbolic coding or where the symbol resists knowing nature. Hence the frontier of ideas (and of the body) is where the coding of abjection is found. What the body linguistically expels is also what represents the limit between inside and outside (Kristeva, 1982: 70). Aesthetic discourse would then be more prosperous to the 'metaphorisation' of the abject as it permits the linguistic coding of the irrational that rational discourse does not convey. In the case of borderline personalities, Kristeva suggests a pronounced manifestation of the inside/outside opposition within symbolic production. This opposition is constituted of contents that would 'normally' be repressed in neurotic patients and would manifest themselves as condensations or displacements. She thus is putting forward the co-presence of two oppositions: on the one hand, the split conscious/unconscious is evidenced in the conscious subject's ability to judge (and censor) their utterances. This ability to differentiate the 'good' and the 'bad' is formative of the 'I' (the verbalised *I*) in opposition to 'other' (the unverbalised, the not-*I*, the unconscious). On the other hand, Kristeva also finds, within both the conscious and the unconscious, contents referring to the inside/outside and which are not subjected to the conscious/unconscious operations of the symbolic subject. If there is a co-presence of two modalities within language, then psychoanalytic practice is faced with the challenge of differentiating between these modalities within the one patient discourse. In this lies a growing difficulty for psychoanalytic theory and has brought about a split. On the one hand are traditional practitioners who, by abiding to the one (Freudian) model only, risk confusing modalities pertaining to the real and those concerning the imaginary. On the other, a more progressive approach has opened new terrains of investigation and renewed the potential for psychoanalysis as method of cure. The difficulty for contemporary psychoanalysis now is to highlight the mechanisms that permit the recovery of the abject alongside the interpretation of unconscious contents.

The co-existence of the two structures is especially evidenced in the analysis of moods. As 'the *psychical representation of energy displacements* induced by external or internal traumas' (Kristeva, 1987a: 31), moods are of particular interest. ne step beyond the manifestation of affect and one step before the conscious recognition of mood. Consider 'sadness' and a potential scenario of the historical path followed from stimulus to its expression: an event (the death of someone) excites the body causing affective discharge (emptiness for instance), the psychical apparatus records the affective response to event (sadness). Mood is recognised in the verbal association *I am sad.* As moods stand at the frontier between affect and representation, Kristeva is particularly curious as to whether moods belong to the domain of affect or to the domain of language, or both (Kristeva, 1987a: 31), whether the presence of affects on a symbolic level are symbols in their own rights. In the Freudian model, energy displacements are the foundation of symbolic representation. They are associated with linguistic signs and subjected to the censorship of the super-ego. In the Kristevan model, these energies are also subjected to the censoring of the super-ego, but are seen as 'fluctuating', that is not sufficiently stabilised to allow associations into verbal signs. Instead, these energies are transferred in the form of 'moods' affecting '*the whole of* behaviour and all sign systems (from motricity to elocution and idealisation) without identifying with them nor disorganising them' (Kristeva, 1987a: 32). Kelly Oliver notes the fluctuating quality of moods when she describes how '[a]ffective energy' can be transferred from one person to another. In her view:

> The idea that we can transfer affects through contact and conversation resonates with most people who have had the experience of a conversation with a loved on in which s/he is upset during the conversation and after the conversation s/he feels much better but now the other party to the conversation is upset. This kind of situation suggests a transfer of affect. (Oliver, 2000: 10)

Although Oliver could be accused of trivialising psychoanalytic terminology by mixing two registers as if they were of equal value and meaning (affect and feeling, transfer and transference: psychoanalytic jargon and popular psychology), her example has the merit to attempt to highlight how mood takes its place in interpersonal symbolicity.[7] In Kristeva, 'mood' is present within the symbolic, it is not an object of identification: it is not a symbol. The presence of a non-symbol would entail a rationale based on negativity with the non-symbol acting as an anti symbol disruptive of the symbolic chain: for instance sobs interrupting speech. Yet, 'mood' does not disorganise sign systems and cannot therefore be explained within the Freudian dialectic of the return of repressed unconscious contents: sobs are not the symptom (displaced or condensed) of repression.

---

7 The attempt to illustrate theory with everyday examples is rarely found in Kristeva's work. In her early work, she tends to focus on theory, practice being solely literary practice. In the 1980s, we find more examples pertaining to psychoanalytic accounts of patients' predicament. Yet again, Kristeva's reporting tends to remain highly jargon-laden. A feature of her most recent work (1990s) is the general tendency to make her work more accessible by accepting to discuss more mundane cultural issues.

Moods (in particular sadness in depressive states) not only mark the presence of energy displacement but more importantly signify the rupture of this energy. In the case of melancholia/depression, the presence of sadness (voice, gesture, etc.) points to the Thing of loss (the maternal) that does not evolve into its representation (the maternal as *object* of loss). The subjectivation process is arrested (rupture of energy) at the level of separation and the social subject bursts forth into the symbolic as a mirroring of affect, in this instance sadness: '[t]he melancholic Thing interrupts the metonymy of desire, like it opposes the intrapsychic elaboration of loss' (Kristeva, 1987a: 23). In other words, there is a separation loss/affect but no differentiation loss/object. Identification is mimetic of the Thing, that is the maternal loss: *I* is like the other (here sadness) and the other (sadness) is like *I*. In this echolalic representation of the other, the boundary separating the inside of the subject and its outside fails to evolve into a boundary differentiating subject/other, that is an Oedipal subject.

The term 'other' refers then to two related concepts. On the one hand, the other is that which the pre-subject will identify with: the subject of enunciation, *I* is other than what it really is. In this instance, *I* equals other. The other is also that which is not the speaking subject: what is other refers to what the pre-linguistic subject was and really is, an other than *I*. In this second instance *I* is the opposite of other. The encounter of the other (the pre-verbal other) reminds the symbolic subject (*I*) that its identity is other than the other it really is. In other words, on a pre-symbolic level, the other is that which threatens the subject in its unity with the maternal: the paternal. On a symbolic level, the other is that which threatens the subject in its identification with the paternal realm: the maternal. The absence or failure of the paternal function on a symbolic level then equates with a menace upon identity, an absence or failing of this other that *I* is, and a return to and of the other than *I*, the maternal.

The Maternal: Between Nature and Culture

Within the symbolic function, the abject is recalled each time the subject is exposed as other than its symbols. Abjection is an experience located at the point where the body meets the outside: an outside menace is experienced internally and triggers an ab-jection, a throwing out of, at once an instinctual re-action (excess matter affecting the body is expelled causing relief), and a symbolic one (the throwing out symbolises the re-enactment of separation subject/maternal). Abjection is thus at once a bodily act and a symbolic act of subjectivity,[8] testifying

8 If abjection can be construed as a symbolic act, it does not mean the abject is a symbol. Abjection involves two protagonists, the subject and the maternal. Kristeva proposes that in attempting to voice the sadness of separation, the child calls upon a third party (the father of individual pre-history) to help them identify with something other than [the ma]ternal (Kristeva, 1987a: 34).

as it occurs of the encounter, exchange and conversance biology/symbol. It is this encounter that is increasingly lacking in the contemporary subject. Because language is the prime site of the social, a metaphor of the encounter symbol/affect or of the paternal and the maternal, the failure of the paternal function in the individual is signalled in linguistic enactment. If we follow Kristeva's argument, the connecting of symbol and affect in utterances occurs on the condition that 'this father of individual prehistory is able to play its role as an Oedipal father within symbolic Law' (Kristeva, 1987a: 34). The increasing absence of the paternal function as agent of differentiation on the symbolic level causes the deficiency of the paternal function in the maternal on a pre-symbolic level. Absent or deficient, the paternal function no longer represents the site of the unified, stable self. Theorists invested in explicating the symptoms of the deficient father (psychoanalysis, social sciences, politics, etc.) at a loss to define what 'paternal functions' could be connected on either side of the Oedipal phase. If we follow Kristeva's numerous accounts on the paternal function, definitions of 'paternal' range from the paternal as absence to the paternal as multiple. Increasingly, we appear to be moving from the former to the latter: absence is being compensated by a multiplicity of socio-political measures attempting to provide the individual some paternal presence (State, education system, police, social workers, etc.). Like we have a multiplicity of paternal functions, we now have also a multiplicity of scenarios vis-à-vis the subjective process, depending upon the paternal agency accorded to each individual. Kristevan theory tends to encapsulate the variety of symptoms of paternal failure into a model whereby the disconnection pre-symbolic/symbolic, translating in a linguistic disconnection symbol/affect, is discussed. The individual is described as increasingly subject to a deadened language. The purpose of discourse is to convey information, to supply the symbol in isolation from its affective charge, in a manner similar to computer language.

If the paternal function is failing on the symbolic level for the symbolic subject, it is then also failing within the maternal realm for both mother and infant. A big part of Kristeva's work has been to attempt the formulation of subjectivation especially the passage from the maternal to the paternal function. She is calling for a 're-connecting' of the symbolic subject to its archaic history, located at the point where this subject has now lost its biological roots. In *Pouvoirs de l'horreur* (Kristeva, 1980), she pointed out that psychoanalytic and semiologic theories still do not precisely explain the modalities of psychical representations and the displacement of energy. No science has yet proposed an adequate framework to account for these pre-verbal representations and displacements from system φ to ψ. The reassignment of the paternal function to the maternal would indicate an effort at re-connecting the symbolic to the biological. However, this reassignment does not mean that the 'maternal' is being reconsidered in the Kristevan sense of a theorising of abjection. Although post-Freudian research has been expanding towards understanding the modalities of the maternal function, researchers, with at the forefront Anglo-Americans, tend to understand the maternal function as the mother's role and the paternal function as the father's role. These two roles are analysed as two disconnected moments of subjectivation. Moreover, this research is stunted on the one hand because of a discouraging climate privileging the symbol over its connected affect,[9] and on the other because any scientific discourse rests upon a system of abstractions and fails to represent the 'illogic' of the maternal within its symbols. Since scientific discourse can be envisaged as a metaphor for the displacement of energy, from body to psyche to representation, the chances of sciences (especially neuroscience) of ever succeeding in reconciling the body/psyche with abstraction should be questioned. The difficulty is to formulate a theoretical framework capable of negotiating the pre-verbal within the symbolic. Hence, there remains Kristeva's appeal for a retheorising of the maternal, that is the recognition of pre-symbolic contents within the symbolic, a linking social/biology.

Oliver (2000) reconsiders the link social/biology in her essay 'Conflicted Love'. She uses Kristeva's idea of the maternal as protosocial but suggests further that if the maternal 'cannot be reduced to antisocial nature, we might go two steps further than Kristeva and suggest that matricide is necessary only to maintain patriarchy' (Oliver, 2000). In Kristevan logic, it is indeed the quality of the paternal function, whether symbolic or archaic which decides of the subject's predicament while the maternal, as much as it prepares the paternal/subject encounter, remains a threat for subjectivity. Much of the criticism her notion of 'abjection' attracted derives from the difficulty to consider a maternal function as both pre-social and anti-social: a social 'programming' function that must be ultimately abjected. Oliver supports her argument by demonstrating how the paternal and the maternal functions are construed by Freudian theorists:[10] males would have mastery over their aggressive instincts and through this control and repudiation of their biology gain dominance and sociality; females are subjected to their biological destiny and have no choice in the matter but to remain anti-social and cast out. Men and women are then construed by traditional psychoanalysis as diametrically opposed, natural woman against social man. Oliver believes that it does not have to be so and that the construction of the parent (and the subject to be) could be organised around a mother recognised in her social function rather than sacrificed to culture and a father valorised for his part in the making of culture without repudiating his body.

---

9 On the one hand, psychotherapeutic practices are often oriented towards refining the psychotherapeutic 'tool' towards a speedier, more efficient service, on the other hand, social systems (in the West) also favour those public services that can demonstrate productivity. In both cases, the aim is to achieve a better control of the emotional subject and facilitate its insertion in the socio-symbolic sphere.

10 Freud bases his theory upon the relationship between primitive Man and fire. Men can choose to destroy the fire by urinating on it or to own the fire through the control of their aggressive urge; women on the other hand can only keep the fire going and have no choice in the matter. Hence, the biology of the one permits him to master nature while the biology of the other only enables her to be subjected to nature.

To respond to Oliver's suggestion, Kristeva insists that what is important is that there are three terms to the subjectivation equation. It may be, in Freud the mother/father/child traditional family, in Klein the breast/penis/child phantasised family, in Kristeva the paternal/maternal/child triangulation. What matters is that a third term be introduced in the dyad maternal/child, so that the process of differentiation can take place. In her essay, Oliver does not precisely account for this process, nor does she suggest how her loving mother/ embodied father/ child could modify the patriarchal setting. In fact, her triad does not step away from sexual categories: the maternal is the mother while the paternal is the father. Furthermore, her construction of the parents' gender identities suggests the erasure of sexual difference, with a more social mother and a more natural father. In such a context, the erasure of sexual difference may be a contemporary factor of crisis in subjectivity but does not prove that a fundamental shift in subjective organisation is at work. Rather, Kristeva envisions that the erasure of sexual categories translates in the manifestation of differentiation upon a different 'object' than gender, race for instance, with the rise in racist acts in society. If its objects are changing, differentiation occurs nevertheless. Where supporters of difference denounce the dominance of one sex over another, they equally point the finger at the unfair treatment of one race over another instead. Hence, it appears more interesting to consider how maternal and paternal functions are distributed within the social sphere and what motivates an infant to move from being undifferentiated to being other.

The Paternal and the Maternal Revisited

Kristeva's theorising of parental categories steps away from the traditional biological categories mother/father. Language is constituted of two modalities, each pertaining to a function of the paternal/maternal but not exclusive to a biological reality. The maternal is neither solely the privileged function of the mother nor is the paternal function reserved for the father. Rather, both functions can exist within any one parent and are the source of the double-connectedness of the linguistic subject. More than a subject in relation with its symbols, Kristeva's subject is represented in its link to the paternal and the maternal. Both symbolic and abject co-exist within language production. The measure of subjectivity depends upon the subject's negotiating of this paternal/maternal legacy. In 'unravelling the double-bind' of the contemporary subject (Oliver, 1993), Kristeva finds an increasing imbalance between language modalities traced back to the maternal and those connected to the paternal. The failing of the paternal function translates in the subject's inability to create bonds with sites of the paternal, for instance, the fragmentation of the nuclear family. Following Freud, Kristeva posited the life drive (Eros) as the creator of social bonds, the aim being to seek an object to satisfy the drive. The death drive (Thanatos) on the other hand would equate with the disintegration of bonds, arresting the move towards any object.

Kristeva's work also emphasises the correspondence between the paternal function and Eros on the one hand, and the maternal and Thanatos on the other. The paternal function would have a cohesive function, enabling the containment of destructive impulses present at birth. In language, the symbol is the representer of this first modality of language containing the subject's psychical activity: for instance, if the impulse is hunger, I do not bite into the first object present to immediately satisfy oral deprivation but contain the hunger in its expression 'I am hungry'. If this capacity to offer containment and cohesion is today weakened, the second modality present in language is by the same token becoming more prominent. The increase in violence could be connected to the expression of the abject maternal: a certain form of art displaying contents representing the abject (Cindy Sherman's disgust pictures), the increasing violence of televisual narratives (videos, films, cartoons, etc.), the enactment of violence in the social sphere (killings in American schools, child murders in Britain, etc) are markers of the symbolic subject's 'possession' (Kristeva, 1996d) by the maternal. A weakened paternal to contain the maternal translates in a weakened boundary between archaic phantasy and symbolic activity, resulting in the stronger presence of the abject maternal within the symbolic. Although this can have a positive effect in the case of emerging forms of art, the increasing enactment of destructive impulses is not acceptable when this destruction is geared towards the social fabric. For this reason, Kristeva is interested in finding new methods to restore the subject's capacity for 'imaginary matricide' (Kristeva, 2000: 218) over its actual enactment. Such work rests on a re-theorising of the maternal function, which itself means the necessity for theorists (in the wider sense: analysts, social workers, academics, etc.) to re-visit their own connection with the maternal.

In her own field, Kristeva believes that such work will necessarily involve a reconsidering of transferential processes between analyst and patient, and the adoption of a non traditional 'neither forbid nor repress' stance. In attempting to reach out to a new subject bearing towards the maternal, paternal castration is no longer the preferred method. Yet, Kristeva is also aware that a loosening of the analyst's distance equates with a more invested attitude that could translate in a confusion of transferential boundaries. Having been analysed and thus firmly anchored in their symbolic role, the analyst 'playing dead' was a guarantee that the material presented in analysis was a product of the patient's transference upon them. No longer a blank screen, with Kristeva the analyst now shares traditionally unshared counter-transferential material with the patient. The risk lies in rendering the boundary between patient narrative and analyst narrative permeable, to the point that some theorists are today questioning the very distinction between transference and counter-transference. Robertiello and Schoenewolf (1987) define the current understanding of counter-transference as two-fold:

> [...] objective countertransference, which is induced by the patient and which the therapist feels, without the temptation to act on it; and subjective countertransference,

> which represents an irrational response to the patient rooted in the therapist's fixations. (Robertiello and Schoenewolf, 1987: 4)

They believe that 'virtually every error a psychotherapist is likely to make is traceable to its countertransference and counterresistance' (Robertiello and Schoenewolf, 1987: ix). For this reason, theorists like Maxwell Gitelson suggest 'abolishing the term *countertransference* and calling it instead 'the analyst's transference to the patient.'' (Robertiello and Schoenewolf, 1987: 7) thus levelling the response to the patient/practitioner encounter to one shared term. Thus, the possibility of contamination of patient discourse by the analyst's more invested presence becomes an issue in the theorisation of the maternal.

The Maternal: Psychoanalytic Artefact or Archaic Transference?

A Subject Pre-disposed or Disposed to Social Bonds?

Around 6 months, the pre-subject's relationship with the maternal changes. While from birth, the infant had experienced the maternal as the provider of all its needs, the maternal is now a source of frustration/gratification. The locating of an early Oedipal scene from that age is explained incompletely by several factors.. Upon observation, psychoanalytic researchers (like Freud, Klein, Lacan, Kristeva) construe infant psychology as entering the primary narcissistic phase, traditionally the phase during which the baby moves away from simply existing, and begins to perceive its separation from objects encountered in its surrounding. Lacan will magnify this separation phase with his coining of the Mirror Stage: around 6 months, the baby is for the first time able to see its image in the mirror because it perceives its separateness from that image. Klein insisted on the schizo-paranoid position of the baby and its capacity for relating to objects shortly after birth. Kristeva added her suspicion that the Kleinian understanding of deprivation as source of a love/hate psychical dualism, and thus the Kleinian logic of an earlier form of subjectivity, may be found even earlier in the prototypical source of loss: birth. Some contemporary researchers, like Bowlby (1998) and Stern (1985), go further in suggesting the existence of an innate capacity for social exchange and propose a different infant development. Stern believes infants 'experience a sense of an emergent self from birth. They are predesigned to be aware of self-organizing processes' (Stern, 1985: 10). Stern believes infant experience is never symbiotic or completely undifferentiated. Instead, the baby would be born with a core self, predestining it for interpersonal relationships. Effectively, the existence of an innate core self is the pre-condition to relating to others. Hence Stern views subjectivation in reverse from Freudians: instead of a symbiotic being learning differentiation, the baby's is differentiated in the first place and learns to organise interpersonal relationships. However, Stern also maintains the 6 months old threshold as the time around which the infant has finished consolidating 'the sense of core self as a separate, cohesive, bounded, physical unit, with a sense of their own agency, affectivity, and continuity in time' (Stern, 1985: 10). The period after that is spent developing independence, autonomy and individuation from the maternal realm. Similarly, John Bowlby proposes 'attachment behaviour' as innate and on a par with survival mechanisms: 'attachment behaviour is conceived as distinct from feeding behaviour and sexual behaviour and of at least an equal significance in human life' (Bowlby, 1998: 39). The capacity for social bonds would rest on this instinctual behaviour and attachments would be learnt from birth through means of goal-corrected experiences. Bowlby's suggestion is thus opposed to the Freudian and post-Freudian understanding of attachment (or love) as a learnt process, the logic of which would be a transferential re-actualisation of early relationships with parental figures. Kristeva's work remains based on the Freudian understanding of social exchange. She remains attentive to contemporary findings such as those mentioned above. Her interest in Melanie Klein's work points to her interest in humans' pre-disposition to narration (pre-narrative envelope) while at the same time insisting that such phantasmatic narratives depend upon their verbalisation. Only the intervention of some paternal agency will bring narratives to symbolic existence. Hence, her theorising on pre-subjectivity still locates its onset in 'primary narcissism' at around 6 months of age while suggesting that this model may be exceeded by contemporary research.

From Maternal to Paternal: Narcissism

Freud gave two understandings of 'narcissism'.[11] He first posited the existence of a stage of development between auto-eroticism and object-love. During this narcissistic phase the infant would for the first time acquire the capacity to unify its sexual impulses by taking itself as object of love. Later, the capacity for love will be re-enacted on a social plane by taking others as love objects. Narcissism would then be a stasis or fixation of the infant's libidinal investment, turning towards itself as opposed to engaging with the other. In a second stage, Freud further differentiated narcissism into primary and secondary narcissism, to explain the move from the choice of self as love object and other as love object. Primary narcissism would refer to the baby's anobjectal world, that is a complete absence of exchange with the world outside itself. Secondary narcissism would then be the stage of development where the pre-subject learns social exchange through a series of identifications with significant others such as parental figures. The question Freud did not fully address and that Kristeva will seek to answer is how the baby successfully moves from a closed structure (primary narcissism) where the other does not exist to an open structure (secondary narcissism) permitting socio-symbolic exchange. Classical psychoanalysis draws the line that separates the two stages of narcissistic investment in the intervention of the paternal function in the

11 Laplanche and Pontalis, 1991: 261-5. The final chapter will describe and discuss Freud's two models for the individual's narcissistic economy.

maternal/child dyad. Paternal castration is what permits the change of love object from maternal to paternal. Libidinal investment of the maternal is an archaic form of identification, in the positioning of the child in the place of maternal desire for the paternal. However, this early triangulation and differentiation is not strong enough to represent identification proper and should thus be considered proto-social rather than social.

Locating the onset of an Oedipus prime at 6 months old is arbitrary and dependent upon two factors: it is first supported from a physiological viewpoint. 'For this necessary stage to occur, the child must have been separated from its mother's body (weaned) and must be able to turn around and see someone else *as* someone else' (Sarup, 1992: 64). With weaning, the child is effectively able to sustain its survival from food supplied by sources other than the maternal caregiver. Second, the baby's motor development now permits it to concentrate its attention on objects other than those in immediate focal proximity and to investigate a world beyond the maternal. Separation from the maternal realm is then construed as the threshold between two stages in subjectivation, mediated by new sensory and psychical experiences. The construction of archaic contents constitutes the second point highlighting the discoveries but also limitations of psychoanalytic interpretative abilities. Kleinian discoveries did not indicate a change in infant behaviour but a breakthrough in methodology, discovering for the first time material that was already there.

Are we then seeing a change in human psychopathology, from Oedipal to narcissistic or were those pathologies already at work for instance in Freud's days as Blanck and Blanck (1986) suggested? Freud himself partly answered this question when he questioned the 'choice of neurosis' (Nasio, 1992: 70) and proposed that the age at which trauma occurred would decide on the neurosis. Although his explanation supports the thesis of a change in human pathology, other theorists like Kristeva remain critical of too hasty an explanation, which, in the case of Freud's, clearly puts the 'responsibility' on the patient. In line with the contemporary psychoanalytic trend in reconsidering the role of counter-transference in analytic setting, Cooper and Maxwell (1995) point to the psychoanalytic group called 'the Independents' and suggest that 'today, there is a growing trend which explains impasse in terms of treatment error and puts the responsibility on the analyst' (Cooper and Maxwell, 1995: 122). Robertiello and Schoenewolf believe that 'virtually every error a psychotherapist is likely to make is traceable to its countertransference and counterresistance' (Robertiello and Schoenewolf, 1987: ix). Similarly, Kristeva's work attempts not only to theorise the transference from maternal to paternal sites but also insists on the role played by the counter-transference of 'the other' (the analyst, the mother, the father, etc.) in understanding the process of symbolisation. More precisely, she suggests that such new (Kleinian) theoretical construction of the infant might be the response of a psychoanalytic body in jeopardy in the face of untheorised patient material and compensating for a theoretical void with its own imagined constructs:

Is the confrontation with this primary phantasmatic universe an artefact of the

> psychoanalyst's regression? Could it be the result of a theoretical lack jeopardised by the enigmatic functioning of a baby or a psychotic defying verbalisation and that the imagination of the therapist compensates? (Kristeva, 2000: 241)

The role of compensatory counter-transferential modes, as integral or arbitrary part of the process of symbolisation, is at the core of contemporary psychoanalytic debates. What Kristeva, along with other above mentioned researchers, are arguing that the function of the analyst, as guarantor of the paternal or symbolic function, is threatened in the encounter with patients offering pre-symbolic or maternal contents. Within a counter-transferential dynamic the risk is for the analyst to be either 'possessed' in turn by those destructive impulses and risk psychosis themselves or to adopt a defensive castrating attitude and thus fail to meet the psychoanalytic demands of a patient hindered by the maternal. Some theorists (Stern, Bowlby) by-pass the question by positing the existence of a self or capacity for social exchange *à priori*. If human beings already possess a kind of pre-programmed ability for social bonds, then the question of the baby moving from anobjectal (maternal) to object oriented relations (socio-symbolic, paternal) changes in status. The fate of social exchange would not depend upon the subject's healthy transfer from maternal to paternal but on encountering identificatory models, who would act as triggers of the subject's social programming and whose profile would decide of the future success and limitations of the subject's social bonds. If on the other hand human socialisation rests on acquiring such 'program', then the answer lies in the elaboration of the infant's experience of the maternal and paternal functions. Differences in contemporary theories testify to the debate over the onset of an archaic type of symbolisation that can be interpreted as disagreements over the onset of an archaic relationship with the paternal function. Theorists agree on the six months threshold, but disagree on the interpretation of that threshold. A comparison of Jacques Lacan's and Françoise Dolto's understandings of what primary narcissism represents in the process of subjectivation sheds further light on the debate.

Lacan describes the baby's experience of newly found skills, which he terms the 'Mirror Stage', as inaugurating later symbolisation. He finds a discrepancy between the baby's capacity to apprehend itself in totality for the first time, its visual maturity and independence, and the immaturity of its ability for locomotion rendering it powerless and dependent upon maternal care. This premature experience of its totality is both fascinating, with the baby wishing to grasp this image of its self, and alienating since it cannot reach it. The baby's image in the mirror thus becomes an ideal image of itself, an image constituting 'what Lacan calls the primordial identification to an ideal image of one's own' (Nasio, 1992: 84). The Mirror Stage imprints in the baby the experience of a visual power that the body denies it and from which it derives a jubilatory pleasure. Lacan's use of the term 'mirror' refers to the image of the baby seen as other in an actual mirror but also in the more general experience of separation and otherness the baby is beginning to experiment in its relations with others: 'the desires of the child go first through the specular other. There, they are approved, disproved, accepted or rejected.' (Nasio, 1992: 102) The Mirror Stage marks the onset of socio-symbolisation, anticipating the later apprehension of the subject in the linguistic 'I'.

On the contrary, Françoise Dolto's mirror Stage 'confirms a primary narcissistic individuation already at work in fundamental narcissism' (Dolto and Nasio, 1992: 62). Where Lacan saw the experience as primary and jubilatory, Dolto analyses it as a painful confirmation that the move towards symbolisation equates with the baby's castration. The baby realises that it is separated from its image. While in Lacan there is identification with the image ('I am my image'), in Dolto primary narcissism results from the realisation that the child is not its reflection.

Both Lacan and Dolto analyse the process of subjectivation as constituted by an early encounter with the pre-symbol in the mirror within the maternal. However, Lacan describes the 6 months old threshold as the primordial time of the pre-subject's first identification, while Dolto suggests the same experience as the end of fundamental narcissism and the onset of primary narcissism. In identifying a third narcissistic phase, 'fundamental narcissism', before primary and secondary narcissism, Dolto is closer to the Kleinian idea of pre-narrative envelopes which would be present before 6 months. Similarly, Kristeva believes in a kind of pre-programming of the baby, possibly genetic and undoubtedly inherent to parental functions. Instead of viewing primary narcissism as the onset of an archaic form of symbolisation, primary narcissism or Lacan's Mirror Stage would then be the painful realisation by the infant of what Kristeva termed 'an already there of language' (Guberman, 1996: 21). However, Kristeva tends to view the debate in a different way. Instead of attempting to locate a cut off point from which to consider some form of symbolisation, she prefers to discuss the importance of the analysis of pre-narrative contents as part of symbolic activity. In other words, both sides of the debate maternal or paternal are for her the expression of a pre-existing internal conflict, traces of which she finds in the discourse of the speaking subject. Short of theorising maternal contents, these will remain unknown to symbolic representation. The existence of a pre-subjectivity rests less on its observation in babies than upon its recognition and symbolisation in the mature subject. Thus, the recognition of the subject's experience of and difficulties with the maternal depends upon its transfer to the paternal function.

Archaic Transference

Kristeva envisages the child's capacity for an archaic form of symbolisation of the maternal through some paternal agency. From 1991, the 'imaginary father' is clearly identified as an agency within the maternal enabling an early transfer from the maternal to the imaginary father. Paternal presence (reduced to the penis) 'remains in Melanie Klein a maternal *imago*, a kind of other maternal breast, malevolent and competing, but not a third party' (Kristeva 1996a: 174). Although the Kleinian model posits an early form of Oedipal triangle, her model does not allow for the transfer from maternal to paternal sites, since both are two sides of the same *imago* (the breast). Kristeva's theorising of the paternal within the maternal is a return to the Freudian 'father of individual pre-history',[12] whose more pronounced function permits to imagine an early Oedipal triangulation and better explains the infant's primary identification.

> Before any Oedipal evidence of the love of or for the father, the analyst finds, when he listens to patients recalling narcissistic wounds, or better, subjects constituted by the narcissistic wound, a very illusive and yet solid presence of the father. This archaic mirage of the paternal function, which rises at the onset of primary narcissism as the ultimate guarantee of identity, could well be called an imaginary Father. (Kristeva, 1993: 182)

The imaginary father is an imaginary construct of the baby, whose imaginary presence introduces a third term in the mother/child dyad and enables first the baby's distanciation from the maternal and second its transfer onto the paternal. Kristeva is then proposing an early triangulation and archaic identification with an archaic or imaginary paternal function. If this paternal function is imaginary for the baby, it is however rooted in the reality of the mother's own relationship with the paternal function. It is conditioned by 'the mother's desire for another than the child - her own father? the child's father? an extra familial or symbolic instance?' (Kristeva, 1996: 117). The figure taken by the paternal agent for the mother matters less than the fact that she desires something other than the child. It is this desire for an other rather than the actual other which sets up, between the mother and the child, a gap or third party, acting as separator. The baby notices this gap and endeavours to fill it in order to close the mother/child dyad. In doing so, it attempts to occupy the place of the other in the mother's eyes, that is to transfer from maternal to paternal sites. This transfer is both constitutive of archaic identification and regulated by the maternal function. For the baby, Klein has demonstrated that the maternal function, and the paternal function within it, are not the actual mother and father but phantasmatic figures created by the baby and offering a possible insight into the baby's archaic representations, that is the archaic representation of its biological reality. Moreover, these phantasised maternal and paternal figures persist within the subject even after they have left the maternal continent and entered the socio-symbolic sphere and also offer the analyst the possibility to interpret the move from biological to social:

> Maternal power and paternal authority would then be like artefacts of a phyto- and ontogenetic memory made of biology and representation, hidden within us, subjects of psychoanalysis, and that we have the possibility to deconstruct: with the help of certain mothers sufficiently satisfactory and sufficiently distant; finally and above all, thanks to

12 Kristeva tends to equal the following terms: 'Imaginary Father of pre-history', 'Ideal Father' and 'kindly father' (Kristeva, 1993: 103, 158).

> transference and analytic interpretation. (Kristeva, 2000: 381-2)

This is where Kristeva introduces a second aspect of the paternal function. She believes that the good functioning of the maternal function (the transfer from maternal to paternal) depends on maternal (mother, analyst, etc.) counter-transference.

> Kleinian and post-Kleinian clinic, which revealed the existence of this narrative thinking included in proto-phantasy, was built not on the coining of a precocious narrative logic, but really on the coining of *primary anxiety* which becomes the condition to thinking if -and only if- it is recognised and replayed by the object (by the mother or better by the analyst). (Kristeva, 2000: 238)

Kristeva is insisting that the interpretation of pre-narrative phantasies can only be performed by an interpreter who is also knowledgeable in their own primary anxiety and has successfully operated the transfer from maternal to paternal.[13] In this, she is advocating the advantage of the psychoanalytic setting because the completed analysis of the analyst normally guarantees their ability and conscious knowledge of the transfer from maternal to paternal. However, as we mentioned earlier, this ability is not the sole apanage of psychoanalysis but can also be 'performed' by other people (mothers, social workers, intellectuals, etc.). Hence, where Klein introduced the concept of pre-narrative envelopes, Kristeva emphasises that these pre-narrative contents, witness to the maternal/child dyad, exist solely under the condition that they are mediated by the introduction of a third term, the paternal function. Without the transfer from maternal to paternal site, the recognition and representation of the child's pre-narrative would not exist. It is the paternal function that validates the existence of the maternal.

The psychoanalytic understanding of 'maternal' has then changed. It is now doubly theorised with on the one hand the insistence on its disruptive aspect, effectively antinomic to 'paternal', threatening social organisation. This reading of the maternal elicited by French psychoanalysts, such as Lacan and Kristeva, is today at the heart of British psychoanalysis.[14] They emphasise the part of Klein's

---

13 In this sense, the maternal function can only be performed by another human. Its encoding (for instance television increasingly replaces parental role) would render the maternal function void as the counter-transferential process does not happen. To put it crudely, a TV set knows nothing of primary anxiety, can neither recognise nor replay it, because it cannot sense. Research has demonstrated that the absence of human interaction causes infant death or at best irreversible mental retardation (Spitz, 1946) and cases of hospitalism and anaclitic depression; sensory deprivation experiments also provoke, in less than forty-eight hours, adult hallucinations or delusions (Berne, 1973).

14 The Tavistock Clinic is one of the international focal points of post-Kleinian research. Figures of post-Kleinian psychoanalysis include Winnicott, Bion, Balint, Fairbairn and Bowlby.

work pointing to the importance of the death drive within the socio-symbolic sphere and concentrate on further theorising its mechanisms, that is the part played by the maternal in the process of socialisation. But Kristeva also criticises a second reading of Kleinian theory. Theorists such as Michael and Margaret Rustin insist on the notion of reparation of the maternal elicited by Melanie Klein. Klein observed a reparative tendency in the child (and later the adult) as a defence against anxiety and destructive phantasies. Imagining the child's predicament, she explains:

> 'My mother is disappearing, she may never return, she is suffering, she is dead. No, this can't be, for I can revive her.' (Klein, 1988b: 75)

These reparative powers are experienced in phantasy and protect the child against the loss of the maternal object: the 'bad mother' (anxiety) is repudiated while the 'good mother' (reparation) takes over.[15] Reparation, or the adoption of good over bad, is given validity by the social environment, encouraging the child in its efforts to overcome the loss of the maternal and move into the social sphere. With this reinforcement by what we would term the paternal function (social, interacting with an other than the maternal), the child moves from maternal to paternal sites. Klein observes the same transfer in adult patients suffering from depression: the intervention and support of a paternal agency (the analyst to begin with then a changed relation with the outside as analysis progresses) motivates the adult to leave the maternal experienced in the depressive position and enter the realm of the paternal experienced as hope. Although the role of the paternal function can be extracted from this Kleinian logic, we are not dealing with an Oedipal paternal. Klein envisages the role of the Oedipal father as secondary to the earlier Oedipal scene shared by mother and child. A comparison of Klein's views with both Freud's and Kristeva's, shows that the idea of a paternal function within the maternal is already tentatively present in Klein's work. However, it will be Kristeva who theorises the full economy of such an early triangulation. The part of Kleinian logic and specifically her notion of reparation, is today being emphasised without the theorising of an archaic triangulation. Beyond archaic anxiety (or because of it), the subject succeeds in establishing relations with objects other than the maternal object. It chooses identification with the symbolic other instead of an undifferentiated proto-symbolic identity with the maternal. The part played by the death drive, with its associated anxiety, hatred and violence, is minimised in favour of the subject's ability for social contract. This second reading is contrary to the idea of the maternal as transgressive. Instead of a maternal function equated with

---

15 For instance, in the film *Anne Trister* (Pool, 1986) a child observed by a psychoanalyst repeatedly attempts to destroy toys and the analyst: she tears a soft toy, covers it in red paint, insults the analyst, attempts to hit her. As the analysis progresses, the child begins to 'heal' the toy with bandages and becomes more compassionate towards herself and other human beings.

the disruption of paternal sites (social), it magnifies the second aspect of the maternal and its paternal function. However, the lack of focus on archaic triangulation means that only the child/mother dyad is given consideration. Kristeva sees such tendency as the benevolent trivialising of the maternal as content in favour of the maternal as symbolising strategy. In other words, the maternal is reduced to a loving, nurturing function closer to social learning while its relation to the abject is ignored. In this Kristeva sees a form of socialism through which psychoanalysis is transformed into social work and even secular religion (Kristeva, 2000: 375). Considering the wide range of theories that have emerged since Klein's study of the maternal, the construction of the maternal function with the reassignment of the paternal function to the maternal has become the corner stone of contemporary psychoanalytic advancement, transferring the frontiers of subjectivity to more archaic territories.

Conclusion

Kristeva, Stern or Klein's contention that humans have an innate ability for symbolisation presents psychoanalysis with the invalidating of its own theory on the process of subjectivation. Indeed, since Freud, socio-symbolic membership rests on a process of learning and maturing of the human psyche that takes the individual from its natural origin to its cultural belonging. In short, the psychoanalytic subject, represented in their symbols, is the antithesis of the natural subject. Yet Kristevan theory reconciles these two seemingly mutually exclusive views.

According to her, even if human possess a competence for symbolisation at birth, the process of subjectivation takes place only on the condition that parental functions activate this natural skill. The newborn responds not so much to a natural programming but to parental wish for what the child will be. From birth, the individual is subjected to parental desire for it to become a member of its society. Desire for socialisation, Kristeva argues, is both trans-generational and inherent to the human species' history and reality. The question of a biological or cultural disposition to narration thus remains unanswered and unanswerable. It may be that the evolution of humans into a speaking species created a genetic reality. Or it may be that a given biology caused the species to acquire language. The Kristevan framework proposes instead to begin with a traditional psychoanalytic understanding. The child, eager to keep parental interest for itself, positions itself in the place of parental desire. In doing so, it also initiates the process of becoming an other than itself and in utilising symbols representing itself becomes a subject. Kristeva's idea is further reinforced by accounts of children brought up by other species (the so called 'wild children') who do not develop the ability to symbolise. Furthermore, Hamilton's study (1993) shows how the object of maternal desire is what the child will thrive to become. The case of baby Tanya for instance describes how maternal desire for the family dog translated in the child's efforts to become 'dog'. Kristeva's contention is then that the process of subjectivation remains embedded in an exchange between the natural and the cultural, with the one reinforcing the other. The analysis of this exchange, found in particular in *Pouvoirs de l'horreur: essai sur l'abjection* (Kristeva, 1980) constitutes the originality of her work.

Although Kristeva's answer to the nature/nurture question remains anchored within the psychoanalytic framework, her views on parental desire as initiating the process of subjectivation can be interpreted as a distancing from tradition. Motivated by paternal threat of castration, the Freudian subject (male) represses the maternal and chooses social membership. Lacan's subject is born out of the loss of the maternal. Both theorists construe the subject within paternal logic. In positing parental desire, in the pre-oedipal phase, as the place where the socio-symbolic contract is first established, Kristeva also proposes the maternal function as foundation of the subject. It is in fact the maternal that organises separation from itself and identification with the pre-Oedipal paternal function. This separation begins much earlier than Freud's Oedipus or Lacan's Mirror Stage. Indeed, birth can be seen as the founding moment of separation between the maternal body and the infant. From birth to language acquisition, the individual will experience a series of separations, from physical to psychical, which will lead to symbolicity. In this, Kristeva is indebted to the Kleinian school. The measure of success of 'subjectivation' rests with maternal ability to separate while containing the child. Containment is part of the function associated with the paternal. But the paternal function, absent or corrupted, can be described today as withering away, creating a situation of crisis for the contemporary subject. Kristeva's work shows that the failure of the paternal function on an Oedipal level is in fact a repetition of the earlier failure of the maternal function. In the pre-Oedipal move from maternal to paternal, the maternal function is failing to contain the child and thus is failing to facilitate separation towards subjectivity.

If the paternal function is failing, or if the contemporary subject's ability for containment is failing, contemporary society is then faced with a return to and of maternal contents that Kristeva terms 'the abject'. If the Kristevan maternal represents the move from nature to culture, the abject represents the boundary between nature and culture that the subject crosses in the process of symbolisation. It is what reminds the subject of its natural origins and that subjectivation is the repression of their nature. The abject then exposes subjectivity as contractual rather than inherent. In other words, encountering the abject is to face the knowledge that the social is a construct, the existence of which is arbitrary, unnatural and ultimately fallacious. In reverse, it is what threatens subjective survival. More concretely, Kristeva believes that anything reminding the subject of their dissolution will be experienced as abject: reminders of birth (menstruation for instance), of death (decay such as corpses, nail clippings, etc.) and of the permeability of boundaries (bodily waste: sweat, faeces, etc.). These provoke in the subject a reaction of disgust or 'abjection' as a defence against subjective death. Abjection is then two things: on the one hand it is a strong bodily reaction against subjective annihilation and as such is an archaic assertion of the subject's connection to the symbolic; on the other, abjection is also abjection of the subject's naturalness, of its origin and of its death. The importance of ignoring one's origin in particular is a theme we will find again in the myths of Oedipus and Narcissus.

Kristeva thus defines abjection as both anti-symbolic and symbolic. In constructing such a theory of the abject, she proposes a framework to analyse subjectivation from a Kleinian angle. Loyal nevertheless to the Freudian spirit, she terms 'Oedipus prime' the phase during which the child becomes an archaic subject. This phase begins from birth, birth being the prototype of the maternal/child separation, and finishes with 'Oedipus proper', that is the Freudian Oedipal phase. However, Kristeva does not suggest the two phases she identifies as a simple sequence of events. Rather, the experience in Oedipus prime is carried over into Oedipus proper, testifying to the subject's pre-history. Indeed the idea of a co-presence of two modalities, semiotic and symbolic, within symbolic production is to be recalled here. The subject's separation from the maternal is not as complete as Freud or Lacan saw it. On the one hand, symbolic production is born of a logic of negativity, whereby the symbol is always other than what it really is. But on the other, symbolic production is also the carrier of a pre-symbolic reality, the semiotic, that bursts forth into the symbolic virtually unchanged. Neither a symbol nor a no-thing, the object of this second modality is the abject. Abjection then is the marker in the subject of the co-presence of the two functions that constituted them: the maternal and the paternal.

Kristeva's premise that symbolicity is constituted of elements belonging to both maternal and paternal has repercussions in analysing the crisis of the contemporary subject. She suggests the failure of the paternal function as the root of later crisis. Effectively, failure is found in the disconnection between paternal and maternal, beginning in pre-Oedipality with the non-containment of maternal contents and re-enacted on the symbolic level with the disconnection symbol/affect. This is evidenced in a cultural tendency to suppress the link between the symbolic subject and their biological origin. The natural subject is transformed into a total symbol (say a genome or a psychological and behavioural type) leaving no room for the advent of subjective singularity. Symbolic production has become an increasingly deadened discourse, aiming at presenting information in isolation from its affective or emotional charge. In suppressing maternal contents from symbolic economy, contemporary society is effectively discouraging imaginary matricide and encouraging their enactment.

Analysing the co-presence semiotic/symbolic initiated earlier is, for Kristeva, a way forward. This co-presence is not subjected to the Freudian dialectic and therefore repression does not preclude the presence of a second modality alongside symbolic production. Indeed, Kristeva finds that however deadened the discourse of the contemporary subject, the co-presence symbol/abject remains. If the abject and abjection testify to the subject's pre-historical experience with the maternal, an analysis of the abject necessarily leads to a reconnection of the symbol to its origin.

Kristeva's solution out of crisis posits difficulties. If the symbolisation of the maternal abject is possible, it is only on the condition that the paternal is enabled to play its containing and separating function. Yet, Kristeva sees this function failing on both accounts: the maternal fails to contain the pre-Oedipal subject and the paternal fails to separate the oedipal subject from the maternal. Contemporary research suggests a sliding of the psychoanalytic tool away from Oedipus and towards an analysis of Narcissus. This change of interest suggests a change in pathology, from Freud's neurotic to contemporary 'narcissisms', and a change of analytic framework. Narcissus is becoming the new gauge against which subjectivity and its shortcomings can be analysed. But this shift in interest also has socio-cultural connotations. For most part, the understanding of crisis tends to put the emphasis on the mother's accountability for crisis (rather than the maternal); the paternal function is assimilated to the father's and thus scarcely considered. Hence the absence or failure of the paternal, and the misrepresentation of the maternal, is replayed in social discourse. Kristeva's framework also allows a socio-cultural criticism of crisis. First, a three-term framework must be rehabilitated. Second, those terms should be considered from a metaphoric base. There is a need to re-visit parental categories and in particular to re-define the boundary that separate the maternal from the paternal function. This boundary is the locus of subjectivation, the place where the individual moves from their natural origin to his/her cultural becoming. Finally, following Kleinian logic, Kristeva believes that in reassessing the triangulation explaining the process of subjectivation, researchers should consider its dynamic from birth.

Current debates appear to have stalled in the place of parental definition. On one side of the debate those who prefer to abide to the Freudian Oedipal model stick to the Oedipal subject and resist the consideration of an earlier triangulation. On the other, those who recognise the importance of pre-Oedipal history could offer a different outlook, but tend to insist on a dyadic and non-metaphoric mother/child viewpoint that emphasises the social dimension of 'maternal' rather than its transgressive potential.

Since Klein, the likelihood of an archaic form of Oedipality existing before the Freudian Oedipal phase is justified. Klein put forward that the capacity for a dualistic (love/hate) apprehension of the maternal stems from the maternal imposing this dualism upon the infant through deprivation and containment. Kristeva added her suspicion that birth can be construed as the prototype for separation and thus dualism. She also conceives of parental desire as a form of transgenerational programme pre-destining the child for symbolicity. Furthermore, other researchers consider that the capacity for symbolisation is innate. Stern believes that the individual is born with a core self upon which processes of organisation of the self are super-imposed. Bowlby showed the existence of an attachment instinct, distinct from other instinctual behaviours, the needs of which are satisfied through goal-corrected experiences. Although some of this research invalidates aspects of the psychoanalytic model crucial to an understanding of the Kristevan model (transference and primary narcissism in particular), it is nevertheless useful in that it re-enforces Kristeva's views on early symbolisation from another (narcissistic) base.

Narcissism was first described by Freud to describe a stage in child development between infant auto-erotism and object-love that he locates around 6 months of age. He later divided narcissism into two distinct moments: primary narcissism pertaining to the baby's anobjectal world and secondary narcissism relating to the individual's ability to form identifications with significant others. The move from the one to the other is initiated by the paternal whose castrating function forces the child to give up on the maternal as love-object and choose the paternal instead. What Freudian theory does not develop, and that other theorists do, is how the baby moves from a closed structure (anobjectal) to an open structure (objectal).

Freud also posited that the 'choice' of pathology is dependent upon the time at which trauma occurred in childhood. Contemporary records of a changed pathology in adults suggests a change from Oedipal conflicts to narcissistic conflicts, traditionally located around 6 months old. This traditional timing of narcissism corresponds to the moment theorists believe the baby's bodily functions are sufficiently developed to enable the child to be weaned, turn its head at will and have long distance vision. Where the maternal was the only accessible point of contact with the outside world (in sight, food and locomotion) the advent of these three aspects of the baby's physical development means that it can now focus its interest beyond the realm of the maternal.

Post-Freudian research offers different viewpoints as to the timing of a cut-off point from which the baby is construed as an archaic subject. Lacan for instance sees the 6 months old threshold as the starting age of primordial identifications in what he terms the 'Mirror Stage'. The baby would for the first time be able to see its image in a mirror and conceive of the separation between itself and the image. For Lacan, the baby can but be subjected to this separation. Because it does not have the ability to physically grasp its own image (limited locomotion), it remains bound physically and psychically to the maternal for the apprehension of itself. However, the fact that it can visually grasp its own totality and recognise it as its own is enough for Lacan to believe that the Mirror Stage constitutes the stepping-stone towards symbolisation. Dolto, on the other hand, believes that 6 months marks the moment the baby realises its separateness from its image and that its reflection is not itself. Hence Lacan's construction of the 6-month-old baby equates the image with the individual while Dolto's makes them mutually exclusive opposites. Kristeva's research bypasses this issue in the sense that, instead of analysing actual babies, she prefers to analyse the dualism maternal/paternal in its repetition on the Oedipal level. In this instance, she too notices a change in adult pathology, from Oedipal to narcissistic conflicts.

This change in human pathology calls for a change in methodology enabling the analysis of this 'new' human. In this new psychoanalytic venture, a diversity of suggestions are found to be the cause of treatment failure: at one end traditionalists analyse failure as the analysand's resistance to treatment (and to the analyst in the transference); at the other, theorists like the Independents believe that failure in analysis means failure of the analytic tool (in the counter-transference), putting the omen on the analyst. Amongst those differences, one common ground emerges: whether failure is the analysand's or the analyst's, it is nevertheless located in the inter-personal relationship shared by both protagonists. In other words, the debate regarding psychoanalytic treatment is centred round a re-assessment of the transference and more importantly counter-transference, the very tool of the psychoanalytic scene. This is a debate Kristeva will return to in suggesting that new pathologies mean new transference requiring new counter-transferential 'skills'.

As a pathology, narcissism refers to the individual's arrested development at the point where they can choose themselves as object of love but not recognise themselves as other. Based on this Freudian premise, Kristeva proposed that narcissism in the adult is rooted in a failure of the archaic triangulation. In a 'successful' setting, the maternal, as a symbolic entity, defines herself in her relation to the paternal function (a partner, a job, etc.). The child notices that they are not the sole focus of maternal interest. In a symbiotic attempt to keep that interest, the child endeavours to occupy the place of this third party and in doing so attempts to become this third other. Kristeva believes that this changed position is how the baby transfers from the maternal (natural) to the paternal (social). However, this move from maternal to paternal is effected only on the condition that the maternal interprets the baby's experience. The function of the maternal is partly to recognise the baby's reality and repeat it on a symbolic level, a function not dissimilar to the interpretative work of the analyst in the counter-transference.

Today, the maternal function is then doubly theorised. On the one hand, it is construed as disruption of the social sphere, effectively opposed to the ordering function of the paternal. In this instance, paternal refers to the Oedipal paternal. Kristeva's work suggests pinpointing and interpreting such maternal contents as a means to overcome failure in the process of subjectivation: re-tracing the subject's developmental path, from pre-Oedipal to Oedipal. Such a 'method' points to a second aspect of the maternal, one of containment. This second aspect of the maternal can be described in terms of a pre-Oedipal paternal function within the maternal. The theorising of new pathologies calls for a new approach to analysis, beginning with the reparation of the link paternal/subject. The term 'reparation' was initiated by Klein to describe the baby's defence mechanism against its own ambivalence towards the loss of the maternal: the phantasy of the maternal as bad, causing the child's anxiety, is repudiated and replaced with a phantasy of the maternal as good (reparation). The baby's efforts to leave the maternal are motivated by the reward it gets from paternal agencies (father, society, etc.).

For Kristeva, both disruption and reparation co-exist within the maternal function. She thus advocates the theorising of both and remains dubious about practices leaving one aspect of the maternal out. However, she also remains aware of the difficulties such new theorising causes. For if the baby's transfer from maternal to paternal sites is effected only through the interpreting maternal, then the success of this maternal mediation is dependent upon its own successful transfer to the symbolic. In other words, the failure of the Oedipal triangulation on the maternal level translates in the failure of the pre-Oedipal triangulation. In time, this failed pre-Oedipal triangulation will repeat itself on the Oedipal level and so on. The change in human pathology, the crisis of contemporary subjectivity and the difficulties faced by psychoanalytic theory can be explained in those terms. The failure of the paternal function on a social plane translates in a failure of the maternal function on a pre-Oedipal level, giving rise to a new type of subject and culture, essentially narcissistic.

Chapter 6

Narcissism

In 1914, Freud 'depicts adult narcissistic love as disturbance in libidinal development leading to seeking oneself as a love-object' (Cooper and Maxwell, 1995: 77). Anna Freud put forward the difference between transference neurosis symptomatology and narcissistic disorders, and alerted analysts that to treat narcissism like neurosis (Oedipal conflicts) would lead to an impasse (Cooper and Maxwell, 1995: 20-21). Today, Kristeva recalls this Annafreudian understanding of the difference between Oedipal and narcissistic disorders. If imaginary scenarios evoked by the subject in the context of analysis appear to refer to the narcissistic stage of development, then one should be careful to avoid automatic assumptions of realism, believing that 'the risk would consist precisely in under-estimating the metaphoric sense of phantasy; to hear only the reality of named objects, without the metaphorised part; in short, in denying imaginary metaphorisation and settling for a form of psychological realism' (Kristeva, 2000: 239). Imaginary contents are not a symbolic representation of the real but a 'symbolisation degree zero'. The symbol is the metaphoric incarnation of the imaginary. Hence to confuse the imaginary for the real (to take imaginary contents for symbolic contents) would equate first with not addressing the 'true' real and second with constructing the imaginary as the subject's psychological reality. This would effectively displace the analysand's narrative from pre-history and pre-verbal experience to accomplished subjectivity in the symbol. In short the analyst would be transforming narcissistic economy (maternal function) into an Oedipal one (paternal function) and fail to recognise and interpret the locus of the subject's arrested development: the move from maternal to paternal within the maternal function rather than within the paternal function.

Anna Freud and Kristeva's concerns are today found in other clinical accounts judging the prospect of cure of narcissistic states uncertain. Cooper and Maxwell (1995) sum up the reasons why the psychoanalytic field remains doubtful vis-à-vis the possibility of cure of narcissistic states. Freud blamed the patients' unconquerable resistance, Bion points to the untouchable nature of the narcissist's primary object. Finally, 'the prognosis of these patients is poor. [...] The analyst may invest a lot of energy over a long period of time, but he or she has to be prepared for the fact that it may well turn out to be an analysis that goes nowhere as a result of the patient's early childhood experience of non-containment' (Cooper and Maxwell, 1995: 124). Resistance to transference to the paternal site, the refusal to renounce the idealised maternal object and the failure of the imaginary father form the three pillars around which the contemporary psychoanalytic field understands and investigates narcissism. Cooper and Maxwell's pessimistic views are increasingly tempered by other less dramatic accounts and testify to the present investment of psychoanalytic circles in understanding and treating an increasing amount of narcissistic patients. Psychoanalysts[1] agree with Anna Freud that '[t]he narcissistic transference is different from the ordinary transference because it involves the revival of archaic objects rather than the instinctual investment of Oedipal concerns' (Cooper and Maxwell, 1995: 124- 5). They add that '[t]hese patients are trying to re-experience the missing connectedness of their primary attachment. [...] In the repetition of earlier 'smashings', the patient is trying to find the original unbroken contact.' (Cooper & Maxwell, 1995: 124- 5). This echoes Kristeva's belief that the crisis in contemporary society has translated into a collective desire to return to a time anterior to the symbolic contract. Her work points to the importance of theorising the maternal as operating the passage from pre-symbolic to symbolic. There is a need to further search for the original place prior to social crisis and for rebuilding the social stratum from that point. In *Histoires d'amour* (Kristeva, 1983), Kristeva put forward narcissism as the 'new dementia' (Kristeva, 1983: 131-53) of contemporary subjectivity. Ovid's account[2] of the Narcissus myth has frequently been analysed in terms of 'the morbid, narcotic, subterranean signification of this legend' (Kristeva, 1983: 134). But a more incisive reading can better apprehend the predicament of the contemporary subject:

> But it may be more interesting today to insist on the originality of the narcissistic figure, and the quite singular place it holds, first in the history of Western subjectivity and second, considering its morbidity, in examining the critical symptom of this subjectivity. (Kristeva, 1983: 134)

Thus narcissism is today construed as the new psychical mode of social and individual organisation for contemporary men and women. Before considering the increasing interest given to narcissism, in both Kristeva's recent work and other

---

1 Some theorists, in using psychoanalytic discourse understand narcissism as secondary narcissism. Christopher Lasch for instance does not locate the difficulties of narcissistic personalities within primary narcissism: 'Pathological narcissism, 'which cannot be considered simply a fixation at the level of normal primitive narcissism,' arises only when the ego has developed to the point of distinguishing itself from surrounding objects.' (Lasch, 1979: 79). But Lasch's understanding does take into account the contribution made by Melanie Klein. Since Klein, secondary narcissism or the accomplished differentiation self-other has been shown to be secondary to the earlier experience of part differentiation and that Lacan described as the Mirror Stage. What Lasch (and other theorists sharing his understanding) terms 'narcissistic pathology', and which appears at the level of symbolic economy, effectively arches back to an earlier difficulty in the subjectivation process.

2 I am referring to Ovid's 'Echo and Narcissus' and 'Narcissus by the Pool' (Ovid, 1968: 83-87).

works (object relation theorists in particular), a return to the theses Freud proposed in his readings of Narcissus will highlight the change in perspective.

Freud addressed the theme of narcissism in two texts (collected in Freud, 1991) which have become the corner stones of a Freudian understanding of the subject: *Formulations on the Two Principles of Mental Functioning* published in 1911 and *Narcissism: An Introduction* published in 1914. The two texts differ in their approach to the question; considered side by side, they do not offer a logical narrative of either narcissism as a theme or of Freud's thought progression from 1911 to 1914. In fact, the difference between the two texts is characterised by a change of framework, a move from 'Freud's great biological myth' (Laplanche, 1976: 72) to 'the submission of the drive to desire' (Mitchell, 1990: 31). In 1911, Freud believes that the negotiation of instincts, not the least survival instinct, would be the trigger towards socialisation, while the 1914 text, biological motivations are deemed inadequate to account for human behaviour and Freud privileges psychical motivations (albeit founded upon biological imperatives).

Formulations on the Two Principles of Mental Functioning

In *Formulations*, Freud proposes that the individual's developmental path is double: the ego and the libido evolve according to two different modes. Succinctly, the ego would go from a logic of pleasure seeking ('pleasure principle') to a logic of reality testing ('reality principle') while the libido would go through various phases with auto-erotism at one end of the developmental path and object-love at the other. Freud considers that the move towards object-love is motivated by instinct luring the (male[3]) individual towards attachment in the service of procreation.

In more details, at birth, Freud envisions the infant's psychical system as a 'copy' or prolongation of intrauterine experience. The infant presents a self-sufficient psychical system almost completely closed to the outside world. It derives satisfaction from a 'state of psychical rest' (Freud, 1991: 36). This pleasurable state is 'disturbed by the peremptory demands of internal needs' (Freud, 1991: 36) such as hunger. Faced with such disturbance, the infant compensates by hallucinating what it wishes for. Based on a logic of pleasure/unpleasure, the infant 'probably hallucinates the fulfilment of its internal needs; it betrays its unpleasure, when there is an increase of stimulus and an absence of satisfaction, by the motor discharge of screaming and beating about with its arms and legs, and it then experiences the satisfaction it has hallucinate.' (Freud, 1991: 37). However, hallucinations do not always lead to the infant's satisfaction of its needs and out of a recurring disappointment, it abandons 'this

3 In his 1914 essay, Freud states clearly that while men are capable of fully developed object-love for a woman, women overall display a narcissistic type of love in their attachment to their (male) partners or to their offspring.

attempt at satisfaction by means of hallucination' (Freud, 1991: 36). The psychical apparatus stops working on the basis of the pleasure principle and moves on to the reality principle, thus developing a 'new principle of mental functioning' (Freud, 1991: 36-7).

In the reality principle, the psyche 'decides' 'to form a conception of the real circumstances in the external world and to endeavour to make a real alteration in them' (Freud, 1991: 36). This is evidenced for instance in the way children use emotions (or manifestations of unpleasure) to impact their environment. 'Later, as an older child, it learns to employ these manifestations of discharge intentionally as methods of expressing its feelings' (Freud, 1991: 37). Freud also describes the difference between these two functions (pleasure/reality) as a move from the infant appreciating the qualities of pleasure/unpleasure to also appreciating the qualities of sensory information (what we could call 'reality testing') (Freud, 1991: 37). In this new mental state, another sub-function develops, that of attention to the outside world and that of notation. The child observes and memorises its observations; these memory traces are at the basis of later beliefs about the self and the world. The aim is to store a catalogue of data that the child will recognise as familiar and use when internal needs require it. Freud insists that this process is not conscious and its use without compromise - as opposed to the later role of the super-ego, the 'little judge' with which the individual must constantly compromise. When internal needs require it, the child decides 'whether a given idea [is] true or false - that is, whether it [is] in agreement with reality or not - the decision being determined by making a comparison with the memory traces of reality' (Freud, 1991: 38). Freud believes that repression would start with the reality principle. In the pleasure principle, repression would have caused tension (or unpleasure) and is thus excluded at that stage. Instead of uncoordinated motor discharge, release is now provided by purposeful action aimed at modifying the outside world, source of frustration. The child's empowerment to act implies the use of thought in comparing reality with memory traces of similar events and deciding the best course of action. Thinking further empowers the child to further delay motor discharge into action and thus to restrain from action (or acting out). 'Thinking [is] endowed with characteristics which made it possible for the mental apparatus to tolerate an increased tension of stimulus while the process of discharge [is] postponed' (Freud, 1991: 38). Freud believes that because 'the later care of children is modelled on the care of infants, the dominance of the pleasure principle can really come to an end only when a child has achieved complete psychical detachment from its parents' (Freud, 1991: 37). However, he also says that the introduction of the reality principle is never total and that a part of ourselves is 'kept free from reality testing' (Freud, 1991: 39) and remains 'subordinated to the pleasure principle alone' (Freud, 1991: 39): 'phantasizing' in the child, day-dreaming in the adult. These two activities are for Freud the sign of abandonment of the person's dependence on a real object.

While the ego-instincts develop from pleasure to reality principles, the sexual instincts become detached and follow a different path. The first stage is auto-eroticism, followed by a brief period when the child seeks the sexual object (onset of Oedipal phase) soon followed by a long period of latency (fear of castration) until puberty when the adolescent seeks again a sexual object. Because of auto-erotism and the latency period, Freud believes that the development of the libido is delayed and not subjected to the same frustration as the pleasure principle and would explain the connection between sexual instinct and phantasy:

> The continuance of auto-erotism is what makes it possible to retain for so long the easier momentary and imaginary satisfaction in relation to the sexual object in place of real satisfaction, which calls for effort and postponement. (Freud, 1991: 40)

Religion, with the renunciation of earthly desires for a reward afterlife, science, with the promise of practical gain, education, which rewards the child with parental love, art, making of the artist a creating hero are all examples that Freud puts forward to sustain his idea. Pleasure is postponement in exchange for stronger social belonging.

Formulations is an important milestone in the theory of narcissism. Freud states that neurosis would be 'a forcing of the patient out of real life, an alienating of him from reality' (Freud, 1991: 35). His essay describes two courses of development of the psyche.

> If we are right in thinking that each step in these two courses may become the site of a disposition to later neurotic illness, it is plausible to suppose that the form taken by the subsequent illness (the *choice of neurosis*) will depend on the particular phase of development of the ego and the libido in which the dispositional inhibition of development has occurred. (Freud, 1991: 42)

These two points, the alienating of the individual from reality and the choice of neurosis in the adult founded upon the arrested development in the infant or child, form the corner stones of an understanding of Freudian (and Kristevan) narcissism. Although Freud does not strictly speaking equate alienation from reality and narcissism in this essay (neurosis is not narcissism), his 1914 essay will deal with this aspect of human behaviour and explicate the different scenarii such alienation underwrites in both neuroses and psychoses.

Furthermore, in this 1911 essay, Freud is giving an early definition of narcissism as constituted by a structure closed to the outside world. As Laplanche has put it:

> Expressed in its *manifest content*, this thesis would reconstitute the evolution of the human psyche starting from a kind of *hypothetical initial state in which the organism would form a closed unit* in relation to its surroundings. This state would not be defined by a cathexis[4] of the ego, since it would be prior even to the differentiation of an ego,

4 'Economic concept: the fact that a certain amount of psychical energy is attached to an idea or to a group of ideas, to a part of the body, to an object, etc.' (Laplanche and

> but by a kind of stagnation in place of libidinal energy in a biological unit conceived of as not having any objects. Whereby reference is made either to the prototype of intrauterine life or to the state of the nursling. (Laplanche, 1976: 70, footnote mine)

At this stage of his work, Freud envisions the narcissistic structure as a closed unit and an uncathected ego (the ego is not invested with any sexual energy). Freud will later modify this aspect of his theory and describe how libidinal energy is present within the narcissistic structure. Hence, in this 1911 text, Freud describes narcissism as a structure closed to any object relation whereas his 1914 text will beg the question of narcissism as an early form of subjectivity. However, in his reading of this early attempt, Laplanche exposes some inconsistencies vis à vis the individual's passage from closed unit to open unit:

> Freud, in his reconstruction, persists in wanting to derive, in genetic terms, the appearance of certain 'reality functions' - first of all perception, judgement, communication, etc. - from the biological monad. […] The internal needs which cause a rise of the energy level in the system and would threaten its equilibrium find their outlet in 'hallucinatory satisfaction'. It is 'the persistent absence of satisfaction' alone which would provoke - we know not how - the monad to abandon so convenient and apparently impregnable a position. (Laplanche, 1976: 70)

Freud constructs a scenario of infant to child development extrapolated from the apprehension of the human biological model. Here, Freud could be criticised for mixing two registers and making of biology a psychical reality. Second, if we follow in Freud's 'biologico-centrism' in development after birth, it does not follow that the 'lack of hallucinatory satisfaction', elucidates how the move from a monadic system to a dyadic or triadic one is biologically equated. And Freud does not offer further biological models in this essay. Thirdly, even if as Laplanche does, we ignore the question of equation between biology and psyche, the question remains:

> In these thoughts, Freud has, of course, no intention of presenting a concrete description of the prenatal or neonatal state, just as we have no intention of denying or affirming the effective existence of monadic biological states (the bird embryo in its egg, provided that the latter received heat), or dyadic states functioning as a quasi-monad (mother and foetus), or of far more imperfect dyadic states (mother and child). The question is rather one of knowing whether we can assert the existence of a *real genesis* of the object relation by virtue of the internal pressure of need and of the path of 'primal hallucination' alone. (Laplanche, 1976: 70-1)

In other words, Laplanche is wondering several things: do infant's hallucinations

---

Pontalis, 1988: 62). Object-cathexis can be likened to the concept of symbolisation when it involves the discharge of affect or language as symptom.

represent that which precedes the object? Is the frustration of need, due to the imperfection of hallucinatory tactics, the real motivation, as Freud believes, for the move from pleasure principle to reality principle (and towards the external object)? Could these hallucinations be the site of early object relations and the source of symbolisation, rather than the frustration of need? The answer for Laplanche lies in the meaning we give to 'hallucinatory satisfaction'. He highlights two: the 'hallucination of satisfaction' and 'satisfaction through hallucination'.

The 'hallucination of satisfaction' corresponds to 'the reproduction of the pure feeling of discharge even in the absence of discharge' (Laplanche, 1976: 71). For instance the hallucination of satiation through feeding reproduces the real feeling of satiation but in the absence of food/satiation. In this first instance, the infant's psychical apparatus is self-sufficient and completely closed to any outside element. Both Freud and Laplanche point out that the infant could not survive and would 'be destined - without any possible escape - to destruction' (Laplanche, 1976: 71). Infants clearly do not remain in a self-destructive closed unit but move on to an open structure allowing symbolic exchange. With regards to Laplanche's initial queries, such an interpretation may answer the question of what motivates the child to move to a more open structure. The imperfection of hallucination, in this case leading to death, means that compensating need through hallucination must be abandoned if the individual is to survive. Although it gives a possible motive to symbolisation, such an interpretation does not explain the actual mechanism by which the individual moves from a closed to an open structure. Laplanche's second interpretation, 'satisfaction through hallucination' offers more scope in this respect.

In satisfaction through hallucination, satisfaction comes 'by virtue *of the very existence* of the hallucinatory phenomenon' (Laplanche, 1976: 71). In this second instance, Freud puts hallucinations on a par with wish fulfilment, dreams, etc. Laplanche points out that should this be the case, then the hallucination would be in place of the real thing, that is it would be 'metabolized into an 'object', into a sign that can be introjected in its place' (Laplanche, 1976: 71). This second interpretation is indeed crucial to an understanding of post-Freudian theory and in particular to a Kleinian and post-Kleinian stance. Freud's views, at this stage of his work, are contradictory. On the one hand, narcissism is envisioned as a closed unit in which no symbolic exchange, even archaic, is possible. On the other, Laplanche's interpretation of 'hallucination' points to an archaic form of object-relation. For Freud, however, this archaism is not significant. Symbolisation, or the move out of narcissism, is born out of the frustration of the individual's needs. Originally founded upon a pleasure/unpleasure logic, the individual finds themself no longer fulfilled by hallucination. The closed structure then opens up onto a different structuring where reality is the new commanding principle. Freud's work explains why but not how humans exchange pleasure for reality. We must then, as Laplanche does, agree to an inconsistency and a missing link in Freudian thought. In this case, a second scenario can be envisioned, one proposed by Klein, that the human psychical structure is open at least from the beginning of life to some form of symbolic exchange with internal and external objects. Laplanche believes that '[p]rimary narcissism, as a psychical reality, can only be the primal myth of a return to the maternal breast, a scenario that Freud on occasion explicitly classifies as one of the principal primal fantasies' (Laplanche, 1976: 72). But again, Freud will not emphasise this aspect of his work. His 1911 attempt at a thesis explaining the genesis of the symbolic subject will be his future bias and what Laplanche calls 'Freud's great biological myth' (Laplanche, 1976: 72) will become exclusive in the post 1920 work of Freud.

On Narcissism: An Introduction

Freud's 1914 attempt to describe 'narcissism' leaves aside the question of biology and concentrates on the psychical formation of the ego. By reducing the meaning given to 'primary narcissism', Laplanche believes that Freud 'partially avoids the contradictions of the preceding thesis' (Laplanche, 1976: 72). However, Mitchell (1990) disagrees and proposes that from 1914 on, Freud's work increasingly moves away from biological concerns, finding biological explanations inadequate to explain human behaviour. Instead of an avoidance of the biological issue, *On Narcissism* is for Mitchell an extensive description of 'the submission of the drive to desire and the subsequent sexualization of even the knowledge of the self' (Mitchell, 1990: 31). Hence, in the Freudian construction of the submission of the biological to the social, the biological motive disappears, or rather is transformed into its representation. For Mitchell, Freud's essay and future work define 'human' as the negotiation of one's natural instincts and the manner and degree in which different individuals achieve the submission of biology to the social. Regarding narcissism, the submitting of instinct to social imperatives is a direct answer to the infant's need 'to direct its energy to discovering itself' (Mitchell, 1990: 30) while autoerotism is its physical enactment.

In his 1911 essay, Freud had established that subjectivity is founded upon a dualism opposing the libido to the ego. The libido follows one path while the ego moves from pleasure principle to reality principle. For Freud, this early picture, although incomplete in places, could provide an explanation for neurotic disorders. Its logic, however, did not hold in the case of psychosis, or 'paraphrenia' as he termed it. Freud had noticed that 'Narcissism [...] would not be a perversion[5], but the libidinal complement to the egoism instinct of self-preservation' (Freud, 1991: 66). Freud explains that narcissistic patients display two fundamental characteristics:

5 'Perversion' 'connotes the whole of the psychosexual behaviour that accompanies [...] atypical means of obtaining sexual pleasure' (Laplanche and Pontalis, 1988: 306). Typical references in Freud are to heterosexual intercourse whereby orgasm is achieved through vaginal penetration and for reproductive purposes. In the instance of narcissism, the turning of libido onto the ego is not precisely a deviation from the norm but rather a 'natural' but atypical response from the instinct for preservation inherent to the ego.

> [...] megalomania[6] and diversion of their interest from the external world people and things. In consequence of the latter change, they become inaccessib influence of psychoanalysis and cannot be cured by our efforts. [...] The paraphrenic seems really to have withdrawn his libido from people and things in the external world, without replacing them by others in phantasy. When he *does* so replace them, the process seems to be a secondary one and to be part of an attempt at recovery, designed to lead the libido back to objects. (Freud, 1991: 66)

Freud had noticed that what characterises neurotic patients, in mourning for instance, is a re-orientation of the sexual drive from outside objects to internal ones. Put bluntly, the individual withdraws interest from the outside world and turns to fantasy to compensate[7] for loss. In the instance of neurosis, the libido withdraws from outside objects and turns to internal ones. In the instance of psychosis, the libido is also withdrawn from external objects but is not directed towards internal objects in fantasy. Instead, the libido is turned back onto the individual's ego:

> The libido that has been withdrawn from the external world has been directed to the ego and thus gives rise to an attitude which may be called narcissism. But the megalomania itself is no new creation; on the contrary, it is, as we know, a magnification and plainer manifestation of a condition which had already existed previously. This leads us to look upon the narcissism which arises through the drawing in of object-cathexes as a secondary one, superimposed upon a primary narcissism that is obscured by a number of different influences. (Freud, 1991: 67)

Freud is stating that secondary narcissism, that he witnesses in neurosis, is a superimposition, a secondary symptom so to speak which both masks and marks the existence of the earlier stage that is primary narcissism and which Freud believed marked psychotic states. The common trait between the two stages of narcissism is the withdrawal from the outside. But where secondary narcissism is typified by the cathexis of internal fantasmatic objects, primary narcissism is typified by the cathexis of the ego taken as object. The difference is in the locus of object: internal but outside object (fantasy) in secondary narcissism; internal and inside object (ego) in primary narcissism. This is a significant leap in Freud's work. In *Formulations* he describes the ego as a closed structure following a path separate from the libido, an asexual ego incapable of attachment. In *On Narcissism*, the ego is now charged with libido, a partly open structure capable of attaching to itself. So, contrary to his 1911 definition, whereby narcissism

---

6 Megalomania: here, a display of one's grandiosity and belief in one's own omnipotence. For instance, in 'primitive' people, the magical belief that the Shaman can 'make rain' through the invocation of spirits.

7 This is reminiscent of the infant's hallucinating as a means to compensate for internal needs. So in neurosis, Freud proposes the adult's withdrawal from the reality principle and return to the pleasure principle. Freud will return to this throughout

describes the closed structure of infant world, narcissism now describes a state where the ego, on a par with external sexual objects, is taken as love object.[8] As Mitchell puts it:

> In other words, at first, the self loves the self (or the ego), only later does it 'put out' some of this self-love on to other objects. It is this primary narcissism that re-expresses itself in psychosis, and it was this that was hidden from psychoanalytic investigation whilst it concentrated on the neurosis whose problematic attachment (but attachment none the less) to objects other than itself obscured this situation. (Mitchell, 1990: 33)

If we follow Mitchell's comment, the narcissistic ego is an intermediate between the objectless and object relating individual, in short, an archaic form of the future object. Moreover, this archaic object, or narcissistic ego, is the starting point towards full socialisation.

From his observations,[9] Freud categorises humans' attachment to objects. First, he finds that there are two arching types of attachments: narcissistic (ego-libido) and anaclitic (object-libido). Narcissistic and object love are antithetic, following

---

8 This leads to the second image of narcissism, popularly and arguably wrongly assimilated to the individual who 'falls in love with himself'. Michell notes that Freud was never able to expand on this aspect of his work. First, 'psychotic material' (psychotic patients) was not readily available to him as those individuals tended not to seek the private consultation of psychoanalysts but were generally 'directed' towards the local psychiatric asylum. Freud's examples (organic illness, hypochondria, being in love, children and primitive people) indicate that his findings are founded upon deduction rather than direct observation. For instance, Freud finds that children and primitive people display characteristics of megalomania that is: 'an over-estimation of the power of their wishes and mental acts, the 'omnipotence of thoughts', a belief in the thaumaturgic force of words, and a technique for dealing with the external world - 'magic' - which appears to be a logical application of these grandiose premises' (Freud, 1991: 67). From these observations, Freud deducts that there is 'an original libidinal cathexis of the ego, from which some is later given off to objects, but which fundamentally persists and is related to the object-cathexes' (Freud, 1991: 68). Note the objectionable assumption that western subjectivity is a higher, more advanced form of subjectivity while 'primitive people' show a stage of arrested development by contrast. The editor to the 1991 republication of Freud's essay points out that this theme recurs in Freud's work and refers the reader to *Totem and Taboo* (Penguin Freud Library no 13, 141-8) for a more comprehensive explanation. For a criticism of Freud's view, see Gayatri Spivak, in particular 'Echo' in the *Spivak Reader* (Landry, Donna & Maclean, Gerald (edd) (1996))

9 Again, one should note that the 'formation' of cathexes, or how the libido is allocated, still eludes Freud at this stage of his work (it remains 'hidden and unknown to him'). His findings are based upon the observation of the effect of attachment (cathexes) as seen in neurotic symptoms. Mitchell, Laplanche and others extrapolate from Freud's work what he did not develop.

an 'economic model'[10] the more of the one, the less of the other. Freud further subdivides narcissistic love into four categories and object love into two:

> A person may love:
> (1) According to the narcissistic type:
> (a) what he himself is (i.e. himself),
> (b) what he himself was,
> (c) what he himself would like to be,
> (d) someone who was once part of himself.
> (2) According to the anaclitic (attachment) type:
> (a) the woman who feeds him,
> (b) the man who protects him,
> and the succession of substitutes who take their place. (Freud, 1991: 84)

In the ideal Freudian scenario, the developmental path of the individual will see them give up their narcissistic attachment by transferring the libido onto outside objects (anaclitic type). However, Freud also believed that part of the narcissistic libido still remains even after a 'successful' transfer of the sexual drive onto outside objects. In the less ideal but more realistic scenario found in adults, narcissism has been dampened down and the ego-libido appears to have passed into object-cathexes through processes of repression: 'libidinal instinctual impulses undergo the vicissitude of pathogenic repression if they come into conflict with the subject's cultural and ethical ideas' (Freud, 1991: 87). Freud envisions that repression 'proceeds from the self-respect of the ego' (Freud, 1991: 87) and depends upon the environmental framework of each individual. But repression is never total and the individual's idealisation of themself remains, under a different guise. This was defined by Freud as what they are, were and would like to be.

If out of a situation of crisis, a narcissistic type of subjectivity prevails, then the four constructs of narcissistic types listed by Freud would be becoming more

---

10 The expression is borrowed from Laplanche. He wonders what advantages there are in considering the narcissistic ego within economic terms when it is the site of feelings and passions. Although the ego (and external objects) cannot be quantified in terms of measurements (of libido, feelings, etc.), Laplanche believes that Freud's economic model enables clinical observations and descriptions of an economic bias: the cathecting of internal (ego) and external objects or of the ego and internalised fantasmatic objects shows equivalences, exchanges and antagonisms. 'Thus, in the theory of narcissism, it allows for a description [...] of a veritable energy 'balance' [...] since the individual disposes of *relatively constant quantity of libido*' (Laplanche, 1976: 73). The idea follows that of banking with the individual 'owning' a certain fixed capital of libido which they distribute onto objects. When one object is invested with libido, the other is depleted. However, Laplanche also points out that the ego cannot be totally deprived of sexual energy, 'the ego remains the site of a permanent stasis of energy, perpetually maintaining in itself a certain minimal level' (Laplanche, 1976: 73). There is then no absolute symmetry in the cathecting of the ego and of external objects.

present than the two allocated to anaclitic type. Following Freud's logic,[11] it appears the issue of the individual's capacity for idealisation is at stake. In theory, alongside the ego, the individual sets up an ego ideal against which they measure the actual ego. 'For the ego the formation of an ideal would be the conditioning factor of repression' (Freud, 1991: 88). Narcissistic love enjoyed in the child by the ego is in the adult displaced from the ego onto the ideal ego. The ideal ego is then the remnants of the narcissistic ego and, as such, is endowed with perfection. For Freud, the formation of the ego-ideal/super-ego is motivated by the cultural/social pressure and personal critical judgement. Tension between individual and environment force the maturing individual to partly forego their narcissism. Mitchell reminds us that the ego-ideal/super-ego is not formed out of a vacuum. It is the result of the subject's effort to comply with the social system and is effected by family, class, national pressures, etc. 'But ideals periodically fail and the predicament of Narcissus takes over' (Mitchell, 1990: 36). As a defence against giving up narcissistic enjoyment, 'his ideal is the substitute for the lost narcissism of his childhood in which he was his own ideal' (Freud, 1991: 88). Mitchell's comment points to the relationship between primary narcissism and socialisation. More importantly, she highlights the 'nature' of failure, leading to the narcissistic predicament contemporary society would be faced with. This aspect of failure is developed by Chasseguet-Smirgel (1999) and Kristeva.

Chasseguet-Smirgel finds that narcissism is founded upon the child's discovery that their genitals can never satisfy maternal genital desire.[12] In this lies the rift (de-

---

11 Freud uses two expressions to refer to that part of the ego founded upon the narcissistic ego: 'ego ideal' and 'ideal ego'. Laplanche and Pontalis (1988) note that the 'ego ideal' is an agency distinct from the ego, constituting 'a model to which the subject attempts to conform' (Laplanche and Pontalis, 1988: 144). In the move from primary narcissism to identification with significant others, the ego ideal is set up to 'keep watch' over the individual's behaviour and is used by the individual both as a model of perfection and as a self-censoring agency. The ego ideal will later become the super-ego. The 'ideal ego' is an '[i]ntrapsychic formation which some authors distinguish from the ego-ideal and define as an ideal of narcissistic omnipotence constructed on the model of infantile narcissism' (Laplanche and Pontalis, 1988: 201). The difference between the two expressions lies then in the agent upon which the individual models their ideal: the infantile model for the ideal ego and significant others for the ego ideal. Janine Chasseguet-Smirgel (1999) further locates the difference between ego-ideal and super-ego as two different moments of the Freudian oeuvre: ego-ideal (1914) is 'the successor to primary narcissism' and the super-ego (1923) 'that of the Oedipus complex' (Chasseguet-Smirgel, 1999: 11). To be clear, the (anachronistic) pair 'ego-ideal/super-ego' will be used to refer to the individual's effort at complying with their social environment and 'ideal ego' to mean the agency recurring in the individuals when the role of the ego-ideal/super-ego fails.

12 Chasseguet-Smirgel insists that, contrary to what Freud believed, children have the knowledge of what adult sexuality entails and a desire to satisfy the mother sexually. Consequently, the male child also knows the difference between the father's genitals and his own undeveloped organ, while the girl angrily realises that she is deprived of any organ that would have enabled her to satisfy the mother.

fusion) that separates the child's desire for unity with the mother and the mother. Narcissism rests on 'an insatiable thirst to find again one's lost unity' (Chasseguet-Smirgel, 1999: 5). The child seeks to find a solution to such dissatisfaction. 'This implies an eternal pursuit for this part of narcissism that primary defusion had torn away from him [man]' (Chasseguet-Smirgel, 1999: 14). Boys[13] understand that they cannot immediately satisfy their desire to re-unite with the mother but will be capable, in the future, to realise this fantasy. Between the pre-genital moment 'and the one, projected into the future, when incest is supposed to take place, the whole of psycho-sexual *evolution* is found' (Chasseguet-Smirgel, 1999: 161). In 'normal' development, the father becomes what the boy needs to become to achieve his goal, his ideal. This is the expected superseding of narcissism by Oedipus. In cases where idealisation fails, Chasseguet-Smirgel finds that psychosis does not necessarily ensue. 'If I began studying the relationship between the ego-ideal and perversion, it is because perversion seems to me to represent a solution enabling the subject to keep primary megalomania without tumbling over into psychosis' (Chasseguet-Smirgel, 1999: 6). For Freud, 'the formation of an ideal would be the conditioning factor of repression.' (Freud, 1991: 88) In the tension opposing the (megalomanic) ideal ego and the ego-ideal, rather than repressing pre-genital reality, perversion allows its integration into the ego. Instead of idealising the father, pre-genitality is idealised and, with the help of the deceitful mother, believed to be equal if not superior to full genitality.[14] 'But as a solution,

---

13 The girl's path is, in Chasseguet-Smirgel's account, as problematic as it is in Freud. Because the satisfaction of the mother rests on a phallic economy, the girl initially knows that she is not a satisfactory object for the mother and stays in a kind of frustrating limbo. Secondarily, the father appears as her 'true' sexual object, but because of the delay, the girl is never quite convinced that she can be a satisfactory sexual object for 'her' object, the father (Chasseguet-Smirgel, 1999: 20). The impact such a theory of sexual development has on feminist thinking will not be developed here. First, it follows a Freudian logic that has already been criticised, rejected and reassessed in debates opposing Anglo-American feminists (in particular radical feminists) to post-feminists (post-structuralist generation). Second, what interest us in Chasseguet-Smirgel's account is not the gender divide but her belief that 'perversion' is the symptom of the failure of the paternal function that avoids psychosis.

14 Chasseguet-Smirgel illustrates with many examples but two in particularly anticipate the idea of a narcissistic society:

- First, what Kristeva sees as euphoric discourses aimed at flattering the subject's ego into passivity: 'the Leader rocks the masses with the Illusion that they can have access to absolute happiness, re-united with plenitude, a 'complete man' again, all needs satisfied' (Chasseguet-Smirgel, 1999: 163). The leader repeats what the pervert's mother elicited: there is no need to repress pre-oedipality and become like the father; there is no need to deal with Oedipal conflicts and castration; satisfaction of fantasy can happen right now.
- Second, perversion is a matter of performance: 'The pervert will be a man of taste, an enlightened amateur, an aesthete, more often than a real artist, the production of art being hindered by the impossibility of paternal identification necessary to the process of sublimation' (Chasseguet-Smirgel, 1999: 27).

perversion tends to substitute [the subject's] evolution the way I describe it, the slow and painful process of identification to the father' (Chasseguet-Smirgel, 1999: 6). To sum up, in cases where the paternal function is failing, perversion substitutes the move from narcissism to Oedipus for a narcissistic subject, while by-passing the risk of psychosis.

Kristeva intimated the emergence of narcissism as society's new dementia. Within Freudian logic, the individual's effort to fit the social system means a collision between the ego-ideal/super-ego and narcissistic demands. The subject is subsequently faced with a sense of personal loss of a once more perfect state in order to fit the system. There is a need, on the subject's part, to grieve for the lost object. It entails a withdrawal of libido from the object back onto the ego, the very definition Freud gave of narcissism. Either the subject mourns and redirects the sexual drive onto other external objects or, in the case where the object of loss cannot be given up, mourning fails and psychosis sets in. The failure to mourn the lost object is where Kristeva's idea of narcissism as a new dementia can be located. In defining this new dementia, she does not equate contemporary narcissistic states with those contemporary of Freud's. In Freud's understanding, psychical illness follows the collision between narcissistic reality and social imperatives. That is, narcissistic types of attachment are witnessed after the individual's move from primary narcissism to object relation. Freud was not in a position to directly observe psychotic states, but built a theory of narcissism from what he construed as logical deductions. Mostly, narcissistic types are signs of a neurosis secondarily and temporarily returning to narcissistic defences to protect the ego against damage.

In the different order described by Kristeva, social imperatives are failing in the first place. The paternal function is either not present or intangible. We are then faced with a different picture whereby the individual shows difficulties, even cannot, move away from original narcissism. The difference between the social reality of Freud's time and this social reality bears the question of what happens to the subject's developmental path when one essential parameter of the Freudian equation has withered away? Is the Freudian edifice (and Kristevan logic with it) now based on an outdated logic? On what base can psychoanalytic thought reconstruct itself and its new subject? If idealisation is the key to identity and the failure of ideals has become the norm, against what social reality will the individual counter-balance their narcissistic demands? Finally, can we deduce from Kristevan logic the emergence of a new narcissistic type of social organisation? These questions will form the basis of the concluding chapter.

Conclusion

Theorists from different theoretical backgrounds have complained about the 'narcissisation' of society. While narcissism is becoming the new frontier of psychoanalytic discussions, the divide over what the term actually means, how it takes effect and what is to be done about it has been growing. The debate comes down to an interpretation of its cause and effect. From the perspective of intellectuals such as Anna Freud, Kristeva, Cooper and Maxwell or Zizek, theorists who seek the cause of narcissism in the symbolic realm and reparation from the symbolic are mistaken. Their complaints, an exacerbated individualism, the pull towards a general *laisser-faire*, the loss of traditional values, etc., are well founded. Yet, these are not the cause of narcissism but its cultural effect, its symptoms. If reparation is to be sought, then theorists must turn to the 'real' source of the narcissistic puzzle, the pre-symbolic. A return to Freud's original studies of narcissism, *Formulations on the Two Principles of Mental Functioning* (1911) and *On Narcissism* (1914), is then essential to a better understanding of the current debate.

In 1911, Freud is focused on finding a biological motivation for human socialisation. The individual begins life with a 'self'-centred organisation aimed at preserving a near constant state of pleasure. Freud imagines pleasure as the avoidance of unpleasure, that is keeping at bay any great source of stimulation (hunger, pain, isolation, etc.). The retreat from unavoidable moments of unpleasure is achieved partly through the use of hallucinations of satisfaction (satiation, well-being) bringing the return of sensory quietude. Yet, the infant grows to understand that frustration is unavoidable, and that hallucination is not a fully satisfactory mode of compensation for lacking the real thing (death would ensue). It then moves on to a reality-centred organisation of itself whereby the outside world can be and is impacted in order to obtain release from frustration. In so doing, the child moves from a closed self-sufficient mandate to a more open, other-oriented one. Such a move implies the development of thought, intentionality and understanding of delayed satisfaction.

The narcissistic position, in this early Freudian attempt, is expressed in terms of its ambiguity and contradictions. Freud viewed primary narcissism as the individual's early experience of itself as a completely closed unit. Yet, in *Formulations*, Freud gives no tangible justification for such hermetically bound space. First, the boundary between biology and psychical activity (between stimulus and the perception of stimulus) is crossed from the beginning of life, implying that the biological motivation, although it may be prime, is not enough. Second, hallucinations of satisfaction suggest some form of thought sequence (on the lines of: *I perceive hunger so I hallucinate feeding and then hunger vanishes*). While such capacity to organise events remains within the closed unit of infant psychical activity, it also equals the ability to project oneself onto a time frame, permute and exchange internal objects, an ability that would constitute the essence of socialisation. Finally, Freud's reality principle implies exchange with outside objects. There seems then to be no indication in Freud's 1911 attempt that narcissism could be considered a completely closed unit. On the contrary, *Formulations* suggests, as Klein and Object Relation theorists emphasised later, that from birth, the individual is engaged in exchanges with some form of object. In retrospect and thanks to the work of those post-Freudian theorists (Klein, ORT, the British School) who contextualised it, Freud's 1911 attempt shows remarkable insight. But at the time, Freud abandoned the hope of finding biological motivations to socialisation. Instead, he turned his attention to the theory of the drive, its aim and objects.

In *On Narcissism*, Freud explains the passage from biology to socialisation as a submission of instinct to social imperatives. Whether this change of focus is motivated by the wish to avoid the contradictions of *Formulations* or whether Freud deemed the biological motive insufficient is not clear. Still, *On Narcissism* states that the individual's adherence to social organisation necessarily implies the submission of instinct (biology, the drive for pleasure) to psychical development. In an objectless world, the baby is now driven to discovering its self and in doing so, the developing ego becomes its privilege 'object' of interest, an internal 'object', indeed its first 'object' and its first cathexis. The individual's relation with this not-yet-object but archaic object nevertheless typifies primary narcissism: a moment in individual development between the objectless and the social. Hence, in 1914, primary narcissism is no longer the objectless world of the infant but an 'object'-oriented moment, a transition towards socialisation. But socialisation is fully achieved only on the condition that narcissistic attachments are repressed at best, or at least dampened down, and the libido transferred from ego to outside objects. This part of development is the ultimate gesture guaranteeing the submission of instinct to social and the individual's ticket to societal membership. Yet, the outcome is never fully accomplished.

With secondary narcissism, Freud describes how the individual, reluctant to give their primary love object, the ego, finds a way to save this narcissistic ego while evolving towards other anaclitic attachments. The narcissistic ego is transformed into an ideal ego and represents the individual's primary or infantile model of being. Its existence testifies to a mishap in the socialisation process. Correspondingly, another agency is founded during the passage from narcissistic to anaclitic-type relations. The ego-ideal emerges out of individual negotiation and assimilation of social law. It becomes the ultimate arbiter of the subject's right and wrongdoing, the representative of the individual's social perfection. In the context of the failure of the paternal function, the formation and preservation of the ego-ideal is compromised and the relation to the paternal impaired. Secondary narcissism, as pathology, refers to the temporary desertion of anaclitic-type attachments (paternal) and a return to narcissistic attachments (maternal), of which the ideal ego is the prototype.

Chapter 7
Narcissus

The myth of Narcissus[1] tells of a fate in sharp contrast with Oedipus's. Where Oedipus's tragedy recounts a man's quest to know his origins and fate, Narcissus is condemned to die should he ever know himself. The essence of the tale presents Narcissus going to a pond to quench his thirst, discovering the existence of his reflection in the water and falling in love with it. Attempts at forming an erotic relationship with this image fail, causing Narcissus to understand aspects of his forming subjectivity. First, the image is his own, not an other's he can exchange with. He is denied the intersubjective exchange he covets: touching the image in the pond destroys it and he cannot be touched by it. Second, Narcissus realises that the image, the sight of which initially fulfils him, is not stable, not even as mere vision: his falling tears cloud his eyes, make the surface ripple. Narcissus is then left with a quivering reflection of himself and discovers the instability of the specular image. Finally, he is unable to bear the separation between his body reality and his image reality and commits suicide.

Interpretations of the Ovidian narrative vary. Within psychoanalytic thought, the view that narcissism is a normal stage of development and the later mark of a defined pathology prevails. The overarching image is that of Narcissus, the prototypical character who gives his name to a psychical phenomenon. Other characters are left in the shadow if not obliterated from analysis. In particular, feminist thinkers (Mitchell, Spivak, Nouvet, Lichtenberg Ettinger) have recuperated the tale to challenge psychoanalytic narratives by focusing on the role of Echo. Gayatri Spivak (1996) emphasises the motivations for the erasure of Echo's narrative in more traditional psychoanalytic readings. Indeed, Spivak's reading re-locates Narcissus: no longer the typified hero of a stalled process of (phallic) subjectivation, Narcissus becomes the account of the subject's search for a lost origin, whose internal conflicts tell of the difficulty to testify to a narrative of the maternal within a phallocentric economy. Spivak's opposition Narcissus/Echo, where Narcissus fixes and Echo disseminates, is reminiscent of Kristeva's own symbolic/semiotic opposition. Indeed Spivak's opposing of the two characters carries the image of narcissism as developmental and pathological stage between an objectless and object relating individual. For Narcissus, Echo is an invitation to relate to an other than himself, an invitation he rejects. Both Spivak and Kristeva

---

1 See: Ovid's account; Kristeva, 1983: 131-4; Hamilton, 1993: 19-25; Cooper and Maxwell, 1995: vii-x and 36.

insist on verbalising the lost voice of that 'other scene' which Echo can be said to represent, the one who disseminates or the voice of the maternal. While Spivak insists on bringing Echo's narrative out of the shadow, Kristeva will tend to side with a more traditional reading.

Narcissus: The Suppression of Echo

Unlike traditional psychoanalytic accounts of the myth, Spivak's essay, *Echo*, points not to the arrested development of Narcissus, but to the invitation to socialisation that Echo represents. More importantly, Spivak highlights the motivations she imagines exist behind the suppression of Echo's narrative in psychoanalytic discourse, namely, Freud, Lacan and Green. Echo is the epitome of the silent listener, the blank wall upon whom the other can project their story. As such, Echo occupies a place of tremendous power, that of the one who is supposed to know all truths. By virtue of her silence, any expression is possible or rather, no expression is impossible and no story cannot not be told.

> In my ethically instantiated reading of the Ovidian narrative, the traces of Echo occupy the position of something like an analyst. Under the broken rebus - legendary bones and paradoxically absent voice, connected by nothing at all - that is her mark or guarantee that she will be around, the mastership of truth [...] *is* the experience of the impossible [...] (Spivak, 1996: 186).

Putting this in relation to Freud's reading, Spivak states that 'Freud is part of the precomprehended scenario of 'An Impossible Response'' (Spivak, 1996: 191)[2] and challenges his 'ignoring of Ovid's staging of (Narcissus and) Echo' (Spivak, 1996: 191) by returning to her idea of Echo as the voice from somewhere else. Spivak implies that the foreclosure of Echo and the absence of consideration for her narrative in male (Freud, Green, Lacan) readings of Ovid's text, is really a foreclosure of 'an unreachable desired mother of the homosexual son' (Spivak, 1996: 193). Put less bluntly, Spivak is suggesting that male theorists, eager to abide to paternal law, have foreclosed the trace of maternal presence in the process of subjectivation. If we believe Freud (*Totem and Taboo*), paternalistic society is essentially founded on a homosociality that he describes as the outcome of the original 'totemic meal' of the primitive horde. The sons jealous of the father's appropriation of all the women kill and eat him. Consumed with remorse, they decide to forbid themselves any further parricide and renounce access to the father's wives. The brotherly pact becomes the quintessential social contract: a homo-social contract founded on the exclusion of women, the recognition of parricide and incest as fundamental taboos.

2 Narcissus as the 'impossible response' is an idea borrowed from Claire Nouvet (1991). We will return to Nouvet later on in this chapter.

Spivak expresses her surprise that such homosocial organisation should not recognise that its economy of exclusion/totalisation necessarily leads to its own doom. 'Who can deny that, in the construction of the subject's history, the driving force of the symbolic is a desire for self-knowledge, even though full self-knowledge would mean an end to symbolicity?' (Spivak, 1996: 193). In foreclosing Echo, Freudian analysis shows a paradox. On the one hand the foreclosing of Echo is the pre-condition to the creation of the symbol, on the other, the eradication of this side of the Freudian dialectic, necessarily leads to the eradication of symbolicity. Hence, the drive to obliterate the inimical maternal and search for the absolute symbol is a self-destructive enterprise that leaves Spivak perplexed: 'Why, in spite of so many hard lessons to the contrary [...] do we still cling to the rotarian epistemology of *advancing* from the Imaginary to the Symbolic?' (Spivak, 1996: 193). Echo's knowledge of a place beyond truths could steer symbolicity beyond the dialectical deadlock it creates.

Spivak finds the economy of the maternal in symbolic discourse is an illogical outcome. In his work on narcissism and the structuration of the ego, Freud had envisioned that the nascent ego is not innate but formed in stages. First the ego is a structure closed to the outside world and attempts to suffice to itself through psychical operations such as hallucinating satisfaction. The failure at self-sufficiency forces the ego to turn outside itself for support and develop into a unit open to social exchange. Spivak constructs the Narcissus/Echo narrative according to this Freudian logic: 'Narcissus immobile, Echo from elsewhere' (Spivak, 1996: 192). This enables her to articulate the Narcissus/Echo myth differently. The baby, totally emerged in the present moment cannot be effecting the passage from a closed psychical apparatus (ego libido, primary narcissism) to an open one (object oriented libido). This function is performed by an 'elsewhere', that is the maternal mirroring (or echoing) of the baby's present described by Winnicott. Narcissism is then symptomatic of an absence of mirroring causing the arrested passage from a libido directed inwards (at the ego) to a choice of sexual objects outside the self.[3]

> Our reading proposes a shifting of the stakes. For us Narcissus is not necessarily a stalling of/in the self where there should be a passageway to others or the other. There is access to the founding dilemma of ethics if we read the Narcissus-Echo *pair* as an icon (or, more accurately, a graph) of the passage, crossed easily and imperfectly in the exchange of everyday life. (Spivak, 1996: 193)

3 Juliet Mitchell's analysis of Echo is opposed to Spivak's. Like Spivak, Mitchell recalls Winnicott's work, positing that in order to become a person, the baby must find and identify with its image as it perceives it in the eyes of another. Mitchell thus sees Echo as 'the absolute *other*' (Mitchell, 1990: 39) because she is unable to listen to others and because she repeats the other's fascination with his self. Hence Narcissus never escapes the circle of his own intra-subjectivity because he cannot direct his libido outside of himself. So Spivak's reading of Echo is one of endless opening onto the outside, while Mitchell's reading sees her as impasse.

So, rather than describing a state of arrested development, Spivak's Ovidian tale proposes a description of intention or invitation by Echo to move from ego to object libido that stalls with Narcissus.

Psychoanalysis enhances the fact that Narcissus would rather die than give Echo power over him. Weber (1982) sees this resistance of Narcissus to Echo's invitation as 'the power of narcissism' within psychoanalytic discourse. Put differently, narcissism becomes a powerful construct at the service of psychoanalytic representation of the subject. 'The power of narcissism, then, would entail not simply the symptom of an individual subject, 'Freud': but rather the theoretical project of psychoanalysis itself, putting its limits into play' (Spivak, 1996: 194). The theoretical construct 'narcissism' would be even more powerful than Freud posited narcissism as a necessary moment, organising the self, while remaining ambiguous in his construction of narcissism. The ambiguity stems from Freud's ambivalence regarding the 'maternal continent' which he could never fully theorise. Hence some of his theories, such as narcissism, implicitly record the presence of the maternal at work but stop short of full explanations. Weber provides us with an explanation as to the reasons for such a stalling of the Freudian ocuvre (and of psychoanalysis as a whole) before the question of the maternal.

> [I]f Freud's initial stories deal with men, betrayal, and ingratitude, death enters the scene with - as? - the passive female [...] The *Schicksalzug* (trait of destiny) that Freud asserts it represents, is [...] a recurrent fatality linked to the female: she either eliminates the male or is eliminated by him. [...] The activity of the subject, in this final story, consists indeed of a repetition, but what he repeats, actively, is the narcissistic wound that never heals without leaving scars [*LF*, 134]. (Weber, 1982: 134) (Spivak, 1996: 195)[4]

Freud hinted repeatedly at this 'other scene' than the phallic construction of the subject.[5] But while his work testifies to repeated attempts at articulating a framework to explain the other, the different, the foreign, the same texts also testify to his recurring return to more phallocentric interpretation. Spivak concludes 'Narcissus is fixed, but Echo can disseminate [...]. Whales, those paleo-mammals that were once creatures of the earth, *echo*-locate objects and other inhabitants in

---

4 In this quote, Weber refers to a romantic epic, *Gerusalemme Liberata*. But his point applies to numerous stories. Weber explains:

> But nothing is more difficult to do away than this persistent female: you kill her once, and her soul returns [...]. The activity of the subject, in this final story, consists indeed of a repetition, but what he repeats, actively, is the narcissistic wound that never heals without leaving scars.
>
> Freud tells the story of these scars, but instead of reading these stories as the signal of something else, he sees them as more of the same, as the manifestation of a new and more powerful *authority*. (Weber, 1982: 134)

5 Bracha Lichtenberg-Ettinger's work on the 'matrixial encounter' attempts to define a subjectivity that would not be solely subjected to phallic logic.

the sea world, which is not their home but merely their makeshift dwelling place' (Spivak, 1996: 196). So, beside the narcissistic narrative of self-searching, Echo intercepts or locates Narcissus's 'other scene' and proposes another narrative of origin-searching.

Narcissus: A Distant and Unstable Symbol

In psychoanalytic terms, Ovid's account describes the fate of an adolescent who discovers that the object of his love is his own image. Kristeva sees the narcissistic moment in Narcissus understanding that he lives in a world of signs that he must decipher. This leads him to knowledge and especially to self-knowledge, which she sees as the epitome of Narcissus's tragic fate: he is at once himself and his image and fails to dissociate his body and his self:

> Only a little water keeps us apart. [...] I am myself the boy I see. I know it: my own reflection does not deceive me. [...] How I wish I could separate myself from by body! A new prayer this, for a lover to wish the thing he loves away! (Ovid, 1968: 86)

Out of Narcissus's fate, Kristeva draws two important conclusions: Narcissism is a normal stage of human development and narcissism is a 'dis-ease' of the modern man and woman.

Narcissus: The Ignorance of Origin

Narcissism is a necessary stage in subjectivation to be transcended. It corresponds to a learning stage of development during which the subject learns to operate the passage from being to symbol. For Kristeva, this makes of Narcissus 'logically, and quite normally, the obliged creator of the world' (Kristeva, 1983: 135). Why 'the obliged creator'? Because through the narcissistic moment, the subject in formation learns that 'I', or the conscious subject, is a reflection of its being through signs. Being is the origin but the creator is the one who links being to its image, a step first achieve, albeit archaically, in narcissism. Narcissus 'the obliged creator' adheres to a generally monotheistic and in particular Christian understanding of the creator as the beholder of the unitary and unifying symbol: 'In the beginning was the Word and the Word was with God, and the Word was God' (John 1,1). If we hold on to this paternalist view of Narcissus, self-knowledge is a deadly curse because Narcissus must, but fails to, recognise himself as the origin of knowledge. He has no other base to construct himself from.

Claire Nouvet (1991) elucidates that part of Narcissus's make-up is indeed the ignorance of himself as origin. Following a Derridean logic, Nouvet proposes that Narcissus and Echo cannot be regarded as characters endowed with a speaking consciousness. Instead, both protagonists epitomise the dynamic of text that we, the readers, construe as the mark of consciouness. She explains:

> Although it is described as dialogue between self and other, the exchange between Narcissus and Echo in fact *inscribes* another description, that of echo which inhabits the voice as soon as it utters a sentence. [...] As soon as it appears, language 'echoes', that is diffracts into a potentiality of alternative meanings without providing us with the means to decide on any true, proper meaning. Although presented as the 'other side' of a dialogue, Echo remarks in fact the original lateral sliding of language into contingent meanings. (Nouvet, 1991: 107)

Echo's narrative is in fact a repeat of Narcissus's, staging narcissus as the 'true' speaker of Echo's words. This leads Nouvet to believe that Echo cannot be regarded as a character in her own right because she is but the voice of Narcissus. Furthermore, Nouvet finds that narcissus is the 'speaker who does not hear himself speak. This failure to recognize his own speech is especially disconcerting since such a recognition seems to be the distinctive characteristic of a speaking consciousness' (Nouvet, 1991: 108). Narcissus cannot then be regarded as a 'true' character either. In fact, Nouvet posits Echo as that which renders consciousness impossible. 'The echo which inhabits language not only severs it from the control of a consciousness, it also defines this 'consciousness' as covering the unrecognized otherness which, from the very beginning, speaks in place of 'I'' (Nouvet, 1991: 108). For Narcissus to become a character (or a consciousness, a subjectivity), he would need to recognise Echo as an echo. In other words he would need to know himself as creator of the echoed narrative but also know Echo as that which he has lost in recognising it/her. Echo represents 'the feminine as derived and secondary' (Nouvet, 1991: 109). She is thus not an effect or afterwards of Narcissus's narrative but truly, as Kristeva elicited, an originally and originary of his self.

One could then conclude that the true 'image maker' is indeed not Narcissus but the Oedipal subject. Freud's work leads us to believe that the structuring of the personality culminates with the resolution of the Oedipus complex. Through the taming and re-orientation of human desire towards object-choices other than the parent, Oedipus is one step further than Narcissus who incompletely manages a two-some with his own image. Indeed, in both traditional psychoanalysis and revised accounts like that proposed by Kristeva, Oedipus appears to recount that part of the subject's story that Narcissus did not finish. In other words, Oedipus begins where Narcissus ends. Yet, both characters also share a common history often left out but a psychoanalytic tradition eager to separate and categorise its pathologies and their actors. Both stories tell of a tragedy humans universally share, Freud believed,[6] and form part of the human subjectivation process. Oedipus and Narcissus's fate are born with a prophecy announced before their conception. Both suffer the consequences of the passage between maternal and paternal

6 More cautiously, Kristeva or Lasch suggest that although narcissism as a stage in human development may be universal, narcissism as pathology would be the marker of contemporary Western society.

functions. Oedipus kills his father and unites with his mother; Narcissus rejects his many suitors, not the least Echo and turns his sexual interest onto himself. In failing to separate from the maternal and to identify with an other than their own kin, both characters reject the paternal function. The absence of a third party locks their choice of a sexual object within a self/maternal economy. In this, the link between the maternal and the death drive - or the de-linking subject/symbol - is recalled. Indeed, Narcissus dies, leaving as a marker of his passage a flower needing no cross-fertilisation for its seasonal regeneration. As for the blind Oedipus, his progeny will carry out the curse of their 'maker'. One after the other, Oedipus's descendants will fail to take a successful place in the symbolic continuum, like their father did.[7]

If the histories of Oedipus and Narcissus may be similarly construed, the outcome is what sets them apart, and what psychoanalysis magnifies in its effort to categorise human structuration. While Oedipus is punished for knowing his origin, Narcissus dies for knowing his symbolic self. For Narcissus, the failure of the paternal function is also the failure of the life drive to regulate the maternal and leads to the death of the subject. On the awakening of his adolescent libido, Narcissus finds himself deprived of the structure that would empower him to choose a love-object other than himself. On the contrary, even a cursed man, Oedipus survives because the knowledge of his origin leads to conflict. It is conflict that psychoanalysis sees as the marker of psychical life and the motive for symbolisation. The conflict that agitates Oedipus is an inner battle between the impulses of the drive (id) towards the maternal and the censorship of the super-ego, previously constituted by the subject's internalisation of paternal law. To sum up, the outcomes of both tales are opposed: Oedipus has choice, Narcissus has not. Oedipus can choose between maternal and paternal. Narcissus cannot choose because the third term of the equation is missing from his psychical structure. Hence, Narcissus cannot become an other, he cannot 'step outside himself' so to speak, and recognise the two 'beings' that constitute him: one instinctual and one social. The absence of a triadic economy means that Narcissus fails to see himself as origin of the image and fails to see the image as symbol. Conversely, Oedipus succeeds in knowing his origin (fusion with the maternal) and in choosing to be something other: through permanent errand away from the site where his mother lives and self-inflicted blindness he doubly ensures separation from the maternal.

Narcissus: A Pathology

If Kristeva first sees Narcissus as a necessary stage of subjectivation, she then also points to a second understanding of the tale. Narcissism is a pathology by which

---

7 The House of Labdacus (of which Oedipus was third generation) was, in mythology, cursed. See the fate of Antigone, Ismene, Eteocles and Polynices, the children of Oedipus and Jocasta.

the subject does not acknowledge symbolic subjectivity as reflection and holds onto the belief of its solid reality instead.

> The error consists then in ignoring that reflection only sends one back to oneself: in short, Narcissus is guilty of ignoring himself as origin of reflection. (Kristeva, 1983: 137)

Kristeva's suggestion is that Narcissus fails to know himself because he fails to know that his reflection is his own: he believes that his mirror image is truly another than himself. We could argue that Narcissus acknowledges the separation between his body and his body image but fails to form a psychical connection between the two. More precisely, his path is, as Kristeva put it 'normal', since he knows he is but a reflection. His demise, and the birth of Narcissus as pathological hero, is two-fold. In Hamilton's words:

> The element of the mirror is important to my interpretation of the myth, since it suggests the particular stage in the process of early differentiation at which Narcissus is arrested. His relation to the mirror image indicates the emergence of identity formation. The mirror is ambiguous; it is both a third term and a symbiotic object. The mirror is 'magic' - both me and not-me - [...]. (Hamilton, 1993: 130)

Narcissism as pathology, or the arrest of subjectivation in the narcissistic moment, is first effected by the recognition of separation. Second, it becomes a refusal to envisage the specular image as other; that is, Narcissus refuses the alienation brought about by the symbol. Finally, narcissism is the failure to see oneself as the creator of the link self-image. Narcissus dies because he knows (and subsequently censors that knowledge) that he is the illusory other in the symbolic image. Why does Narcissus censor such knowledge? Because, unlike Oedipus, his tragedy is not to find in his mirror image a symbol that would sufficiently represent him and sustain the disconnection subject-maternal for a connection subject-symbol. The image, Ovid tells us, ripples, grows dim, disappears and returns only to be disturbed again by Narcissus's anxious gaze.

Narcissism is a pathological ignorance that reflection originates in the subject. This premise brings us back to the earlier suggestion that the crisis of contemporary subjectivity is located in the narcissistic moment of transfer from maternal to paternal site. Narcissus sees in what separates him from his image the annihilation of himself, the 'not-me' suggested by Hamilton, but does not see representation as the marker of his origin: Narcissus does not make the connection self-image. This failure to see or to make the connection is the failure of the paternal function: the contemporary subject's discourse is marked by an absence of affect on a symbolic level, an increase in compensatory psychosomatic illnesses and anti-social 'acting-out'.

> Nowadays, analysands suffer from the *abolishing of psychical space*. Narcissus in want of light as much as of a spring allowing him to capture his proper image, Narcissus drowned in a cascade of false images (from social roles to the *media*) and thus deprived of substance or place: those modern characters testify that today we do not know how to elaborate primary narcissism. (Kristeva, 1983: 464)

In an environment where the figures of the paternal function have been displaced from the father to depersonalised paternal 'devices' (media, institutions, etc.), the link to the paternal function is changing, causing the genesis of a different symbolic subject. The rise in narcissistic-type of subjectivity can be interpreted as an adaptive mechanism protecting the subject from annihilation while allowing a new form of symbolisation. In other words, where the Freudian Oedipal moment marked the genesis of the traditional (neurotic) subject, narcissism, or the passage from maternal to paternal site, has become the new moment initiating contemporary subjectivity and offering a new terrain of investigation and ministration.

A Kristevan reading of contemporary subjectivity suggests this society is sliding away from the Oedipal model elicited by Freud in the first part of the twentieth century and towards a narcissistic type of subject. The return to the Freudian model necessitates, as Spivak explained, the foreclosing of 'Narcissus's other scene'. As in the reading of the Narcissus tale narcissism is both a normal stage of development, provided this stage is transcended, and the marker of an arrested development when it is not. But in the light of Kristeva's belief that the failure of the paternal function is bringing about an increase in narcissistic type pathologies, Narcissus need be re-considered in a light closer to that proposed by Spivak. We are dealing with a cultural Narcissus, the new prodigal son of the turn of a century if we believe Christopher Lasch's vision of a narcissistic society driven by the market economy, counter-acted by the Narcissus of psychoanalysis. Indeed, psychoanalysis sees itself as the last bastion still fighting for the recognition of the subject is the resolution of the Oedipal tale and pointing to Narcissus as the sign of a dis-eased society. Although she has been very vocal in her call for a return to a more traditional paternal function, Kristeva's psychoanalytic discourse does not simply propose Narcissus as the type of a failed phallic subjectivation. Beyond her attachment to the work of Freud, Kristeva is also closer to the feminist analysis of Spivak or Nouvet when she insists on hearing Narcissus's other story, the subject's search for a narrative which could translate the forfeited maternal.

Conclusion

Freud borrowed the term 'narcissism' from the Greek tragedy of Narcissus, commonly described as the story of a boy who falls in love with his own image and who, unable to form a meaningful relationship with that image, dies of despair.

Freud focused his analysis on Narcissus's incapacity at forming attachment with an other than himself. Since Freud, other theorists have counterbalanced his one-sided vision by analysing not only the role of Narcissus, but also that of other 'minor' characters and they have shed new light on the concept of Narcissism. The analyses proposed by Spivak, Weber, Nouvet and Kristeva show how they illuminate and sometimes contradict the Freudian narrative.

Spivak (1996) believes that the character of Echo rescues the narcissan narrative from its doom. Echo repeatedly invites Narcissus to leave the claustrophobic world he has created for himself and to relate to another than himself, namely Echo. Repeatedly, Narcissus rejects her invitation. Echo is a character cursed never to speak her own words and to eternal repetition of the words last spoken by Narcissus. In spite of her fate, Echo succeeds, through repetition, in expressing her desire for Narcissus.

Spivak first proposes that Narcissus and Echo's predicament should not be read in separation but as a pair. Narcissus's development is arrested between an objectless and an object-oriented stage. The paternal metaphor is not motivation enough to pull him out of this in-between, but Echo is. She embodies the voice from elsewhere, the one who repeats some of Narcissus's words and verbalises hidden meaning. What is hidden is Narcissus's fear of losing the maternal 'image' in exchange for the symbol. Spivak sees Echo as the maternal mirroring of Narcissus's closed structure engaging him to leave his ego libido, by recalling his narcissistic persona through her narrative. From the perspective of the Echo/Narcissus pair, the tale is then the 'narrativisation' of the lost maternal voice inviting Narcissus's development beyond loss. If Echo is 'forgotten' in the analysis of the story, then Narcissus becomes the tragic hero who, fearful of loss, prefers to halt his psychical development before the symbol. The subject's arrested development and refusal to choose the paternal metaphor is the psychoanalytic definition of narcissism. This leads Spivak to a second point.

The Freudian and post-Freudian psychoanalytic body as a whole has tended to ignore the presence of Echo in its interpretation of narcissism. Spivak, but also Weber (1982) are suspicious of such *en masse* foreclosure of the character's narrative. They conclude that the presence of Echo threatens to destabilise the psychoanalytic narrative. Narcissus's arrested development serves the purpose of the Freudian and post-Freudian phallic economy. What is economised is the potential of the maternal voice to disseminate phallocentric discourse: either phallic discourse eliminates the maternal and the subject triumphs or the maternal eliminates discourse and psychosis ensues. The primacy of the phallus is the backbone and the strength of psychoanalytic narratives. But its safeguard against threatening aspects of the process of subjectivation is also limiting psychoanalytic theorists in their dealings with contemporary issues and may prove to be its downfall. It points to the difficulty, within psychoanalytic logic in finding answers to unresolved aspects of subjectivity, such as the rise in narcissistic pathologies.

It seems then that one answer to the 'narcissus predicament' psychoanalytic theory faces is in the reconsideration of the subject's connection with the pre-symbolic 'other scene' that Freud had tended to avoid. Kristeva (1983) and Nouvet (1991) both come to the conclusion that Narcissus's 'problem' lies in his ignorance of the importance of origin. Spivak established that Echo's narrative invites Narcissus to recognise himself as other than the narcissistic hero locked in a narrative fusion with himself. Nouvet emphasises Narcissus's refusal to follow Echo's lead. She points out that in order to recognise himself as other, Narcissus would need to know that Echo's words are but a repetition of his own. In recognising himself as origin of the echo, he would establish Echo's narrative as secondary to his own and become the other of origin. Hence, the recognition of origin constitutes two aspects of otherness: one symbolic (the Lacanian *I am other than what I am*), one original (*I was other than what I am*). Nouvet concludes that Narcissus is a character without consciousness and Echo the impeding element. He neither recognises the otherness of origin, nor the otherness of the symbol. In positing the knowledge of origin as the key to overcoming narcissism, Nouvet offers an interpretation of the tale closer to Freud's than to Spivak's. It follows that, for psychoanalysis, Narcissus is doomed to developmental arrest while Oedipus, in finding his origin, becomes a more solid archetypal figure for subjectivity.

Kristeva also suggested that Narcissus's error lies in his ignorance of origin. But analysing Narcissus's interaction with his image rather than with Echo, she adds a further dimension. Narcissus recognises the reflection as his own but subsequently censors the knowledge of himself as origin of the image. There is a refusal on Narcissus's part to separate and then form a link with objects he authored, his reflection, his echoed words. Kristeva sees a parallel between Narcissus's story and the contemporary subject's story. What is lacking in both cases is a symbol, be it words or images, solid enough to guarantee the subject's stability and to justify the risk of forsaking dependence on the maternal. Ironically, while Kristeva does not take on board the role of Echo like Spivak does, she sees escape from the narcissistic puzzle initially in a maternal function reminiscent of Spivak's vision of Echo: a voice who echoes the narcissist's reality, offering the symbol while retaining the link to individual pre-history.

Chapter 8

Narcissistic Society

In proposing the existence of an increasingly narcissistic society, the term 'narcissism' is frequently ill defined and used to refer to different and often incompatible meanings. Even within the bound of the psychoanalytic frame, the term is far from pointing towards a meaningful totality. Freud alone did not succeed in proposing a stable definition of the term. In a first attempt at defining the term, narcissism corresponds to the submitting of instinct to reality. The move from a closed unit (narcissism) to an open structure (social membership) is motivated by the instinct for survival that drives the individual to protect the species (the social) over individual interest. Later on, Freud abandoned the idea of narcissism as a physically driven stage and proposed narcissism as a purely psychical process. Upon observation of adults, Freud concludes the narcissist withdraws the libido from outside interests and turns back the sexual drive onto the ego. Narcissism as pathology is now an intermediate stage between the objectless (auto-erotic) and object oriented individual. Freud then begins to categorise human attachment, opposing the narcissistic and the anaclitic type of attachment. The narcissist attaches to the same, the anaclitic type attaches to the different. To sum up, narcissism corresponds to that stage of development between objectless and symbolic.

Freud further differentiated between primary and secondary narcissisms, with the former referring to the baby's anobjectal world, and the latter to the identificatory stage of development. Secondary narcissism will show in the type of object the individual chooses to attach to: narcissistic type, that is attachment to 'the same', where the object is recognised as separate but not different from the individual. Since Klein, Freud's understanding of primary narcissism as anobjectal has been questioned, in particular the difficulty in defining Narcissus as the place between anobjectal and pre-objectal. The crux of the debate is summarised by Laplanche and Pontalis (1988). They find in psychoanalytic circles a separation between two understandings of narcissism, in particular primary narcissism. Primary narcissism always refers to 'a strictly 'objectless' - or at any rate 'undifferentiated' - state, implying no split between subject and external world.' (Laplanche and Pontalis, 1988: 338). They object to this definition on the following two points: first an anobjectal state erases the very possibility of a narcissistic image; second, some research (Melanie Klein, Balint) suggests the capacity for object relation in the newborn baby. To conceive of a narcissistic stage of development, between no-objects and pre-objects, is then illogical. Laplanche and Pontalis consequently suggest 'primary narcissism' as an 'early phase or formative moments, marked by the emergence of a first adumbration of the ego and its immediate libidinal cathexis' (Laplanche and Pontalis, 1988: 338).

Like Laplanche and Pontalis, Kristeva also retains the idea of primary narcissism as an early structuring of the subject.

> Neither a screen, nor a state, primary narcissism is already a structure, anterior to Oedipus, and which operates with three terms. The central axis of linking and de-linking, of full and empty, of positions and losses, represents the instability of the *narcissistic subject*. He remains there, attracted on the one hand towards an imagined loving father, 'father of individual prehistory', onset of the ego ideal; and on the other hand, attracted towards another pole of desire and hate, fascination and repulsion that is the archaic mother no longer the container of needs: neither subject nor object, an *'abject'-mother*, locus of rejection and differentiation, an infection. (Kristeva, 1983: 464)

Following Klein, Kristeva sees the narcissistic phase as an archaic Oedipal moment, Oedipus prime, already presenting a triadic dynamic: the infant and a bipolar maternal function combining the functions of maternal and imaginary paternal. Hence, Kristeva agrees with Laplanche and Pontalis that primary narcissism structures the baby's nascent ego in its relationship with the imaginary father and marks the departure from the baby's auto-erotic stage: the baby's libido is for the first time invested in an other than itself. But Kristeva also adds to Laplanche and Pontalis the role of the death drive the presence of which renders the narcissistic structure unstable. The life drive (libido) is likened to a linking drive that is supported by the imaginary father, while the death drive (disinvestment of the libido), connected to the abject mother, cuts that link. In operating the move from maternal site to paternal function, the subject is then supposedly showing the superseding of the death drive by the life drive. In analysing contemporary subjectivity, Kristeva is suggesting the opposite is happening.

Finally, Freud saw 'proof' of narcissism in adults as a propensity to attach to the same and incapacity to identify with difference. A parallel can be made with the failure of paternal function: in the absence of the paternal function, the third term of the differentiating structure (Oedipus) is missing. The two terms of the maternal-child dyad are thus left intact. What Kristeva is suggesting is this: in narcissism we find separation and sameness but no difference between the individual and the outside world. Reiterating her belief in the crucial role of the paternal function, she elaborates a reading of Narcissus as that of an individual whose encounter with an evanescent paternal function forbids him to become other than himself. Narcissus is able to see his image but unable to transfer his desire to the site of the image. This image in the pond, a metaphor for the maternal[1] (water, the amnion pool) is

1 The pond is a metaphor for Narcissus's father, the river Cephisis. Water, or the retains the hero's image (Kristeva, 1983: 131). This paternal flow is too unstable

still an archaic link to maternal site. Although the pond acts as a paternal third term, it is not a stable enough term for Narcissus to perform the transfer from maternal to paternal symbol. The intervention of a third figure between himself and the maternal, and suggesting the symbolisation of Narcissus, fails to take place as Narcissus conceives of a third party between himself and the maternal as the death of his pre-subjective being. On the socio-symbolic side, the change in the representer of the paternal means the disconnection of the symbolic subject from their affective life, that is the suppressing of the life drive and return of the death drive. If the imaginary father is the pre-cursor of the paternal symbolic, the failure of the paternal function appears later as a disconnection subject/symbol. This disconnection testifies to the subject's encounter with paternal agencies incapable of fulfilling the subject's need for social containment. This leads to a second aspect of the debate, an aspect implicitly present in Kristeva's work but one that she does not explicitly spell out. If this inadequately contained subject is the mother figure, the maternal function becomes impaired also. In turn, the infant is developing in a climate where neither the imaginary father nor the symbolic father offer sufficient hold to permit a harmonious move, in the traditional psychoanalytic sense, from maternal to paternal. In proposing the failure of the paternal function for the crisis in subjectivity, Kristeva has been moving from failure in the socio-symbolic paternal to analysing the role of the paternal function within the maternal. On a pre-symbolic level, the maternal function suffers from failures of the archaic paternal. The failure of the paternal function on both accounts leads to the possibility of a new structuring of the individual, a narcissistic type.

In a first step, Freud's understanding of secondary narcissism as neurotic defences against ego-damage should be reconsidered. Taking up Freud's idea that we choose our 'neurosis', the narcissist is less representative of a pathological defence against the outside than of the historical moment that founded them. In other words, the shift from the 'good old neurotic' to the narcissist as predominant social type may not simply be the sign of an occasional bout of mental illness that practitioners, from Freud to Kristeva are trying to find the cure for. That Kristeva regards narcissism as the 'new dementia' is, of course, a matter of psychoanalytic perspective and categorising. But from other focal points (socio-cultural and literary mainly), and even though they occasionally deplore it, writers such as Kirschner, Cooper and Maxwell, Lasch, etc. put forward the existence of a functioning narcissistic social organisation. Some like Blank and Blank have even put forward the belief that narcissism as organisational force of the subject can be found in retrospect in Freud's patients. Indeed, if one returns to the tale, Narcissism

---

for Narcissus to gain any permanence of himself in its mirroring. Indeed, Narcissus's father is mentioned only as genitor at the beginning of the tale and is subsequently ab[illegible] from the story. But if water represents an early connection with the paternal, it should [illegible] within the maternal function as an imaginary father too evanescent to conta[illegible] image of himself.

can also be constructed as a system in which Narcissus, his family and his companions have social membership and a function.

Hamilton's study (1993) shows that the myth of Narcissus exemplifies the failure of the paternal function on a pre-symbolic level. She explains that Narcissus's mother named her child after herself.[2] 'We may infer from Leiriope's choice of a name that a child represented a strong wish for closeness and even for the birth of a version of herself' (Hamilton, 1993: 111). The myth is then proposing the mother figure as a narcissistic type. The father is given a role only as genitor: Narcissus is thus deprived of a paternal agent capable of counter-balancing this strong maternal presence. Finally, other characters Narcissus encounters also display signs of arrested development. Spivak's interpretation of Echo envisions the foreclosure of Echo's narrative in psychoanalytic readings of the tale as significant of a patriarchal construction of the character fearing Echo and her 'voice from elsewhere'. For Spivak, the erasure of Echo would correspond to the erasure of the maternal and its 'voice' for patriarchal comfort. But Echo can also be construed as a nymph fated to repeat the same words that others uttered. Hamilton analyses her curse as the confinement of the character to the echolalic stage of the young child: she is able to reproduce the sound of others but not initiate her own different, autonomous discourse. Echo can exist symbolically only as a duplicating of another subject. Rejected by Narcissus, she dies of unrequited love for him. Such contemporary analyses of the narcissistic myth illustrate the fact that by today's cultural standards on subjectivity the myth of Narcissus is considered a more adapted tale than that of Oedipus: it proposes narcissism as the new individual, generational and social structuring.

> Narcissism appears realistically to represent the best way of coping with the tensions and anxieties of modern life, and the prevailing social conditions therefore tend to bring out narcissistic traits that are present, in varying degrees, in everyone. (Lasch, 1979: 101)

If narcissism designates a particular pathology, that of a failed structuring of the personality, historically located before Oedipality, Kristeva's work also demonstrates that it describes a social phenomenon pointing towards a changed subjectivity. Different psychoanalytic schools[3] offer differing understandings of

---

2 The narcissus flower is also called 'leirion'. The mother is called Leiriope, literally 'the face of leirion' (Hamilton, 1993: 111).

3 For instance, narcissism is described in Cooper and Maxwell (1995):

1) as a trauma emerging out of environmental deficits. It is 'attributed to caregiver unresponsiveness resulting in the child's ego depletion caused by varying degrees of collusion' (Cooper and Maxwell, 1995: 77): see the ''false self' – [Winnicott, 1967] or arrested development [with] horizontal or vertical splitting between archaic grandiose self and idealised object [Kohut, 1977]' (Cooper and Maxwell, 1995: 77);

2) as a phobia effecting the 'infant's own omnipotent phantasies [Freud, 1991] and envious/aggressive projection of parts of the self onto the relational exchange [Klein, 1946]

narcissism; they also present several common denominators forming a g picture of contemporary subjectivity and society.

The Subject as 'Self'

Narcissism is first a structuring moment set up by the archaic subject as a defence mechanism to support the split subject/object. Melanie Klein put forward the internal hatred the infant experiences during this time, against the mother who represents the object of its dependency, but also represents the object that must be lost. To protect itself against this loss, the archaic subject splits itself from that loss and substitutes the lost object for another idealised one. The internalised idealised object is phantasised as totally good while the lost object is totally bad. The bad object is then the outcome of the subject's internal incapacity to negotiate the loss of the maternal, displaced onto the outside. Through projection, the subject is able to contain its bad objects in an other than itself and exert control over it. Hence there is a split internal/external; the subject now possesses objects to represent itself. However, internal and external objects remain under their power: they have effectively operated the separation inside/outside but not the differentiation subject/object. The other onto whom the internal bad object is projected is not the differentiated other of the Oedipal structure. It is an extension of the self, a mirror in which the subject can enforce its own omnipotent wishes.[4]

This is evidenced in Anglo-American psychoanalytic groups. The reassignment of human disturbance to a pre-Oedipality is concomitant with a reassignment of psychical mechanisms to a healthy functioning of the self. The term 'reassignment' rather than assignment suggests a return to a pre-Freudian or anti-Freudian apprehension of the person as consciousness only. Kirschner (1996: 37) defines the self according to three 'schools': 'a representation within the ego' (Heinz Hartman and Edith Jacobson); 'a separate structure coexisting with the ego' with the one not reducible to the other (Margaret Mahler, Heinz Kohut); 'a structure which, whether called 'ego' or 'self', essentially replaces the classical ego' (British object-relation

---

and grandiose denial of dependency on a projectively idealised object [Kernberg, 1984]' (Cooper & Maxwell, 1995: 77-78);

3) as a mixture of both: 'defensive internalisation of the tantalising emotionally unavailable caregiver [Fairbairn, 1952], pathogenic caregiving causing failure to progress from dyadic to triadic relations [Mollon, 1993], or intentional turning away from the source of emotional life, the internalised 'lifegiver' [Symington, 1993]' (Cooper and Maxwell, 1995: 78) that is the internalisation of the source of life and goodness in order to control it and avoid knowing that it lies outside the subject's control (Cooper and Maxwell, 1995: 71); See also Seinfeld, (1996).

4 Psychoanalytic records of narcissism show that the narcissistic pathology shows most when the patient becomes aware of its dependence upon the external object (a drug addict denying its addiction for instance) or of its difference (the other behaves in a manner different to that wanted by the patient).

theory, Fairbairn, Winnicott, Guntrip). The definitions of 'ego' and 'self' suggested by Laplanche and Pontalis (1988) clarify the difference between a Freudian and Anglo-American (post-Freudian) understanding of the human subject. They note the frequent confusion between the two opposed terms 'ego' and 'self' and advocate their differentiation. The self would be concerned with the proper (in the French sense of 'propre', the personal and clean) of the person in opposition to its objects, while the ego refers to a psychical system 'in contradistinction to other substructures of the personality' (Laplanche and Pontalis, 1988: 131). In Freudian terminology, the ego refers partly to the individual and partly to their psychical apparatus, that is the ego permits the organisation of neurological information into representations (biological activity), themselves subjected to the drive activity (psychical activity) which permits the translation and storage within the psyche of these representations. Thus Laplanche and Pontalis conceive of the Freudian ego as 'a series of shifts [...] a kind of actualised metaphor for the organism' (Laplanche and Pontalis, 1988: 135).[5] In relation to the three definitions of the self proposed by Kirschner, what is modified, even erased in the case of British object relation theorists, is the multi-layered aspect of the Freudian ego. From the organic body to its metaphoric actualisation, the role of the ego in dealing with the successive translations of biological data into psychical data is lost in the formulation of the self. In Kirschner's words: 'Increasingly, in these post-Freudian theories, the primary imperative of reality is no longer considered to be instinctual renunciation, but rather separation and individuation' (Kirschner, 1996: 35).

Her equation of Freudian psychoanalytic 'cure' with patient's renunciation of instinctual drives is questionable within traditional Freudian terminology. It typifies the Anglo-American inclination in understanding mental health as an ability to control pre-Oedipal material for the preservation of a stable, unified reality within which the subject can also be stable. However, her perception of Anglo-American culture is clearly stated: the objective of post-Freudians is both to confirm in theory the current value attached to the subject's ability for separation/individuation and rely on that theory in a practice that will facilitate the subject's access to an improved socio-cultural belonging, namely its separateness and individualism. The reassignment of the unconscious mechanisms formative of the 'ego' to the more consciously malleable 'self' is implemented through a modified conception of the subject. The separation of the self from other objects is in fact a separation and individuation from those pre-objects and their affective charge that constituted the experience of the infant and of its emerging ego. The

---

5 Laplanche further suggested that the notion of 'self' would denote 'a return of the *repressing* rather than that of the repressed: a return masked by nostalgia, a nostalgia for the good old self which could have been lost through too much analysis' (Kirschner, 1996: 61). Laplanche is then suggesting that society would have lost the very ability to repress through too much permissiveness allowing the overdiversification of identities. The present interest in the pre-Oedipal maternal could be a therapeutic tactic to rediscover repressing 'skills' and instruct clients on how to remaster the appropriate part of repression that they lack.

emphasis is then not so much on the reactualisation, on a symbolic level, of a pre-Oedipal dependence from which the subject derives renewal and *jouissance*, as is the case in Kristevan theory, but on a drive for omnipotent control (more commonly termed 'independence') vis à vis preoedipality and its potential for *jouissance*. Albert Ellis[6] (Palmer and Varma, 1997) describes his understanding of 'good' goals in therapy as follows:

> (1) reducing their [client's] presenting symptoms, such as performance anxiety or depression over a serious loss; (2) discovering and reducing their related and more general symptoms, such as anxiety and/or depression in other aspects of their lives; (3) helping them reach a point where they rarely disturb themselves about unfortunate life situations and therefore make themselves less disturb*able*; (4) showing them how, if and when they do fall back to emotional and behavioral upsetness, they can use their previously learned therapy methods to quickly undisturb themselves again and make themselves even less disturbable. (Palmer and Varma, 1997: 5)

Ellis clearly describes that in his view, 'good' therapeutic practices involve the suppression of unwanted symptoms such as anxiety, depression, disturbance, through a prescriptive method aimed at the subject's better control of their affective responses to personal difficulties. Although this type of therapy capitalises on certain aspects of psychoanalytic theory (it uses its terminology for instance symptoms, depression, loss, etc.), it has little to do, if anything at all, with the methodology used in psychoanalysis. Where a more traditional post-Freudian like Kristeva would seek a regeneration of the human subject in the re-actualisation (in the transference) of pre-symbolic, imaginary contents within the symbolic realm, Anglo-American post-Freudians like Ellis advocate salvation in separation and independence from the affective experience of the maternal.

While analysing the pre-Oedipal experience of the infant, Anglo-American psychoanalytic theory seeks to find a new way of measuring the value of the subject now recaptured as 'self'. Far from being a sign of the subject's ability to transcend the imaginary, Anglo-American theorists gather their common attention round a time anterior to the separation of the subject from its objects (symbolic) as a means to better control the contamination of the symbolic realm by the subject's pre-symbolic experience. Kirschner suggests that a Puritan cultural environment translated in 'Americans' zealous adoption of psychoanalytic therapy as a regime of self-improvement.' (Kirschner, 1996: 47) Kristeva sees in this a normalisation of the subject, which marks the decline of psychoanalysis:

> [A] certain type of psychoanalysis, particularly American psychoanalysis, does not view this [psychical] questioning as an open process, but as a normalisation. 'you are a homosexual, I will transform you into a heterosexual, you are unsuccessful in your

6 The founder of therapies such as Cognitive Behavior Therapy and Rational Emotive Behavior Therapy, Albert Ellis is today one of the most prominent figures in cognitive therapies.

> career, the aim of analysis is to become Managing-Director or the boss and earn a lot of money'. I object to this normative vision of psychoanalysis; it is in fact a kind of decline of psychoanalysis. (Kristeva, 1996c)

In its effort to normalise the subject, Anglo-American research and theories in pre-Oedipality have become a device to separate the human subject from the maternal, sustained by a cultural climate encouraging the standardisation of the human self into performance and perfectibility.

Narcissus, A Commodity

Narcissus would not only be the new figure of contemporary subjectivity but also the base upon which a new social edifice must re-organise its survival. Narcissism is a protective mechanism, facilitating the separation from the maternal and access to the symbolic, while keeping the maternal/child dyad. In a 'normal' subjectivation process (defined by Freudian psychoanalysis), narcissism is superseded by the birth of the Oedipal subject, replacing the maternal/child dyad with an Oedipal triangulation. Yet, the difficulties in moving from Narcissus to Oedipus do not mean that contemporary subjectivity is arrested before the individual's access to symbolisation. On the contrary, contemporary society is witnessing the proliferation of highly sophisticated symbolic systems (the media, information technology for instance has ensured a fast diffusion of an ever increasing amount of information). These could be interpreted as a better mastering of the Oedipal phase. Yet a Kristevan analysis of such symbolic proliferation shows that symbolic performance per se is not a sign of a triumphant Oedipus. On the contrary, she views advancement in information technology as 'data collection' which for her does not offer 'the possibility to reject, change, transform. [...] In computers, we keep the data as it is' (Kristeva, 1996c). Data banks are then a sterile ground where the dynamics of subjectivation, the transcendence of the maternal, cannot take place. In fact, one could argue that sophistication in symbolic performance can also be sophistication in masking that which the symbol cannot name: imaginary contents. Symbolisation (and subjectivity) is then operative but not subjective in the Kristevan sense of 'transformative creativity' (Kristeva, 1996c: on line), which include the subject's conflictual questioning and the process of negativity. On the contrary, any attempt at pointing at the non-differentiation subject/object is resisted[7] as an attack upon the link maternal/child. We then have a split: on the one hand the subject denies its difference in order to avoid mourning the loss of its archaism; on the other, it exhibits a competence for social performance. With the noticeable increase in narcissistic structures intrinsic to

---

7 The development of information networks for instance is for Kristeva a 'technocratic ideology supposed to abolish anxiety' (Kristeva, 1996c: on line). In her opinion, anxiety, repulsion and negativity are essential to the subject's capacity for change.

contemporary subjectivity, narcissism is a strategy set up by the contemporary subject to prevent the representation (and knowledge) of loss. As it is shared by an increasing number of people, this strategy becomes the axis upon which a new social organisation can exist.

Anglo-American theorists conceive of the subject's psychical disturbance as a desire for reunion with the maternal and a failed 'movement out of 'symbiosis' (mahler) or 'hallucinatory omnipotence' (Winnicott) or 'absolute dependence' (Fairbairn) towards autonomy and self-reliance' (Kirschner, 1996: 49). The healthy self would have developed 'the capacity to engage in limited and partial experiences of reunion with our objects, but without losing the sense of separate and distinctive identity' (Kirschner, 1996: 49). The new criterion in defining pathology is that the more dependent the subject, the less healthy the self. What Kirschner, along with other theorists[8] is suggesting is that the present socio-political climate driven by the market economy is participating in a process of standardisation of its social members. Governments encourage, through policies, research, the allocation/withdrawal of funding, etc., the growth of an independent, autonomous subject, unfettered by remnants of parental control (actual parents), highly adaptable and perfectible. At the same time, this social subject can be interpreted as having transferred its desire for union with the parent onto the state apparatus, in particular the repression of the mother for the sake of the (father) state and to exercise the capacity for separation and intimacy at will and according to social needs. Hence, the state encourages the development of techniques of socialisation that guarantee the satisfaction of its needs. This (imaginary?) standardised subject, hinted at by Kirschner and Thorne in particular, is closer to that of a tap that can be turned on and off.

Narcissus, the *Doll-in-the-box*

Many contemporary researchers suggest the rise of narcissism as a model of subjectivation in contemporary society that would relocate social genesis and alter the Oedipal model. A genesis of a narcissistic society can be summed up as follows. Analysts first record the absence or failure of the father, 'absent, not strong enough or not asked for help by the mother' (Cooper and Maxwell, 1995: 35), from the triadic equation. Lasch explains the phenomenon of the absent father (the failure of the paternal function) as a historical process pertaining to our Western socio-economic reality.

> The invasion of the family by industry, the mass media, and the agencies of socialized parenthood has subtly altered the quality of parent-child connection. (Lasch, 1979: 291)

8 Brian Thorne in particular wrote a very wry essay making a prognosis that the sickness of his British clients are in fact an endemic social sickness projected onto its members. See 'The Sickness and the Prognosis' in Palmer and Varma (1997).

According to Lasch, we have moved from the patriarchal family where the father worked from the home and passed on his skills to his male offspring to the segregation of children from the parental world in the late eighteen century: Industrialisation led the father (and mother) away from the home to seek work, child care was provided by figures other than the actual parent. Generational continuity thus began to rupture the family setting. Second, where education was passed on from elders to the young, the development of the media has now facilitated the promotion of youth as desirable (and ageing as social failure), leading to a reversal of roles whereby the 'elders' (parental figures) imitate the discourse of the young (jargon, code of dressing, etc.). Finally, parenthood, once considered a 'natural skill'[9] (see maternal instinct for instance) has become an acquired skill that should be perfected if the parent wishes to be a 'good' parent.[10]

Today, the rise in instances of single parent families means that the mother often handles alone her narcissistic involvement with the child, with important consequences for this child's process of subjectivation. The failure of the paternal function to act as third party between the narcissistic mother and her child means she fails to differentiate herself from the child (and the child from her). Within the symbolic, 'The Oedipal triangulation is lacking [...] or reversed' (Cooper and Maxwell, 1995: 36) The child identifies with the object of the mother's desire that Kristeva describes as the imaginary father. As '[t]he separation difficulty seems to be intensified by the lack or inadequacy of either the father's presence or a paternal function within the mother' (Cooper & Maxwell, 1995: 31), the child learns to play the part of the mother's lost maternal object: it reflects the image of her own narcissism. In other words, childbearing re-activates the symbiotic dyad maternal/child of the narcissistic position: the mother's archaic memory of her narcissistic mirroring with her mother is re-activated and the foetus becomes a metaphorical mirror of the maternal image. For both, the boundaries enabling separation and differentiation are dissolved: the 'I' and the other merge into one undifferentiated body. As narcissism is passed onto the next generation, we are witnessing what Leff terms a '*Doll-in-the-box* syndrome' (Cooper and Maxwell, 1995: 83, 86, 87): the child is seen as a *tabula rasa* upon which another inscribes

9 From a socialist and feminist perspective, Michèle Barrett and Mary McIntosh (1982) point out that Lasch's complaint of the opening of the familial private to public scrutiny and policing hides a hidden nostalgia for the loss of authority of paternal figures (the father, priest, 'lawgiver'). The depletion of the paternal function gives rise to 'new forms of domination' (Barrett and McIntosh, 1982: 37) that Lasch sees as less authentic and more damaging than the 'real' family. He is nostalgic for the 'family' values and authority that was 'before', without precisely defining how that ideal family functioned or when it existed. Barrett and McIntosh parallel Lasch's incidental description of such a family with that defined by the psychoanalytic group of the Frankfurt School: late 19th century, bourgeois, natural family. They see in this Lasch's propensity for universalising and essentialising a certain mythical image of 'family'.

10 See: the British government's suggestion that parenthood should be taught at school; the marketing of parenthood through magazines, books, etc.

the child's individuality and humanity, a subjectivity by proxy. This idea is central to imagining the coming of the tailor-made post-subject, imprintable, malleable, belonging to another and above all fulfilling the needs of the former generation.

Kristeva's work does not envisage the possibility of a 'doll in the box' society as feasible. First, she believes the complete erasure of differentiation is impossible. If the symbolic subject is constituted from a dualism whereby the maternal is more or less successfully abjected to enable the subject's existence in the symbol, the disappearance of dualism would equate with the disappearance of the dualistic subject. In an interview with Jardine and Manke (Guberman, 1996), she points out that the blurring of sexual difference between men and women has not lead to the erasure of sexual categories but to the displacement of difference onto another group. She sees for instance the resurgence of racial discrimination[11] as a symptom of humans' need for differentiation from the maternal. In this instance, the 'other' race becomes the object of the death drive, locus of abjection and hatred, necessary for subjectivation, and the mark of a misplaced process. Closer to science fiction, she envisages 'the end of a certain kind of desire and sexual pleasure' (Guberman 1996: 126) and 'a reformulation of difference [...] in other forms' (Guberman 1996: 127). If the maternal is displaced from the mother onto other categories, so will the object of the life drive, the paternal function, be displaced from the mother onto other maternal agencies.

The New Family

If Kristeva does not forecast the erasure of differentiation constitutive of the subject, she does predict its possible replacement by external devices. She has decried the role of the media replacing the contemporary subject's absent desire with ready-made images. She is also concerned about the growing place given to neurosciences[12] 'valorised and recommended as antidotes to psychical discomfort' (Kristeva, 1997a: 22). Neurosciences increasingly relocate the transferential function of social encounters. What is being transferred is interpreted differently according to different 'schools'.[13] However, all theories dedicated to interpreting the interpersonal in the subject attach a great importance to the locus where the subject meets the other, manifest particularly in the context of analysis. Both protagonists connect in the place where the symbolic gives way to pre-verbal contents, and return to the symbolic through language. This movement and connectedness between maternal realm and paternal function is missing within

11 Racism is the projection of one group's 'badness' upon another. The 'good' group inflicts on the 'bad' group internal desires to reduce conflict and achieve harmonious homogeneity. This translates in a punitive treatment of the other for its difference, which in the extreme leads to genocide.

12 In the wider sense: psychiatry, biochemistry, etc.

13 See Laplanche and Pontalis's study (Laplanche and Pontalis, 1991: 497-8).

narcissistic economy because the non-differentiation subject/object arrests processes between archaic contents and their symbolisation. Medical or technical advancement already permit to modify the outcome of a failed representation of the subject's archaism; the modification applies to symptomatological discomfort born with the non-representation of drives and their affects. Even if the human body is increasingly defined and understood as mechanical structure, Kristeva does not believe that the human subject is born a *tabula rasa* upon which others can inscribe their desired 'programming':

> [L]anguage includes a neuronal or quantitative substratum, but it becomes 'language' only when these excitations are articulated with other elements to form with them a structure making sense for the other: the destination-other, also the other that 'I' become when I listen to myself. The neuronal is overdetermined by an organisation that is given to me beyond language, by the *socius*, by those who spoke before me and who speak to me [...]. (Kristeva, 1996a: 81)

She thus cannot fully imagine a 'society' of narcissistic subjects where technique or medication could be the sole source of the *socius*, replacing former and current generations. In other words, Kristeva does not envision social relations without transferential processes, but does see a 'the pill or the couch' (Kristeva, 1993: 52) battle between psychoanalysis and neurosciences, with different processes offered to the subject in crisis: psychoanalysis would propose to facilitate the translation of the drive and affects into language while neurosciences would modify the outcome of its non-representation. In the latter case, subjectivation would then be analysed according to its qualitative conformation, the insufficiency of which could be compensated by outside devices. Returning to an earlier example which stated that the blurring of sexual difference does not erase difference but displaces it, one can further argue that the scientific method may cure a symptom but does not target the problem of non-differentiation. We would instead have on the one hand a performing subject in the Kristevan sense and on the other a scientific 'subjectivity supplement' managing that part of subjectivation that the subject does not manage. In short, we would have a new triadic dynamic for a new form of subjectivity: the subject, a displaced maternal with a changed object of the death and life drives and science as the new paternal function, a science fiction already appearing in contemporary society. Kristeva requests instead that society re-theorise the maternal as a petition to re-instate the paternal function within pre-verbal economy, in an effort to facilitate a more traditional and, in her opinion, more human movement from dyadic to triadic structuring. In this, she believes that psychoanalysis holds a privileged position. However, Kristeva also acknowledges the increasing role of 'helping institutions for early childhood' (Guberman, 1996: 119), that attempt to 'replace the failed mother' (Guberman, 1996: 119). More generally, beyond the specialised field of infantile paediatrics and beyond a psychoanalytic theory and practice still reserved to a select minority, she also advocates the involvement of other agents of the maternal (social workers, intellectuals, writers, etc.) in the rehabilitation of the maternal function. In re-enforcing the move from maternal to paternal lies the hope for transformation of 'what cannot be analysed into some form of creativity. It could be maternity, friendship, teaching' (Kristeva, 1998c: 15). For it is in the celebration of difference, rather than in its eradication, that Kristeva foresees the preservation of psychical life and of human creativity.

Conclusion

The emergence of a new type of subject, the narcissist, can be regarded as an adaptive response to what could be termed a post-paternalistic society. The father is dead, but this has not led to a reorganisation of social structure around a different base. In fact, it is quite the opposite. The loss of the paternal function has led to a clinging on to some form of paternal image and to desperate psychical measures to preserve the primacy of the father. We are now experiencing the era of performance, of deception, but a sincere deception, performance as an act of faith towards the paternal image least it crumbles. Narcissus, this psychoanalytic perversion, is child to the fatherless system. Whether Narcissus is to be regarded as the active agent of his own destiny or the victim of modern society is a question difficult to answer.

Kristeva's work proposes an alarmist analysis of the contemporary subject: the flattening of emotion, the increase in violence, etc., are a direct effect of a dying paternal function and salvation in its rehabilitation. Her complaint thus remains now what it was at her début. Her early work was a response to the tendency in the linguistic field to over-systematise. She believed then that a highly systematic tradition was motivated by a human need to be reassured that our structural make-up could be mastered. Once mastery was achieved, theorists would be ready to leave the refuge of systematic thought and venture in the uncharted territory of the transverbal. Her prognosis was not to be verified if we consider her complaints today over this society of calculations and scientific answers to human problems. On the contrary, today's need for mastery has intensified and systematisation has pervaded most areas of western culture, with advancements in technology, leaving the investigation of transverbal modalities to an intellectual elite, mostly psychoanalytically oriented. So, Kristeva's stance has altered slightly. Transgression of paternalistic discourse is still called for, but in the light of the failure of the paternal function, the urgency to rehabilitate that function becomes more evident. But rehabilitation with a twist for in Kristeva's later work, the maternal has now become the site of salvation and its analysis paves the way for a less systematic, more transgressive answer to crisis. In short, the maternal holds the key to both changing the system while keeping it from crumbling. This necessitates that Freud's 'primacy of the phallus' be preserved. In adhering to the primacy of the phallus while hailing the transgression of the symbol as the way forward, we find Kristeva's position an ambivalent one. While it is agreed that the Oedipal model is no longer enough to account for the newness of contemporary subjectivity, neither are other models such as technological, scientific or 'biologistic' ones. Yet, Kristeva may, in positing the Oedipal subject as the one and only possible reference point, be narrowing the frame too much and missing the point. While the birth of a narcissistic society can be construed in psychoanalytic terms as a regression, it is nevertheless testimony to human psychical ability, if not to overcome crisis, to survive it. In this respect, we should remain guarded against Kristeva's pessimism and shall we suggest nostalgia for the 'good old fashioned neurotic' that psychoanalysis felt comfortable with. Yet, her interpretation of this culture is undeniably tenable. The increase in violence, the withering away of our ability to emote and the prospect of a humanness increasingly reliant upon technological artifice in its search for fulfilment adds up to her vision of narcissism as the new dementia and suggests the superseding of these social difficulties is doubtful under the current climate. To conclude, the belief in the prevalence of narcissism seems well grounded. But the question of whether it is, in a quasi-Darwinist interpretation, the 'natural' outcome to the paternal function's demise or, in Kristevan imagery, the last bastion of a humanity on its way to automatisation, remains at this stage the domain of speculation. Hence, neither perpetrator nor victim, but merely the living chronicle of the turn of the century subject, the venture into Narcissus's sketchy narrative has begun and remains today the new frontier of a psychoanalytic oriented research into subjectivity.

Bibliography

Atkinson, Rita et al. (1996), *Hilgard's Introduction to Psychology*, 12th edition, Fort Worth, Philadelphia, San Diego, New York, Orlando, Austin, San Antonio, Toronto, Montreal, London, Sydney, Tokyo: Harcourt Brace College Publishers.

Babin, Pierre (1990), *Sigmund Freud 'Un tragique à l'âge de la science'*, Paris: Gallimard, Découvertes Gallimard Sciences.

Badinter, Elisabeth (1981), *The Myth of Motherhood: An Historical View of the Maternal Instinct*, London: Souvenir Press.

Barrett, Michele and McIntosh, Mary (1982), 'Narcissism and the Family: A Critique of Lasch' in *New Left Review*, Vol 135, pp 35-48.

Bartal, Leah (1993), *The Metaphoric Body Guide to Expressive Therapy through Images and Archetypes*, London, Bristol: Pa.J.Kingsley.

Belsey, Catherine and Moore, Jane (eds) (1990), *The Feminist Reader: Essays in Gender and the Politics of Literary Criticism*, London: MacMillan; first published 1989.

Berne, Eric (1973), *Sex in Human Loving*, London: Penguin Books; first published 1970 Beverley Hills (Ca): City National Bank.

Blanck, Rubin and Blanck, Gertrude (1986), *Beyond Ego Psychology*, NY: CUP.

Bollas, Christopher (1987), *The Shadow of the Object: Psychoanalysis of the Unthought Known*, London: Free Association Books.

Bowlby, John (1998), *Attachment and Loss Volume 3: Loss Sadness and Depression*, London, Sydney and Oackland: Pimlico; first published 1980 by The Hogarth Press and The Institute of Psychoanalysis.

Boyne, Roy (1999), 'Citation and Subjectivity' in *Body and Society*, Vol 5, No 2/3, pp 209-25.

Chartier, Jean-Pierre (1993), *Introduction à la pensée freudienne: Les concepts fondamentaux de la psychanalyse*, Paris: Payot et Rivages, Petite Bibliothèque Payot.

Chasseguet-Smirgel, Janine (1999), *La Maladie d'idéalité: Essai psychanalytique sur l'idéal du moi*, Paris et Montréal: L'Harmattan.

Contat, Michel (1997), 'Kristeva dans l'intimité des révolté' in *Le Monde*, 6 juin 1997: Le Monde des livres.

Cooper, Judy and Maxwell, Nilda (eds) (1995), *Narcissistic Wounds: Clinical Perspectives*, Northvale, New Jersey and London: Jason Aronson Inc.

Corsini, Raymond J (ed.) (1979), *Current Psychotherapies*, 2nd edition, Itsca, 11.F.E.Peacock Publishers.

Daly, Mary (1985), *Beyond God the Father*, London: The Women's Press.

Deleuze, Gilles and Guattari, Félix (1984) *Anti-Oedipus: Capitalism and Schizophrenia*, London: The Athlone Press.

Denommé, Robert T. (1969), *Nineteenth Century French Romantic Poets*, Carbondale: Southern Illinois University Press.

Dick, Philip K. (1997), *Do Androids Dream of Electric Sheep*, London: HarperCollins*Publishers*; first published in Great Britain in 1969 by Rapp & Whiting Ltd.

Doane, Janice and Hodges, Devon (1992), *From Klein to Kristeva: Psychoanalytic Feminism and the Search for the 'Good Enough' Mother*, The University of Michigan: The University of Michigan Press, Critical Perspectives on Women and Gender.

Dolto, Françoise (1987), *Tout est langage*, Paris: le Livre de Poche.

——— (1991) *La foi au risque de la psychanalyse*, Paris: Seuil, Point Essai.

Dolto, Françoise and Nasio, J.-D. (1992), *L'Enfant du miroir*, Paris: Petite Bibliothèque Payot; First published 1987, Paris: Editions Rivages.

Doolittle, Teri (1995), 'The Long Term Effects of Institutionalization on the Behavior of Children from Eastern Europe and the Former Soviet Union' in *The Parent Network for Post-institutionalized Children*, March 1995, on line 29 March 1999 @ http://www.cyfc.umn.edu/ adoptinfo/ institutionalization.html.

Dryden, Windy (1997), *Therapists Dilemmas* (revised edition), London: Sage.

Elliott, Anthony (1998), *Freud 2000*, Cambridge: Polity Press.

Ellmann, Maud (ed.) (1994), *Psychoanalytic Literary Criticism*, London: Longman.

Erwin, Edward (1997), *Philosophy and Psychotherapy Razing the Troubles of the Brain*, London: Sage.

Fendler, Susanne and Wittlinger, Ruth (eds) (1999), *The Idea of Europe in Literature*, London: Macmillan.

Fletcher, John and Benjamin, Andrew (eds) (1990), *Abjection, Melancholia and Love*, New York: Routledge.

Ford, Donald H. (1998), *Contemporary Models of Psychotherapy: a Comparative Analysis*, 2nd edition, New York: Chichester J Wiley.

Fredet, Francine (1979), *Mais, Madame, vous êtes la mère*, Paris: Le Centurion.

Freud, Sigmund (1966), *Cinq leçons sur la psychanalyse*, Paris: Payot; first published by Payot in 1924; originally conferences delivered in September 1909, Clark University, Worcester under the title *Ueber Psychoanalyse, fünf Vorlesungen*.

——— (1967), *Moses and Monotheism,* New York: Random House.

——— (1986), *L'homme Moïse et la religion monothéiste*, Paris: Gallimard; First published 1938.

——— (1991), *On Metapsychology*, The Penguin Freud Library Volume 11, London: Penguin Books.

——— (1996), *Totem et tabou*, Paris: Edition Payot; previously published by Payot in 1923 and 1965; first published 1912-1913 as Totem und Tabu.

Gambaudo, Sylvie (2000a), 'Absence and Revolt: The Recent Work of Julia

Kristeva' in *Theory Culture & Society: Explorations in Critical Social Science*, Vol 17, No 2, April 2000, London: Sage.

——— (2000b), 'An Introduction to Julia Kristeva' in Twomey, Lesley (ed.) *Women in Contemporary Culture: Roles and identities in France and Spain*, Bristol: Intellect.

Garelli, Juan Carlos (1998), 'Controversial Aspects of Bowlby's Attachment Theory', online 5 November @http:///rdz. stjohns.edu/lists/bowlbyl/controversy.html.

Gelfand, Elissa D. and Thorndike Hules, Virginia (1985), *French Feminist Criticism: Women, Language, and Literature. An Annoted Bibliography*, New York and London: Garland Publishing.

Grosz, Elizabeth (1994), *Volatile Bodies: Toward a Corporeal Feminism*, Sydney: Allen & Unwin.

Guberman, Ross Mitchell (ed.) (1996), *Julia Kristeva, Interviews*, New York: Columbia University Press.

Guy, James (1987), *The Personal Life of the Psychotherapist*, New York: John Wiley.

Hamilton, Victoria (1993), *Narcissus and Oedipus: The Children of Psychoanalysis*, London: Karnac; first published 1982.

Harper, Robert A. (1959), *Psychoanalysis and Psychotherapy 36 Systems*, Prentice-Hall.

Holmes, Jeremy and Jacobs, Michael (1992), *Sigmund Freud*, London, Newbury park and New Delhi: Sage, Key Figures in Counselling and Psychotherapy.

Icikovics, Jean-Pierre (ed.) (1994), 'Les Pères fondateurs de la science: Freud' in *Les Cahiers de Sciences et Vie*, Numéro hors série, No 22, août 1994.

Jacobs, Michael (ed.) (1995), *Charlie an Unwanted Child in Search of a Therapist*, Buckingham, Philadelphia: Open University Press.

Jacobus, Mary (1995), *First Things: The Maternal Imaginary in Literature, Art, and Psychoanalysis*, New York and London: Routledge.

Kernberg, Otto F. (1995), 'Aggression and Transference in Severe Personality Disorders', February 1995, CME Incorporated; on line 5 November 1998 @http://mhsource.com/edu/ psytimes/p950216.html.

Kırschner, Suzanne (1996) *The Religious and Romantic Origin of Psychoanalysis*, New York: Columbia University Press.

Klein, Melanie (1988a), *Love, Guilt and Reparation and other works 1921-1945*, London: Virago; first published in 1975 by Hogarth Press.

——— (1988b), *Envy and Gratitude and other works 1946-1963*, London: Virago; first published 1975 by Hogarth Press.

Kovel, Joel (1976), *A Complete Guide to Therapy from Psychoanalysis to Behaviour Modification*, New York: Pantheon Books; (1977) Hassock: Harvester Press; this edition (1978) London: Harmondsworth Penguin.

Kristeva, Julia (1974a), *La Révolution du langage poétique*, Paris: Seuil.

——— (1974b), *Des Chinoises*, Paris: des femmes.

——— (1977a), 'Hérétique de l'amour' in *Tel Quel*, Winter 77, No 74, pp 30-49; translated as 'Stabat Mater' 1985 in *Poetic Today*, Vol 6, No 1/2.

——— (1977b), *Polylogue*, Paris: Seuil.

——— (1978), *Sèméiotikè: Recherche pour une sémanalyse*, Paris: Seuil; first published 1969.

——— (1980), *Pouvoirs de l'horreur: essai sur l'abjection*, Paris: Seuil; first published in *Tel Quel*.

——— (1981), *Le Langage cet inconnu*, Paris: Seuil; first published 1969.

——— (1982), *Powers of Horror: An Essay on Abjection*, New York: Columbia University Press.

——— (1983), *Histoires d'amour*, Paris: Denoël, Folio Essais.

——— (1984), Interview with Rosalind Coward at the Institute of Contemporary Arts in London during a conference on Desire; first published 1984 in a special edition of the *Institute of Contemporary Arts Documents*; republished in Oliver (1997).

——— (1985), *Au Commencement était l'amour: Psychanalyse et foi*, Paris: Hachette.

——— (1987a), *Soleil noir: Dépression et mélancolie*, Editions Gallimard; this edition: (1995) Edition Gallimard, Collection Folio/Essais.

——— (1987b), *In the Beginning was Love: Psychoanalysis and Faith*, New York: Columbia University Press.

——— (1988), *Etrangers à nous-mêmes*, Paris: Arthème Fayard, Collection Folio/Essais.

——— (1990a), *Lettre ouverte à Harlem Désir*, Paris: Rivages.

——— (1990b), 'Women's Time' in Belsey, Catherine and Moore, Jane (eds) *The Feminist Reader: Essasy in Gender and the Politics of Literary Criticism*, London: MacMillan, pp 1997-217.

——— (1991), *Le vieil homme et les loups*, Paris: Arthème Fayard.

——— (1992), Interview with Jonathan Rée in *Talking Liberties*, Contemporary Philosophy, Part 3, Channel 4.

——— (1993), *Les nouvelles maladies de l'âme*, Paris: Fayard.

——— (1996a), *Sens et non-sens de la révolte: Pouvoirs et limites de la psychanalyse I*, Paris: Fayard.

——— (1996b), 'Julia Kristeva: si vous n'en étiez pas, quel serait votre désir?' in *L'Humanité*, 12 novembre 1996, online 21 October 1998 @ http://www.humanite.presse.fr/ journal/96/96-11/96-11-12/96-11-12-035.html

——— (1996c), Interview with Rainer Ganahl 18 November 1996, New York, Barnard VIP Suite, Columbia University: online 09 October 1997 @ http://homepage.iprolink.ch/ ~invitro/rainer2/inter2.html.

——— (1996d), *Possessions*, Paris: Fayard.

——— (1997a), *La révolte intime: Pouvoirs et limites de la psychanalyse II*, Paris: Fayard.

——— (1997b), 'Julia Kristeva: n''nstitu', interviewed by Arnaud Spire for *L'Humanité* on 02 july 1997; online Wednesday 21 October 1998

@http://www.humanite.presse.fr/journal/ 97/ 97-07/97-07-02/97-07-02-022.html.

——— (1997c), 'Une désinformation', *Le Nouvel Observateur* No 1716, 25 septembre au 1er octobre 1997, page 122; on line 03 March 1999@ http://peccatte.rever.fr/ SBPresse/LeNouvelObs. 2509JK.html.

——— (1998a), *Contre la dépression nationale*, Paris: Textuel, Conversations pour demain.

———Kristeva Julia and Clément, Catherine (1998b), *Le féminin et le sacré*, Paris: Stock.

——— (1998c), 'Dialogue with Julia Kristeva' in *Julia Kristeva 1966-1996. Aesthetics, politics, Ethics*, *Parallax*, Vol 4, No 3, pp 5-16, Taylor & Francis Ltd.

——— (1998d), 'Aux limites de la vie' in *Agir: pour les droits de l'homme au XXIème siècle*, Auteurs: Thèmes: Idées pour respecter les droits des 'sans-pouvoir', 04 december 1998, online 09 November 2000 @ http:www.droitshumains.org/Forum/Unesco/DOCS/KristevaF.html.

——— (1999), *Le génie féminin: Hannah Arendt*, Paris: Fayard.

——— (2000), *Le génie féminin: Melanie Klein*, Paris: Fayard.

——— (2002), *Le génie féminin: Colette*, Paris: Fayard.

——— (2003), 'Intertextuality: An Interview with Julia Kristeva', online 20 February 2003 @http://.msu.edu/user/ chrenkal/980/INTEXINT.HTM; previously published 1985 in *Intertextuality and Contemporary American Fiction*.

Lacan, Jacques (1966), *Le Séminaire, livre I: Les Ecrits techniques de Freud*, Paris: Seuil.

——— (1971), *Le Séminaire, livre II: Les Ecrits techniques de Freud*, Paris: Seuil.

Landry, Donna & Maclean, Gerald (ed) (1996), *The Spivak Reader*, London and New York: Routledge

Laplanche, Jean (1976) *Life and Death in Psychoanalysis*, London and Baltimore: The John Hopkins University Press.

Laplanche, Jean (1999), *Essays on Otherness*, London: Routledge.

Laplanche, Jean and Pontalis, Jean-Baptiste (1973), *The Language of psychoanalysis* , London: The International Psycho-analytical Library no 94, The Hogarth Press and the Institute of Psycho-analysis.

——— (1988), *The Language of psychoanalysis* London: Karnac.

——— (1991) *Vocabulaire de la psychanalyse* Paris: Presses Universitaire de France; first published 1967.

Lasch, Christopher (1979), *The Culture of Narcissism: American Life in An Age of Diminishing Expectations*, New York: Warner Books.

Lechte, John (1991), *Julia Kristeva*, London and New York: Routledge; first published 1990.

Libération (2001), parution du 12 fevrier online 23 February 2001, @http://.liberation.fr/ sciences/genome/20010211une.html.

Lichtenberg Ettinger, Bracha (1992), 'Matrix and Metramorphosis' in *Differences*,

Vol 3, No 4, pp 176-207.

Lindley, Richard (1991), *The Values of Psychotherapy*, Oxford: Oxford University Press.

Malson, Lucien (1972), *Wolf Children and the Problem of Human Nature*, New Left Books.

Masson, Jeffrey (1997), *Against Therapy*, London: Harper Collins; first published in 1989.

Meins, Elizabeth (1998), 'The Effect of Security of Attachment and Maternal Attribution of Meaning on Children's Linguistic Acquisitional Style', in *Infant Behavior and Development*, No 21.

Mitchell, Juliet (1990), *Psychoanalysis and Feminism: a Radical Reassessment of Freudian Psychoanalysis*, London: Penguin; first published in 1974 by Allen Lane.

——— (ed.) (1991), *The Selected Melanie Klein*, London: Penguin; first published in 1986 by Peregrine Books.

Moi, Toril (1985), *Sexual/Textual Politics*, London: Routledge

Monroy, Michel (2000), 'Psychothérapies et processus d'embrigadement' in *Le Jounal Des Psychologues*, No 174, 43-47, février 2000.

de Musset, Alfred (1993), *Les Confessions d'un enfant du siècle*, Paris: Garnier-Flammarion; first published 1836.

Nasio, J-D (1992), *Enseignement de 7 concepts cruciaux de la psychanalyse*, Paris: Petite Bibliothèque Payot; First published 1988, Paris: Editions Rivages.

——— (1994), *Cinq leçons sur la théorie de Jacques Lacan*, Paris: Petite Bibliothèque Payot; First published 1992, Paris: Editions Rivages.

Nouvet, Claire (1991), 'An Impossible Response: The Disaster of Narcissus' in *Yale French Studies*, Vol 79, pp 103-34.

Oates, John and Sheldon, Sue (eds) (1993), *Cognitive Development in Infancy*, Open University, Hove: Lawrence Erlbaum Associates Ltd; first published 1987.

Oliver, Kelly (1991), 'Kristeva's Imaginary Father and the Crisis in the Paternal Function' in *Diacritics* Summer-Fall 1991.

——— (1993), *Reading Kristeva: Unravelling the Double-bind*, Bloomington, Indianapolis: Indiana University Press.

——— (ed.) (1997), *The Portable Kristeva*, New York: Columbia University Press, European Perspectives.

——— (2000) 'Conflicted Love' in *Hypathia*, Vol 15, No 3, 1-18, Summer 2000.

Olivier, Christiane (1980), *Les enfants de Jocaste: L'empreinte de la mère*, Paris: Denoël.

——— (1988), *La psychafamille*, Paris: Denoël.

——— (1990), *Filles d'Eve: Psychologie et sexualité féminines*, Paris: Denoël.

Ovid (1968), *Metamorphoses: Book III*, London: Penguin.

Palmer, Stephen and Varma, Ved P. (eds) (1997), *The Future of Counselling and Psychotherapy*, London: Sage.

Payne, Michael (1993), *Reading Theory: An Introduction to Lacan, Derrida, and*

Kristeva, Oxford (GB) and Cambridge (USA): Blackwell.

Peyre, Henri (1979), *Qu'est-ce que le romantisme?*, Paris: PUF, littératures modernes.

Pool, Léa (1986), *Anne Trister*, co-produit par ONF et Film Vision 4, Canada.

Robertiello, Richard C. and Schoenewolf, Gerard (1987), *101 Common Therapeutic Blunders: Counter transference and Counterresistance in Psychotherapy*, Northvale, New Jersey and London: Jason Aronson Inc.

Rutter, Michael (1981), *Maternal Deprivation Reassessed*, 2nd edition, Harmondsworth, New York (USA), Victoria (Australia), Markham (Canada) and Auckland (New Zealand): Penguin Books; First edition 1972 reprinted 1973, 1974, 1975, 1976, 1977, 1979.

Sarup, Madan (1992), *Jacques Lacan*, New York, London, Toronto, Sydney, Tokyo and Singapore: Harvester Wheatsheaf, Modern Cultural Theorists.

Schacter, Daniel (ed.) (1997), *Memory Distortion*, Cambridge Mass.: Harvard University Press.

Scheper-Hughes, Nancy (1992), '(M)Other Love: Culture, Scarcity, and Maternal Thinking', in *Death Without Weeping: The Violence of Everyday Life in Brazil*, Berkeley Los Angeles and Oxford (USA): University of California Press, pp 340-99.

Scott, Ridley (1991), *Blade Runner: the Director's Cut*, Time Warner.

Seinfeld, Jeffrey (1996), *Containing Rage, Terror and Despair: An ObjectRelations Approach to Psychotherapy*, Northvale, New Jersey and London: Jason Aronson Inc.

Shamdasani, Sonu and Münchow, Michael (1994), *Speculations After Freud: Psychoanalysis, philosophy and Culture*, London and New York: Routledge.

Sherman, Cindy (1995), *Cindy Sherman: Photographic Work 1975-1995*, Schirmer Art Books; first published on the occasion of the exhibition 'Cindy Sherman: Photographic Work 1975-1995' Hamburg (25 May-30 July 1995), Malmö (26 August 1995-22 October 1995) and Lucerne (8 December 1995-11 February 1996).

Smaller, Margaret (1985) *Intertextuality: An Interview with Julia Kristeva*, on-line 27 November 2000 @ http://www.msu.edu/user/chrenkal/980/INTEXINT .HTM.

Smith, Angela Marie, *Kristeva, Sherman, Butler and the* Abjec,t online 24 November 2000 @ http:english.cla.umn.edu/ graduateprofiles/asmith.Sherm4. htm.

Smith, Anna (1996), *Julia Kristeva: Readings of Exile and Estrangement*, Bristol: JW Arrowsmith Ltd; first published London: MacMillan Press Ltd.

Smith, Anne-Marie (1998), *Julia Kristeva: Speaking the Unspeakable*, London and Sterling, Virginia: Pluto Press.

Sophocles (1959), *Oedipus the King*, New York: Washington Square Press, Inc.

Spitz, René A. (1946), 'Hospitalism: An Inquiry into the Genesis of Psychiatric Conditions in Early Childhood', in *Psychoanalytic Study of the Child*, Vol 1, 53-74.

Stern, Daniel N. (1998), *The Interpersonal World of the Infant: A view from Psychoanalysis and Developmental Psychology*, London: Karnac Books; first published 1985 by Basis Books.

——— (1990), *Diary of a Baby*, New York: BasicBooks.

Trinitarian Bible Society, *The New Testament*, London: Eyre & Spottiswood.

Weber, Samuel (1982), *The Legend of Freud*, Minneapolis: University of Minnesota Press.

Wylie, William D.(2000), *The Basic Human Being: The Wild Child*, online 24 November 2000 @ http://members.aol.com/ WDWylie/ Wild.htm.

Zizek, Slavoj (1991), *Looking Awry: An Introduction to Jacques Lacan through Popular Culture*, Cambridge (Massachusetts) and London: The MIT Press.

——— (1999), *The Ticklish Subject: The Absent Center of Political Ontology*, London, New York: Verso.

Index